Lobbyists and Legislators

Lobbyists
and Legislators
A Theory of Political Markets

Michael T. Hayes

Rutgers University Press / New Brunswick

Library of Congress Cataloging in Publication Data

Hayes, Michael T   1949–
  Lobbyists and legislators.

  Bibliography: p.
  Includes index.
  1. Lobbyists.   2. Pressure groups.   3. Legislators.
4. Supply and demand.   I. Title.
JF529.H39   328′.38   80-23430
ISBN 0-8135-0910-6

Contents

To my parents and Candace

Acknowledgments

This book has evolved over a period of several years during which I have accumulated a large number of intellectual debts. It has its origins in my doctoral dissertation at Indiana University, where I benefited enormously from the direction of Professors Leroy Rieselbach and John P. Lovell. Ronald E. Weber served as much more than a third reader for that effort, having planted many of the seeds that later bore fruit in an unusually insightful and provocative graduate seminar in interest representation in American politics. William P. Travis, my outside minor advisor, guided me through much of the economic literature underlying my argument. Finally, I was profoundly influenced by the late John V. Gillespie, who gave me a thorough grounding in the public choice literature. My sense of loss at his recent untimely death brought home to me just how much his thinking had helped to shape my own. Those who knew him will discern his influence throughout this work.

Since that time, my research ideas have continued to center around nagging questions suggested by the typology of policy processes advanced in the dissertation: in particular, the need to explain its underlying dimensions better, to make more explicit the conception of Congress as a political market, and to assess the normative implications of political market failure. Consequently this work bears very little resemblance to the dissertation; I would like to believe the changes reflect growth. In any event, this effort has benefited greatly from the comments of Lewis Anthony Dexter, Randall B. Ripley, Paul Sabatier, and Robert Salisbury. In addition, two colleagues at Rutgers University, Richard Lehne and Carl Van Horn, have been kind enough to read and comment on the manuscript in its entirety. Many other colleagues here and elsewhere have commented on earlier versions of my argument in one form or another; although I cannot acknowledge each of these contributions individually, all have contributed greatly to the evolution of my argument. I am also indebted to those students at Lawrence University and at Rutgers who served in many cases as unwitting sounding boards for many of the ideas expressed here.

The assistance of Marlie Wasserman, Joe Esposito, and Leslie Mitchner of Rutgers University Press was invaluable at every stage of the development of this manuscript. I would also like to thank Phyllis Moditz and Susan Tiller, who typed the final draft. The Research Council of Rutgers University was especially generous in providing two grants that greatly aided in the final preparation of the manuscript.

Chapter Two was previously published, in substantially different form, as "The Semi-Sovereign Pressure Groups: A Critique of Current Theory and an Alternative Typology" in the *Journal of Politics* 40(1978):134–161. Portions of Chapter Five appeared in different form as "Interest Groups and Congress: Toward a Transactional Theory" in *The Congressional System: Notes and Readings*, 2d ed., rev., edited by Leroy N. Rieselbach, pp. 252–273, copyright Duxbury Press, 1979. In each case, these materials are reprinted by permission.

Introduction

This is a study of the role of organized interest groups in the legislative process. As such, it has two primary objectives: first, to provide a counter to the tendency among contemporary political scientists to downplay the importance of such groups by suggesting, quite simply, that their importance varies under different legislative circumstances; second, and perhaps more important, to specify those legislative circumstances, explaining when interest groups are important and why.

In journalistic and popular accounts, lobbyists have long been portrayed as wielding enormous influence, bribing or browbeating legislators to get their way. Within the discipline of political science, so-called pressure groups were traditionally considered the central actors in the legislative process. Some pluralist theorists went so far as to ascribe a largely passive role to Congress, with legislators responding to the sum of a variety of group pressures that together produced an equilibrium. According to Earl Latham, for example:

> The legislature referees the group struggle, ratifies the victories of the successful coalitions, and records the terms of the surrenders, compromises, and conquests in the form of statutes. . . . The legislative vote on any issue tends to represent the composition of strength, i.e., the balance of power, among the contending groups at the moment of voting. What may be called public policy is the equilibrium reached in this struggle at any given moment.[1]

Whether this equilibrium was in any sense just remained subject to question; the existence of such an equilibrium and the central role of groups did not.

1

In recent years this pressure group model has fallen into disrepute, at least among political scientists. In the wake of Raymond Bauer, Ithiel de Sola Pool, and Lewis Dexter's *American Business and Public Policy,* a thorough and insightful case study of business lobbying on the contemporary tariff, interest groups have come to be considered as little more than service bureaus for their legislative allies.[2] Although Bauer, Pool, and Dexter began their study fully expecting to find considerable support for the pressure group model, what they actually saw lent little support to such a view. Consequently they called for a more sophisticated, "transactional" conception of the relationship between legislators and lobbyists. In their view, this relationship was characterized less by pressure than by inter-dependence:

> If pressure politics no longer satisfies as an explanation of what happened regarding reciprocal trade, this is not just because of a change in the times. We are probably also reflecting a characteristic stage in the development of a discipline. The pressure group model was a sophisticated refinement of previously naive views of the Congressional process. It may now be time for a still more complicated view of the process of influence on and in Congress.[3]

Unfortunately the discipline has by and large failed to respond to their call. Instead their volume is remembered chiefly for its devastating critique of the primitive pressure group model, and something approaching a new conventional wisdom has arisen according to which interest groups are relatively peripheral actors in the legislative process. As a consequence, research on interest groups has declined over the last ten to fifteen years, although this trend has lately begun to reverse, as political scientists have sought to explain the recent proliferation of consumer, environmental, and senior citizens groups.

Indeed political science has been almost alone in attributing so little importance to interest groups. In recent years a variety of economists have advanced theories of the legislative process in which self-interested politicians are seen as delivering benefits to pressure groups in return for continued electoral support. Journalistic and muckraking accounts have continued to take pressure group activity as a given, most recently focusing on the alleged capacities of single-interest groups, corporate political action committees (PACs) or the oil lobby to dominate the legislative process. Moreover, participants in the congressional process have found it accurate—or convenient—to point an accusing finger at the multiplicity of group pressures with which they must contend. As recently as 1978, Senator Edward M. Kennedy asserted that "representative government . . . is in the worse shape I have seen it in my sixteen years in the Senate. The heart of the problem is that the Senate and the House are awash in a sea of special-interest campaign contributions and special-interest lobbying."[4] Similarly, President Carter has found the oil companies a convenient scapegoat for his difficulties in obtaining passage of comprehensive energy legislation. Public interest lobbies point an accusing finger at the superior resources of corporate PACs; according to Fred Wertheimer of Common Cause, for example, "It's almost impossible now to create national policy in Congress because you have very powerful interest groups slicing up the pie. What we're headed for is the United PAC's of America."[5] Business lobbyists complain that Congress is controlled by a party heavily indebted to Big Labor. Congressmen reluctant to confront particularly volatile issues, such as federal funding of abortions or ratification of the Panama Canal treaty, complain that single-issue groups are running Washington.

There is a need to reconcile such views with the insights of Bauer, Pool, and Dexter's convincing analysis. If pressure no longer suffices to explain the relationship between legislators and lobbyists, neither, it must be conceded, does the more recent conception of groups as little more than peripheral participants in the legislative process. Common sense would suggest that groups might well be pivotal to certain kinds of issues and largely peripheral to others. The challenge is to specify the circumstances.

Consequently I advance a typology of policy processes in an effort to identify those arenas in which groups play a major role. Inevitably I have built upon Theodore Lowi's seminal effort in which he distinguished three legislative arenas centering around what he termed *distributive*, *regulative*, and *redistributive outcomes*.[6] For my purposes, Lowi's categories ultimately proved to be insufficiently clear and well defined, and I had to draw on a variety of subsequent efforts to clarify his scheme in deriving my own. Because I sought to specify the circumstances under which interest groups would play a significant role in the U.S. legislative process, some of these efforts proved more useful than others. Some elements I had to reformulate; other I simply discarded. Although the intellectual roots of my typology are traced in the second chapter, an assessment of its limits as well as the potential contribution of alternative typologies await the volume's conclusion.

Such typologies are at best useful only for post hoc categorizations. They can be of considerable heuristic value, however, in pointing to important variables meriting further examination. Thus the greater challenge is to go beyond the typology and explain its underlying definitional dimensions. The centering of these dimensions around the demand and supply of public policies suggests a conception of legislatures as political *markets*. As I observed earlier, economists have recently advanced exchange theories of political markets whereby pressure groups are once again viewed as central actors. I review these efforts here as well as the attempts to subject them to operationalization and empirical tests, because they provide considerable support for my typology; in fact their seemingly contradictory findings can be properly understood only in light of that typology. Yet these theories fail to recognize the considerable latitude available to congressmen, which has been observed by Bauer, Pool, and Dexter; thus the theories ultimately rest on a primitive pressure group conception of the legislative process.

By contrast, a serious response to Bauer, Pool, and Dexter requires a *transactional theory*: one that recognizes the interdependence of legislators and lobbyists without underestimating the significance of groups in the policy process. Such a theory must begin by explaining variations in the configuration of demand for public policies. Sometimes, as Bauer, Pool, and Dexter observed, groups do indeed cancel out, leaving congressmen relatively free. On the other hand, group pressures can at times be one-sided and quite overwhelming. Thus the pattern of demand can make an enormous difference in legislative outcomes. Moreover, all groups are not alike. As Mancur Olson has shown, not all groups are represented in the group struggle,[7] nor is there any guarantee that those participating will do so on anything like equal terms. It is necessary to derive a tentative taxonomy of groups to differentiate such widely disparate forms as corporate PACs, labor unions, public interest lobbies, and nascent social movements. Finally, it is essential to recognize a divergence of interests between group leaders and followers. Following Robert Salisbury and James Q. Wilson, it is clear that group leaders face a problem of representation not unlike that confronting congressmen.[8] Both legislators and lobbyists possess considerable latitude in defining their jobs and taking policy positions.

The theory must also explain variations in legislative responses to various configurations of demands. In the public choice tradition, legislators are viewed as rational, self-interested, and reelection minded. Following Anthony Downs, David Mayhew, and Morris Fiorina among others, I advance a rational choice theory of legislative behavior, which I confront with evidence from the case study literature on Congress.[9] The theory is at the same time transactional. Legislators and lobbyists are viewed as interdependent insofar as they both survive by appearing to deliver benefits to their respective constituencies, an imperative that creates the conditions for a mutually beneficial exchange. Congressmen thus retain a great deal of freedom even as interest group leaders obtain—or what is more important, appear to obtain—benefits for their memberships. Typically, then, the relationship is less one of pressure than of symbiosis, as legislators and lobbyists find they have far more interests in common than in conflict.

Finally the normative implications of the theory must be assessed and the prospects for reform examined. Legislatures as political markets must satisfy all the same underlying assumptions for efficient operation as apply to economic markets, such as perfect information and perfect competition on both the demand and supply sides. Unfortunately political markets seem if anything even more prone to violate these assumptions. This fact carries with it disturbing implications for both the efficiency and equity of political markets, in particular, for the size and composition of the public sector and for income distribution. I examine in detail these pessimistic conclusions as well as a variety of proposals for reforming political markets. The prognosis is not good for any of these proposals, as all of them ultimately require politicians to transcend narrow self-interest and behave as public interest maximizers. To say that our troubles will be over when people stop behaving as they do is to propose a solution that assumes away the problem.

Ultimately we are left with little hope but to improve the knowledge base of decisions. Although improved policy analysis is certainly no panacea, it has a real contribution to make, particularly insofar as participants in the legislative process often find it rational to obscure outcomes and employ symbolic reassurances in order to keep the losers unaware of the real stakes.[10] Thus analysts must recognize that information constitutes a potentially powerful force for the "socialization of conflict"[11] and that, as a consequence, their prescriptions may not always be welcomed by policymakers. Moreover, policy prescriptions must be based on a thorough understanding of the policy process. Outcomes cannot be understood in isolation, and policy evaluations that ignore the political realities of the legislative process that gave rise to them will ultimately be of limited value. The real challenge is to explain the flow of policy from the process of agenda formation through policy formulation to implementation and then to examine how this process varies, across issues as well as across political settings. In that effort, policy typologies can be of considerable heuristic value. Because of my focus on the role of interest groups in the American context, I stress some variables while largely ignoring others that might be of real value in a comparative context. In the American context, however, the first step is to clear away the considerable confusion surrounding the role of interest groups in the legislative process.

I

Interest Groups and Congress

The classic works of pluralist theory regarded interest groups as the central actors in the political process and tended to treat Congress as little more than the arena in which the outcome of the group struggle would be ratified. Though not all scholars of the legislative process were this extreme, as late as 1964 Lowi could observe that, "as an argument that groups must be the major unit of analysis, pluralism excites little controversy."[1] More recent research on lobbying has tended to undermine this conception of the importance of interest groups. According to this recent evidence, groups can more accurately be regarded as little more than service bureaus to be used or ignored by congressmen as they see fit. Though useful as a corrective to the earlier obsession with the "group basis of politics,"[2] this new view can be just as misleading in its own tendency to slight unduly the role of interest groups in the legislative process. Ultimately, reconciling the seeming contradictions between these two views requires a more complex and comprehensive theory of interest groups and the legislative process.

THE ROOTS OF THE CONTROVERSY

Through most of the first half of this century, political science theory was essentially group theory, and interest groups were widely understood to be the fundamental units of analysis. Thus to David Truman it was obvious that "we do not, in fact, find individuals otherwise than in groups; complete isolation in space and time is so rare as to be an almost hypothetical situation."[3] To Latham, Congress was little more than a referee in the group struggle: "The legislative vote on any issue thus tends to represent the composition of strength, i.e., the balance of power among the contending groups at the moment of voting."[4] The less extreme proponents of this view acknowledged a role for government in the process but treated government officials just like any other units in the group process: as political brokers with their own interests and resources.[5]

The fallacy in all this, as Lowi insightfully observed, was that

> the pluralist approach has generated case-study after case-study that "proves the model" with findings directed by the approach itself. Issues are chosen for research because conflict made them public; group influence is found because in public conflict groups participate whether they are influential or not.[6]

Such an approach was clearly self-fulfilling. Evidence in support of group theories of politics would be drawn from cases that stood out in the first place because of the prominent place they gave to organized interest groups, as did Latham's study of basing-point pricing legislation or Stephen Kemp Bailey's *Congress Makes a Law*.[7] E. E. Schattschneider's classic study of pressure group activity surrounding the tariff bill of 1930 seemed to demonstrate conclusively the paramount importance of such groups.[8]

By contrast, Bauer, Pool, and Dexter's more recent study of business lobbying on the tariff issue from 1953 to 1962 was self-consciously advanced as a counter to what they saw as a primitive and simplistic conception of pressure underlying these earlier efforts.[9] Many of the findings of this landmark study do indeed appear at first glance to be irreconcilably contradictory to those advanced three decades before by Schattschneider. These contradictions are irreconcilable, however, only if the debate is limited to the question of whether interest groups are important at all and if one is forced to make a single answer to that question and hold to it in all time periods and under all conceivable circumstances. The most important contribution of Lowi's fine review of these two works was his recognition that the findings of the two studies are time-bound, that the nature of the tariff issue has altered drastically over the years, and that the characteristics of a given issue can have a profound impact on the behavior of interest groups as well as on the other relevant actors in the political process.

In examining the legislative process leading to the passage of the

Hawley-Smoot Tariff Act of 1930, Schattschneider found lobbyists to be both aggressive and highly influential. Individual firms appearing before the Ways and Means Committee lobbied successfully for specific protection, so that most of the tariff provisions benefited individual firms; few applied to more than four.[10] As a result of this remarkable specificity, the final legislation proved to be almost two hundred pages in length.[11] Not surprisingly the various producers seeking protection were governed by a prevailing attitude that Schattschneider termed *reciprocal noninterference:* "a mutuality under which it is proper for each to seek duties for himself but improper and unfair to oppose duties sought by others."[12] Lobbyists for protection vastly outnumbered those for freer trade. In fact, Schattschneider argued, the ultimate outcome would not have been substantially different if none of the groups favoring freer trade had been active at all.[13]

> Pressures are formidable and overwhelming only when they have become unbalanced and one-sided. As long as opposed forces are equal or nearly equal, governments can play off one against the other. The strategy, therefore, is to preserve an equilibrium in many cases. The protective tariff was made strong by joining a multitude of interests in one piece of omnibus legislation.[14]

Bauer, Pool, and Dexter began focusing on the tariff issue after 1953 expecting to find considerable support for what they termed the *pressure group model* of the legislative process.[15] Much to their surprise, what they saw tended to undermine this view. Corporations, evidently reluctant to call attention to their size, exercised remarkable restraint.[16] Many firms found their self-interest on the issue complex and difficult to determine with confidence.[17] Firms acted most successfully as catalytic groups, providing information and helping to define the situation for legislators and other lobbyists.[18] Group efforts tended to cancel out, leaving congressmen relatively free to play off both sides.[19] Although a lot of money was spent in the aggregate, individual lobbies proved to be severely underfinanced.[20] They were also poorly organized and by and large quite timid, approaching only those legislators who agreed with them already. Lobbyists were thus little more than service bureaus for those congressmen already sympathetic to their position.[21] As it turned out, interest groups were much more dependent on congressmen than had previously been recognized. Congressmen, no longer perceived as mere referees of the group struggle, in fact retained considerable latitude:

> Congressmen have a great deal more freedom than is ordinarily attributed to them. The complexities of procedure, the chances of obfuscation, the limited attention constituents pay to any one issue, and the presence of countervailing forces all leave the Congressman relatively free on most issues.[22]

THE ONSET OF THE NEW CONVENTIONAL WISDOM

Bauer, Pool, and Dexter were careful to qualify these generalizations, characterizing their study as a corrective to the oversimplistic assertions of the earlier group theorists. They sought to transcend the naïve conception of pressure underlying the group theorists' conception of the legislative process and replace it with a transactional model that would view all political actors as "to some extent in a situation of mutual influence and interdependence."[23]

Unfortunately their volume is remembered less for its attempt to develop a more balanced view of interest groups than for its devastating critique of the primitive pressure group model. The authors failed to foresee that their views would in turn become fashionable almost in caricature, despite their best efforts to elaborate their arguments in subsequent writings.[24] There has been little response within the discipline to their call for a more sophisticated, transactional conception of interest groups.

Lester Milbrath's The Washington Lobbyists provides an important exception in this regard.[25] Seeking to go beyond the traditional case study approach, Milbrath employed surveys to assess a variety of lobbying techniques, asking both legislators and lobbyists which techniques they regarded as most effective. Not surprisingly he found both sets of respondents unwilling to admit to involvement in illegal or ethically questionable practices, whereas all agreed that the traditional avenues (committee hearings, personal presentations of the group position) were the most effective. From these responses Milbrath concluded that the traditional stereotype of the lobbyist buying off or browbeating legislators must be a vast exaggeration. In reality the goal of the modern lobbyist is much more modest: not so much pressure as mere access.

Milbrath saw his study as providing empirical support for Bauer, Pool, and Dexter's conception of the role of interest groups. Appearing so soon after *American Business and Public Policy,* it seemed to clinch their case, although in retrospect Milbrath seems naïve in assuming that congressmen and lobbyists would respond candidly to questions of this sort. The point here is not that there is more bribery going on than Milbrath sees (although more recent disclosures suggest that this is the case), but rather that one is unlikely to find out with such a research design.

A more convincing case for this revised conception of interest groups was provided by Donald Matthews in *U.S. Senators and Their World.*[26] Matthews stressed the dependence of lobbyists on access and the potential advantage this provided legislators in threatening to withhold it. As a consequence lobbyists tended to focus on allies and to confine their efforts to mobilizing sympathetic senators to become actively involved in lobbying their colleagues. This foreshadowed Matthews and James Stimson's more recent research on the extent to which congressmen look to trusted colleagues for cues on roll-call votes.[27]

The extent to which this view had attained something approaching the status of conventional wisdom within the discipline is nowhere more evident than in the major texts on legislative behavior. Leroy Rieselbach's characteristically careful summary of the existing literature as of 1973 is representative:

> To summarize . . . the classic image of lobby activity is highly inaccurate and misleading. The lobbyist, so recent research reveals, is less the master of the legislator, and more his subject. Because the congressman is the target of many groups, and because his constituents are usually unaware of his specific acts, he can define the "pressures" to which he will respond to suit his own aims and opinions. In such circumstances, the lobbyist can merely seek to gain and hold access to influential legislators, access which will permit him to communicate directly with the congressional decision makers. Group representatives prefer direct contact of an informal, low-pressure variety to other means of influencing senators and representatives; they also find these techniques more effective.[28]

That Rieselbach's summary was both accurate and typical of the treatment in the other basic texts is strikingly illustrated in Randall Ripley's more recent *Congress: Process and Policy.* In an effort to stake out a middle ground in the controversy, Ripley suggested a variety of factors that can affect interest group influence, for example, unity (or lack thereof) of the groups seeking benefits, visibility of the issue, and presence or absence of sympathetic ears in key congressional or executive positions. These conditions are all very appealing, to the point of being almost commonsensical. What is most significant about this listing is its striking lack of footnote references. Coming from so thorough a scholar of the legislative process, this suggests that there was nowhere in the existing literature any systematic attempt to specify or study the conditions for interest group influence. Rather, the debate remained bogged down on the misleading question of whether interest groups are important at all.[29]

THE LIMITS OF THE CONVENTIONAL WISDOM

The problem with this new conventional wisdom, unfortunately, is that it is ultimately no more accurate or comprehensive than the old one. Although the pressure group model is no longer fashionable among political scientists, it has not really been invalidated. Case studies of the legislative process still provide occasional evidence that contemporary interest groups continue to exercise something resembling pressure at least some of the time. The politics of special tax provisions and the lobbying success of the oil industry on the issues of water pollution and oil depletion allowances provide notable examples.[30] Similarly the cozy relationships among interest groups, congressional committees, and administrative agencies have been labeled "policy subsystems," "subgovernments," and "iron triangles," and have spawned the term *clientelism*.[31]

One such case involves the lobbying activity surrounding the periodic extensions of the Sugar Act, which prompted Douglas Cater to coin the term *subgovernment*.[32] This issue is particularly relevant here because it tends to be, on the whole, quite representative of an entire class of foreign trade issues not examined by Bauer, Pool, and Dexter: congressional consideration of import quotas. In direct contrast to the contemporary tariff issue, import quotas do not involve the delegation of authority to make real allocations to the executive branch. Although Congress delegated away its authority to set tariff rates in 1934, it has never yielded its authority to fix import quota levels, an authority it continues to exercise over a wide variety of products, including sugar, meat, and cotton textiles. Because the typical pattern of lobbying activity on these issues is so very different from that observed by Bauer, Pool, and Dexter, it is apparent that the tariff cannot plausibly be regarded as typical even of foreign trade issues in Congress.[33]

The act was carefully designed to prop up the price of domestically produced sugar by restricting domestic production and limiting foreign competition. To accomplish this, the amount of sugar to be consumed within the United States over the coming years would be precisely determined and divided into domestic and foreign shares, or quotas. Then specific production quotas would be assigned to individual domestic and foreign producers. These were essentially licenses to produce given amounts of sugar; no one without a quota could produce sugar and expect to sell it in the United States. No one receiving a quota could sell more than his allotment. No one receiving an allotment was required however to produce any sugar at all if a greater return could be obtained from putting the land to other uses, a factor contributing to the shortage of domestically produced sugar in 1974.

By carefully limiting the foreign share of the overall production figure, the act was effectively imposing import quotas on foreign sugar. Throughout most of the life of the act, these import quotas had their intended effect of keeping the domestic price of sugar higher than the world market price. The end result was thus analogous to the imposition of a tariff on sugar. Yet because this end was achieved through the imposition of import quotas, the authority to set precise amounts was retained in Congress and the process bore a striking resemblance to the pattern of tariff politics observed by Schattschneider: a one-sided coalition of firms aggressively seeking protective legislation, the locus of real decision making centered in the relevant congressional committee (in this case, the House Agriculture Committee), and potential conflict accommodated through logrolling.

Indeed throughout most of its life the Sugar Act provided a classic example of the agree-bill phenomenon identified by Gilbert Steiner and Samuel Gove, whereby the principal demanding groups work out their differences in advance and then maintain a united front in support of the legislation.[34] Typically this process would begin with the domestic sugar producers and refiners negotiating a mutually acceptable bill in advance of legislative consideration of the pending extension. During the Kennedy and Johnson years the industry position would then be endorsed by the administration as part of its overall farm program. Any differences arising between the administration and industry positions would be reconciled before congressional consideration of the legislation, and a united front would then be presented.

Initial consideration of the bill would take place in the House Agriculture Committee, which throughout the life of the act remained sympathetic to the industry position. The committee hearings were typically little more than public forums for the legitimation of the proposed legislation. The domestic sugar industry (cane and beet sugar producers and domestic refiners) generally offered either a joint statement of the industry position or a series of witnesses from the various components of the industry coalition. Only token opposition would appear, generally a witness or two from domestic sugar users, usually bottling companies. As Schattschneider observed on the tariff in 1930, the final outcome would not have been substantially different had they not appeared at all. Virtually no one ever opposed the basic outlines of the bill.

Some additional witnesses would then be heard, sometimes at separate hearings. These witnesses appeared, not to question the bill's basic legitimacy, but to lobby for a share of the domestic or foreign quota. The prevalence of small domestic producers and foreign lobbyists seeking production quotas gave the Sugar Act a somewhat misleading reputation as one of the most heavily lobbied bills in any given session. As with the tariff of 1930, and in direct contrast to the pattern observed by Bauer, Pool, and Dexter, the vast preponderance of this lobbying activity was aimed at obtaining a share of the legislative spoils rather than at questioning the legislation itself. As one might expect, the act generally passed both houses without major amendments and with a minimum of conflict.

Although this pattern of one-sided pressure in support of the act may be regarded as typical for the recent period, it did not always hold. In 1964, unresolved conflicts between beet sugar producers and refining interests led to the failure of Congress to extend the act;[35] and with the election of a Republican administration committed to the eventual dismantling of much of the Democratic farm program, the pattern of executive branch-industry harmony was broken after 1969. This, combined with the emergence of a variety of consumer groups active on the issue, industry dissension, and the public outcry over soaring sugar prices, finally led to the defeat of the program in 1974.[36]

Thus reports of the death of the pressure politics model of the legislative process have been vastly exaggerated. Such instances of contemporary pressure politics suggest that the proponents of the new conventional wisdom must still come to grips with the world that Schattschneider described so long ago. Moreover this new orthodoxy has not been without its occasional detractors. Vigorous challenges to the prevailing paradigm have been offered by Lowi and Grant McConnell, both of whom focus on what they see as the continuing devolution of power to private groups in the modern state and the implications for democratic theory.

Even as the pressure group model fell into disrepute among political scientists, Lowi argued that the institutionalization of pluralism had become the operative public philosophy of policymakers. He attacked this philosophy of "interest group liberalism" for its stress on the delegation of broad discretion to administrators, which he termed *policy-without-law*. Such delegations enabled elected officials to avoid hard choices among contending groups. The real responsibility for choice would be passed on to the administrative process, in which some or all of the affected groups would participate. Policy-without-law thus substituted participation for choice and contributed to the devolution of power to interest groups and administrators not subject to electoral sanction.[37]

In *The Decline of Agrarian Democracy*, McConnell provided one example of such devolution in his chronicle of the growth of the American Farm Bureau Federation and its eventual domination of the administration of agricultural policy.[38] He extended this analysis to business and labor organizations as well in *Private Power and American Democracy*, always stressing the near autonomy of such groups, the inevitably political nature of such governmentally sanctioned subsystems of private power, and the generally oligarchic internal structures governing these narrow, but not entirely homogeneous, constituencies.[39]

McConnell's analysis foreshadowed much of the recent controversy regarding the extent of corporate power in the U.S. political economy. Mark Nadel in particular has echoed McConnell's argument that power is no less political for being exercised privately, and he has stressed the enormous advantage in resources available to corporations in blocking unwanted legislation, dominating regulatory agencies, and obtaining governmental benefits.[40]

This view has recently been reinforced by Charles Lindblom in *Politics and Markets*.[41] Lindblom however spends much less time than Nadel documenting the allegedly superior resources of corporations, and his argument is ultimately much less convincing. Rather, he painstakingly demonstrates that none of the world's polyarchies

have adopted anything approximating centralized planning, a phenomenon he attributes largely to corporate resistance. This inference
is not entirely compelling, for one need only point to the widespread
resistance to nonincremental changes (a central assumption of Lindblom's earlier writings) to account for the failure of industrial
democracies to adopt such a radical departure from past practices.
With or without corporate power one would expect such an evolution to be gradual at best; and the evidence from Sweden, Britain,
and other industrialized polyarchies (including the United States) is
entirely compatible with such an interpretation. In the final analysis
Lindblom's argument is less significant on its merits than for the conversion it signals from Lindblom's earlier, almost complete acceptance of the Bauer, Pool, and Dexter service bureau conception of
business lobbies.[42]

Lester Salamon and John Siegfried recently attempted a statistical
analysis of the relationship between corporate power and political
influence and found that a variety of measures of industrial market
structure are related to lobbying success on tax issues.[43] They char-
acterize their contribution as paving the way for rigorous empirical
analysis of the impact of corporate power on policy outcomes in view
of the inherent limitations of the existing anecdotal and case study
approaches to the problem. Actually theirs is only the most recent of
such studies, although it is the first to be performed by political scientists. A variety of economists have addressed this question, beginning with George Stigler's effort to develop an exchange theory of
regulatory legislation.[44] These studies and their inherent limitations
are reviewed at length in Chapter Three.

The problem with all these efforts, however, as Lowi and
McConnell demonstrated, is that corporations are not alone in
obtaining substantial benefits from government or in exercising private power. Lowi and McConnell both stressed the autonomy of
agricultural groups.[45] Studies by J. David Greenstone, Nicholas Masters, and Harry Scoble pointed to the countervailing power of organized labor.[46] More recently, Henry Pratt has chronicled the rise of
the various gray lobbies and their ongoing involvement in no less
than three distinct old-age policy subsystems.[47] Social protest activities by civil rights and welfare rights groups have produced some
limited victories;[48] and even consumers are beginning to overcome
substantial obstacles to organization, as seen in Nadel, Andrew
McFarland, and Jeffrey Berry's examinations of the proliferation of
so-called public interest lobbies.[49]

What is more important, these critics all take for granted the importance of interest groups in the legislative process and merely assault what they see as the naïvete of pluralist ideology. Thus rather than attempt to specify the conditions for interest group influence, they too remain mired in the question of whether groups are important at all. Clearly there is no choice but to reconcile the seeming contradictions between these two views. A new and more complex theory is needed.

TRANSCENDING THE CONTROVERSY

Bauer, Pool, and Dexter called for a transactional view of the legislative process whereby legislators and lobbyists would be viewed as interdependent. The groundwork for such a theory has already been laid by a variety of efforts to develop exchange theories of interest groups, although much remains to be done. In a seminal work, Olson examined the incentives for rational individuals with common interests to organize and lobby for collective benefits.[50] Salisbury extended this analysis, focusing on those entrepreneurs that actually initiated lobbying activity and offered a mix of benefits in exchange for dues.[51] More recently Wilson has advanced a similar theory of organizational maintenance in which entrepreneurs manipulate a variety of incentives to attract and retain members.[52]

These works provide the basis for an exchange theory of interest group formation. Unfortunately they apply only to the transactional relationship between interest group leaders and followers. What is needed for an appropriate response to Bauer, Pool, and Dexter is a comparably rich and insightful exchange theory of lobbying. Although the relationship between group leaders and followers profoundly affects lobbying strategies and although these theories hold promise for explaining the transactional relationship between legislators and lobbyists as well, they were not designed with that in mind.

Fortunately even as the study of interest groups waned among political scientists, it waxed elsewhere. A variety of economists, puzzled by the failure of regulatory and tariff policies to conform to the normative prescriptions of economic theory, sought to explain these deviations by constructing rational choice models of the legislative process. Previously, economic theories had treated policymakers as largely inert public interest maximizers who would faithfully implement the economists' canons; behavior to the contrary typically elicited laments about the ignorance of politicians and recommendations for the hiring of more economists in key governmental positions. A growing number of economists, following Downs, have come to challenge this view, arguing instead that policymakers, like firms and consumers, should be viewed as self-interest maximizers in a more realistic theory of the policy process.[53]

Interest groups occupy a central place in these exchange theories. They approach government in quest of benefits in such forms as tariffs, quotas, subsidies, and licensing authority. For example Stigler posits that industries will actively seek regulation in an effort to shore up cartels, restrict market entry, and avoid antitrust prosecution. In return they offer political support to legislators in the form of money, votes, and campaign activity. Thus the conditions for a mutually beneficial transaction exist, and legislatures can therefore be analyzed as political markets subject to their own laws of supply and demand.[54]

Unfortunately these arguments, though couched in exchange theory terms, too often view the terms of the exchange as quite one-sided. Empirical tests of these theories have focused solely on the relationship between measures of group strength and ultimate lobbying success, thus unwittingly treating Congress as little more than a passive referee of the group struggle, to recall Latham's phrase. For all their promise, these theories ultimately represent a reversion to the naïve pressure group model so effectively refuted by Bauer, Pool, and Dexter. Ironically these economists, not having read American Business and Public Policy, never fell prey to the new conventional wisdom it helped to create; unfortunately they also failed to benefit from its insights.

Clearly what is needed is to build on these efforts to develop a more sophisticated transactional theory of interest groups and Congress. Such a theory, to reconcile the contradictions between the old and new conventional wisdoms, has to recognize that there is not a single, "typical" legislative process to be explained but several quite distinct arenas. In short a typology of policy processes is needed.

II

Does Policy Area
Make a Difference?

The question for future research on interest groups must be not whether they are important, but when. The challenge is to specify the circumstances. A brief review of previous efforts to develop a typology of policy areas shows that the underlying theme of these efforts is that different types of policy outcomes stem from distinctively different policy processes. Thus for some processes, interest groups may be fundamental actors, whereas for others, they may be trivial. The task is to construct a typology that avoids the pitfalls and ambiguities of these earlier formulations.

PREVIOUS TYPOLOGIES

In an extremely insightful review article, Lowi attempted to reconcile the contradictions arising between the findings of Bauer, Pool, and Dexter in *American Business and Public Policy* and those of Schattschneider in *Politics, Pressures, and the Tariff*. He regarded both works as time-bound and atheoretical despite the obvious quality of the case studies.[1] Thus he argued the futility of attempting to derive from such case studies generalizations that will hold for all types of cases. Instead he proposed a typology of policy areas, which he termed *arenas of power*, which would make it unnecessary to choose between these conflicting findings. Interest groups can be highly influential on certain kinds of issues while being largely irrelevant for others. Lowi identified three such issue arenas, which he termed *distributive*, *regulative*, and *redistributive*.[2]

Distributive policies are quintessential pork-barrel or patronage policies characterized by the ease with which they can be disaggregated and dispensed, unit by small unit. They involve highly individualized decisions that can be made, at least in the short run, without regard to limited resources. There need be no losers in the distributive arena because the potentially deprived can always be accommodated by a further disaggregation of the stakes. Examples are the tariff as Schattschneider saw it as well as most rivers and harbors legislation.

Regulatory policies, according to Lowi, are likewise specific and individual in their impact, but are not similarly capable of infinite disaggregation. Regulatory decisions constitute behavioral rules formulated at the level of the economic sector and then implemented on a firm-by-firm, case-by-case basis. Here limited resources begin to pose problems, producing the beginnings of conflict. Much of contemporary business regulation falls in the regulative arena, as does the more recent tariff.

Redistributive policies immediately invoke the transfer of scarce resources. There are clearly perceived winners and losers in this arena, which is thus highly conflictual, with haves battling have-nots in something approaching class conflict. Social security and public assistance are Lowi's examples here.

Lowi fleshes out the political processes characteristic of these three issue arenas in considerable detail.[3] In the distributive arena, for example, individual firms or corporations approach Congress in quest of favorable legislation. Direct conflict of interests among those seeking benefits is generally avoided through logrolling, or what Schattschneider termed *reciprocal noninterference.* Because those approaching Congress are readily able to accommodate their various interests, all potential conflict is easily resolved within the relevant congressional committees so that the committee is the primary locus of decision rather than the floor. In the regulatory arena, where interest groups are the primary political actors, the relationship among these groups is one of bargaining or vulgar compromise, and the potential conflict is too great to be logrolled in the relevant congressional committee. Consequently conflict spills over onto the floor, where roll-call cleavages take on real meaning. In the redistributive arena the norm is ideological conflict between social classes, pitting the indulged against the deprived. Because of the potential magnitude of such conflicts, policy is generally formulated and conflicts are resolved within the executive branch, with the results of the tenuous accommodation generally imposed on an acquiescent Congress.

Lowi goes on to posit a tendency for political issues to pass through a life cycle of sorts, beginning as distributive policies, passing through a regulative phase, and ultimately becoming redistributive.[4] Thus, he asserts, Schattschneider's case study of the 1930 legislation offers an excellent overview of a quintessential distributive policy: logrolling among individual firms focusing their appeals on the Ways and Means Committee. By contrast, what Bauer, Pool, and Dexter observed was a tariff policy in transition from the distributive to the regulative arena. With the passage of the Trade Expansion Act of 1962, Lowi argues, this transition was complete. Passage of that legislation was characterized by lobbying efforts of full-fledged interest groups; an inability to contain conflict in committee and thus real cleavage on the floor; and ultimately the delegation of authority to negotiate tariff reductions on broad, sector-level categories of goods. In short, the tariff was no longer employed to regulate the international economy for domestic purposes, as it had been in its distributive era; it had become "a means of regulating the domestic economy for international purposes" and thus had entered its regulatory phase. "Tariff became a regulatory policy in 1962; all that remains of distributive politics now are quotas and subsidies for producers of specific commodities injured by tariff reductions."[5]

Unfortunately, the lack of any rigorous underlying theory renders many of Lowi's propositions less than convincing. It is not clear, for example, why all issues must originate in the distributive arena or pass through all three arenas. Nor is it clear that all redistributive issues must necessarily originate in the executive branch; that roll-call votes will always take on real meaning for regulatory issues; or that individual firms, rather than interest groups, will be the fundamental actors in the distributive arena. The problem is that Lowi's issue arenas, as they stand, are not really distinct conceptual types at all. He has performed at best a rich and insightful inductive exercise, attaching labels to what appear, from a wealth of case studies, to be distinctive clusters of attributes.

Nevertheless a variety of scholars have found his effort heuristic and responded by attempting to refine his typology. Most of these writers have posited two dimensions underlying Lowi's original framework and then attempted to fill in the missing cell in Lowi's implicit fourfold typology. Each of these authors, including Lowi in subsequent writings, then proceeded to define these dimensions and fill in the fourth cell in an entirely different way, which attests to the lack of conceptual and definitional clarity in Lowi's original effort.[6]

Table 1

Demand Pattern	Decisional System	
	Fragmented	Integrated
Integrated	Self-regulative	Redistributive
Fragmented	Distributive	Regulative

My own typology owes much to two particularly insightful contributions by Salisbury.[7] I have some quarrels with both of these formulations, but they do constitute important theoretical advances. In the first of these efforts Salisbury posited two underlying continua— *demand pattern* and *decisional system integration*—that interacted to yield four basic policy types (Table 1). Demand pattern referred to the degree of unity of the groups demanding a policy decision; an integrated demand pattern would reflect not mere parallelism of interests but organized cooperation. Decisional system integration or fragmentation referred essentially to the degree of centralization of the body responsible for the policy decision.[8] Thus Lowi's three original arenas are preserved and explicitly defined in much the same way,[9] but Salisbury has added a fourth, self-regulation. He asserts that the natural response of a fragmented decisional system to an integrated demand pattern is to grant autonomy to the demanding group in the form of self-administered licensing authority.[10]

Unfortunately these two underlying dimensions are not clearly and consistently defined. For example an integrated demand pattern was defined as one in which the attentive groups are active on the same side of an issue and working cooperatively.[11] This definition would seem to distinguish cases in which groups seeking benefits from government encounter significant opposition, as Bauer, Pool, and Dexter observed, from those in which the pressures are, in Schattschneider's terms, one-sided and overwhelming. Yet this is clearly not how Salisbury applies these terms. On the one hand, one-sided pressures in quest of self-regulatory policies were described as integrated; on the other hand, comparably one-sided pressures seeking distributive policies (tariffs) were paradoxically characterized as fragmented, a distinction that seems arbitrary at best.[12] Moreover Salisbury associated integrated demand patterns with redistributive outcomes, although Lowi expressly characterized them as arousing intense, highly fragmented demands approaching class conflict. Certainly there is nothing sacred about Lowi's original categories, and

Salisbury's formulation as it stands may conceivably offer certain advantages. Nevertheless Salisbury was explicitly trying to retain them, and the confusion he introduces on these points is therefore quite troubling.

Salisbury's second defining dimension poses serious problems as well. By his own later admission his concept of decisional system integration is not clearly defined and is virtually impossible to operationalize. At times it seems to refer to the degree of centralization or hierarchy in the decisional system, for example, strong party or presidential leadership as opposed to devolution to largely autonomous legislative committees.[13] Elsewhere it appears to include the degree of consensus within the system and the extent to which groups seeking benefits perceive potential opposition and thus tailor their demands accordingly. Thus to make matters worse, demand pattern according to Salisbury is not really an independent dimension at all. The type of policy demanded will be a function not only of the relative integration of demand pattern but of the degree of decisional system integration as well.[14] Much of the confusion surrounding the demand pattern variable can be traced to the ambiguities in this second defining dimension and to the murky interrelationship between the dimensions.

In a subsequent article with John Heinz, Salisbury sought to remedy this confusion by revising his framework. The authors began by acknowledging the difficulties plaguing any attempt to operationalize decisional system integration. Because some integration is a prerequisite to any decision, they conceded, the more fundamental question must be how costly it is to achieve the requisite coalition. They therefore suggested a new variable, the costs involved in reaching a decision. These include the costs to the legislator of conferring benefits on some constituency; the costs of acquiring information about an issue sufficiently to develop a position; and the costs in time, energy, and resources in negotiating a winning coalition. Although these costs will vary from issue to issue and from one policymaker to another, it is necessary, according to Salisbury and Heinz, to aggregate them in order to make statements about institutions as well.[15] Unfortunately because the authors offer little guidance on how these variables are to be combined and operationalized, it is not clear that their new second dimension represents an unqualified advance over the original decisional system integration variable.

In any event the two variables are quite different, albeit related. In general, according to Salisbury and Heinz, the more costly it is to

Table 2

| | Costs of Reaching a Decision | |
Demand Pattern	Low	High
Integrated	Redistributive	Self-regulative
Fragmented	Distributive	Regulative

organize coalitions, the more fragmented the decision unit will be.[16] Decision costs will vary from one issue to another; and decision units are not perfectly flexible in adapting to this variation, but the shift in decisional locus from committee to floor to executive branch described by Lowi for different issue arenas suggest that considerable adaptation does in fact occur. So the relationship between decision costs and decisional system is not perfect, and the cross-tabulation of Salisbury's four policy types (Table 2) is thereby altered somewhat.[17] Unfortunately, much of the confusion noted in Salisbury's previous effort remains: distributive policies are still mistakenly associated with fragmented demand patterns, and redistributive policies are linked with integrated demands. Thus, though Salisbury and Heinz make a major contribution in recognizing the importance of the demand pattern dimension, they still do not adequately explain its operation.

Ironically, much of the confusion surrounding their typology can be cleared away by their distinction between what they term *structural* and *allocative outcomes*. Allocative policies confer direct benefits on individuals or groups; structural outcomes are more ambiguous, for they establish authority structures or discretionary rules to guide future allocations. Thus, according to Salisbury and Heinz, distributive and redistributive policies are clearly allocative, whereas regulatory and self-regulatory policies both involve delegations of power, either to new authority structures or to the demanding groups themselves.[18]

Salisbury and Heinz do not treat this structural-allocative distinction as one of their defining dimensions but as a dependent variable because certain kinds of outcomes can be expected to result from the interaction of different demand patterns with different decisional systems dealing with issues involving varying decision costs. Thus they predict that the greater the decision costs for a given issue, the more likely it is that policymakers will opt for an ambiguous structural outcome rather than a more concrete and controversial allocation.[19]

This points to a deeper problem: the confusion as to precisely what kind of classification scheme Salisbury and Heinz have really advanced. It is not entirely clear whether they have a typology of policy processes, of outcomes, of expectations, or of something else. Their confusion stems most likely from ambiguities inherent in Lowi's original formulation, in which he asserted that, "in politics, expectations are determined by governmental outputs or policies."[20] Each type of outcome would thus generate different expectations and a distinctive pattern of political relations. Such a formulation comes dangerously close to being circular. First it employs policy outcome as an independent variable determining expectations, thus process; next it employs policy process to explain outcomes. Salisbury fails to clarify this point, for he follows Lowi in taking actor perceptions, or expectations, as his starting point and in employing policy at different times both as a dependent and as an independent variable.[21]

What is needed is a typology of policy *processes* that will distinguish those processes under which interest groups are likely to exercise influence from those for which they are largely irrelevant. Inasmuch as any policy process is, in Eastonian terms, a conversion of system inputs into outputs,[22] it stands to reason that a typology of processes must be derived from a cross-tabulation of input characteristics with outcomes. When Salisbury and Heinz's distinction between structural and allocative outcomes is introduced explicitly as one of the defining dimensions and when the operation of the demand pattern variable is properly understood, their framework can be reformulated to yield a typology that preserves the essence of Lowi's original issue arenas while substantially clarifying the distinctions between them.

A TYPOLOGY OF POLICY PROCESSES

My typology is thus derived from the cross-tabulation of a reformulated demand pattern dimension with a modification of the structural-allocative outcome distinction, which I term *supply pattern*. The terms *demand pattern* and *supply pattern* are in keeping with an exchange theory conception of legislatures as political markets that forms the basis of a transactional theory of lobbying.

In regard to demand pattern it is worth noting that Bauer, Pool, and Dexter explicitly assumed that congressmen will typically be able to play off a multiplicity of groups facing them on any given issue:

> We do not deny that there were large numbers of pressure groups. We
> are certain that, whatever the outcome, it would have been quite dif-
> ferent if all the organized interest groups on one side had been
> silenced, while all those on the other had remained vocal. However,
> *it is in the nature of the democratic struggle that that does not happen*
> (Emphasis added).[23]

Although they conceded that the legislative outcome would in fact
have been substantially different if the groups on either of the contending sides had remained inactive, they failed to recognize that
often this is precisely what happens.

Ironically, in the course of their assault on the pressure group
model, Bauer, Pool, and Dexter unwittingly adopted one of the fundamental tenets of the pluralist creed: the assumption that all interests affected by a given issue will be represented, which has its theoretical roots in Truman's concept of "potential groups."[24] Olson has
persuasively demonstrated that such "latent" groups cannot be
relied on to form in opposition to established groups,[25] and Salisbury
has shown that group formation will in fact be least likely to occur
when it is most needed—in hard times.[26] These arguments are but-
tressed by a wealth of empirical evidence that interest group activity
need not be balanced on all sides of a given issue. Bauer, Pool, and
Dexter seem to have forgotten their own evidence to this effect: Pro-
tectionists they found in general to be more active and effective
in communicating their views than lobbyists for freer trade.[27]
Schattschneider, of course, found pressures to be even more one-
sided on the tariff legislation of 1930. John Kingdon found interest
groups active on both sides of an issue for only 12 percent of the
cases he examined in *Congressmen's Voting Decisions;*[28] and Robert
Ross, in an analysis of interest group blocs in Congress over a six-
teen-year period, found 55 percent of the hearings he examined to
be noncompetitive. In fact trade policy hearings, along with labor
and housing issues, were found to be atypical in their tendency to be
consistently competitive.[29]

It should be clear from this evidence that Salisbury and Heinz
failed to grasp the fundamental significance of political conflict.
They stressed active cooperation in their definition of an integrated
demand pattern, but more important than active cooperation is the
presence or absence of active opposition to the group or coalition
seeking benefits. A well-integrated coalition may well be less successful in pressing their demands on policymakers in the presence

of a determined opposition than a group of loosely organized and uncoordinated interests that are largely unopposed. Hence I distinguish between *consensual* and *conflictual* demand patterns, thus stressing the importance of political opposition. This distinction is analogous to that drawn in game theory between non-zero-sum and zero-sum conflicts.[30]

The utility of this dimension should be readily apparent from its capacity to reconcile the conflicting findings of Schattschneider and Bauer, Pool, and Dexter on the tariff issue. When Schattschneider studied the tariff there was almost no discernible opposition to it. In contrast, by the 1950s the demand pattern had become conflictual; groups were active on both sides of the issue and tended to cancel one another out, leaving congressmen free to vote as they pleased. Bauer, Pool, and Dexter concluded that interest group influence had been vastly exaggerated and that Schattschneider's findings were largely outdated. What they failed to recognize was the fundamental change in the pattern of demand between the two periods.

In regard to supply pattern Bauer, Pool, and Dexter emphasized the fact that legislative action on the tariff in the 1950s did not actually affect the setting of specific rates at all. With the rate-setting authority resting with the executive branch, the legislative debate was concerned simply with how much latitude to grant the executive in negotiating further reductions in the tariff schedules.[31] Thus they concluded that the legislative process does not typically resolve the group struggle:

> A legislative enactment is seldom a clean decision of important issues. It is normally a verbal formula which the majority of congressmen find adequate as a basis for their continuing policy struggle. It sets up new ground rules within which the issue may be fought out. The ground rules will reflect the balance of forces, but the minority is seldom so weak on a major issue that it has to accept a once-and-for-all decision. The formula must usually offer them the chance of later reversal, keeping the big issue alive.[32]

But it was not always so. In fact at the time of Schattschneider's study the authority to set specific tariff rates still rested entirely with Congress. It was only with the passage of the Reciprocal Trade Agreements Act of 1934 that Congress delegated this authority to the executive branch, a move calculated to reduce the influence of pressure groups on the passage of tariff legislation. Consequently it should come as no surprise that such groups do seem less important in the passage of subsequent tariff legislation. What Bauer, Pool, and Dexter observe as the virtual irrelevance of groups to the tariff issue in the contemporary era may more properly be understood as the virtual irrelevance of Congress to the tariff issue in this period. The politics of the contemporary Sugar Act demonstrates quite conclusively that Congress when it chooses can remain very relevant indeed for such issues.

Thus the heart of this dimension lies in Salisbury and Heinz's distinction between structural and allocative policy outcomes. They recognized the error in assuming that the typical outcome of the legislative process is merely to establish the rules by which the group struggle will continue. Delegation represents only one possible outcome of the legislative process; any attempt to develop a typology of policy processes must come to grips with the fact that interest groups will at least some of the time receive an explicit allocation of tangible benefits.

The issue is not precisely one of allocation versus delegation, however, for delegation can itself be a form of allocation if the guidelines for implementation are sufficiently explicit. The fundamental distinction is the one Lowi has drawn between policy-without-law and rule-of-law. Policy-without-law results whenever legislation grants administrators broad discretion: whenever the categories of jurisdiction are not clearly defined or the standards guiding enforcement are left vague. Rule-of-law results whenever this discretion is removed through clear standards and definitions, so that the choice between indulged and deprived is thus made explicit.[33]

Salisbury and Heinz recognized the appeal of such ambiguity to policymakers and suggested that policymakers would often resort to structural outcomes in order to reduce decision costs.[34] Lowi argued that delegation has become pathological in the modern state because it offers a substitute for the hard choices that ought to be faced by representatives subject to electoral sanction. Through the delegation of broad, discretionary authority, legislators not only avoid having to choose among conflicting interests, with the attendant risk of electoral punishment by the losers, but through the appearance of reform they may successfully appease those demanding change.[35] Murray Edelman has also observed this phenomenon, stressing the symbolic appeal of the administrative system and of legal language in restoring the quiescence of mass publics. He argues that much legislation ostensibly regulating business is ambiguous by design:

The ambiguity is neither incidental nor accidental. For lawyers and their organized clients, it is the most useful attribute of legal language. To those directly involved, the meaning of the law constantly and observably changes with variations in group influence.[36]

Indeed the availability of delegation as a strategy helps to explain why congressmen faced with conflicting pressures on the tariff seemed free to vote as they pleased. Even for well-organized groups active on the issue, the determination of self-interest was by no means as straightforward a matter as had commonly been assumed.[37] In view of the difficulties many firms faced in deciding whether or not to seek tariffs at all, it should come as no surprise that they should find it even harder to assess their interests in an ambiguous delegation of negotiating authority to the Tariff Commission. Thus it was not the multiplicity of interests per se that gave congressmen considerable latitude on this issue; it was the complexity of self-interest and the availability of delegation, with its potential for obfuscating the outcome.

Of course Congress may also respond by passing no bill at all, although in so doing it may be making an explicit choice among contending groups by denying demands for change. There are thus three alternative supply patterns. Congress may respond to a given demand pattern by passing no bill at all, by passing an ambiguous and discretionary bill (structural, policy-without-law), or by making an explicit allocation (rule-of-law).

The two possible demand patterns and three alternative supply patterns combine to yield a typology of six policy processes, as shown in Table 3. Insofar as the categories making up both underlying dimensions are exhaustive and mutually exclusive, these six processes should be quite distinct and comprehensive.

In the distributive arena, a group or coalition of groups seeks an explicit allocation of benefits from Congress and, in the absence of attentive opposition, gets its way. There need be no losers in this arena, as potentially conflicting interests can be accommodated through logrolling. This is the classic realm of pork-barrel politics, or what Mayhew has termed *particularized benefits.*[38] As Lowi recognized, this is the issue arena Schattschneider described for the tariff in 1930. The stakes of the legislative process, for those actively participating in it, are non-zero-sum. Politicians and producers cooperate as benefits to the producers are drawn from outside the legislative game, for example, from inactive and inattentive consumers.

Table 3

| | Demand Pattern | |
Supply Pattern	Consensual (Non-zero-sum)	Conflictual (Zero-sum)
No bill	Nondecision Barrier 1: community values	Nondecision Barrier 2: institutions and processes
Delegation (policy-without-law)	Self-regulation (legitimized autonomy)	Regulation (extension of group conflict)
Allocation (rule-of-law)	Distribution (pork-barrel politics)	Redistribution (resource transfers)

This cooperation is accomplished by passing on the costs of tariff protection to consumers in the form of higher prices or, in the case of subsidies or of rivers and harbors legislation, by raising taxes or inflating the currency.

The key to interest group success in this arena is to keep the relationship among the active participants non-zero-sum and cooperative by drawing the spoils from unorganized groups not active on the issue. The "infinite disaggregability of benefits" Lowi cited as characteristic of this issue arena is really just one way in which this cooperative relationship can be preserved. If n players encounter opposition, the benefit pie can easily be broken up $n + 1$ ways in order to avoid conflict. What makes such an accommodation possible, however, is not simply the infinite disaggregability of benefits; clearly n players opposed by some larger number m players will not take kindly to dividing the spoils $m + n$ ways. Rather, distributive processes are made possible by the exclusion of some potential players from the game so that the benefit pie can be enlarged at the expense of these inactives whenever necessary to accommodate a potential rival. This is the essence of pork-barrel politics.

Examples abound of "subgovernments" or "iron triangles" posing vexing exceptions to the new conventional wisdom regarding interest groups: the Sugar Act, Stanley Surrey's case study of the politics of special tax provisions, Arthur Maass's classic study of the Corps of Engineers and water resource politics, John Ferejohn's *Pork Barrel Politics*, and most import quotas, acreage allotments, and subsidies of all sorts.[39] Indeed Mayhew has presented evidence that in 1972—presumably as typical as any other year—more than 70 percent of all roll calls could not plausibly be regarded as closely contested, which suggests that consensual demand patterns are far more common than Bauer, Pool, and Dexter ever would have guessed.[40]

In the regulatory arena, by contrast, groups seeking legislation encounter stiff resistance from threatened interests. The challenging groups are strong enough to force some congressional response but not strong enough to obtain a clear-cut redistribution of resources. The group conflict is not resolved in the visible public arena; instead it is passed on to be accommodated in the bureaucracy or the courts. The crucial variable is whether the congressional grant of authority permits administrative or judicial discretion, for agencies receiving such discretionary mandates become the scene of renewed group struggle. Whether the ostensible intent of the legislation's original sponsors is actually achieved will be entirely contingent on the outcome of this subsequent administrative struggle. This contingency is made inevitable by the collective decision of Congress to avoid choice; such bills, in short, are ambiguous by design.

Edelman has emphasized the susceptibility of unorganized publics to such symbolic reassurances, observing that, though tangible resources are typically not delivered to such groups as promised in regulatory statutes, they exhibit no awareness of their deprivation.[41] Examples abound in this vein of regulatory "capture" by clientele groups, but the palliative effects of such symbolic delegations of legislative authority are not confined to the unorganized. As noted, congressmen were made free by the activity of organized groups on both sides of the tariff issue only because the considerable ambiguity shrouding the self-interest of most firms made it possible to avoid a clear choice through the delegation of rate-setting authority to the Tariff Commission. Similarly the reluctance of Congress to choose between business and labor interests has resulted in institutionalized representation for each on the National Labor Relations Board. The persistence of the NLRB as an exception to the "capture" theory of administrative regulation is directly attributable to Congress's unwillingness to make even a thinly disguised choice between these two competing and well-organized interests in the granting of discretionary authority to the board.[42]

It must be stressed that, despite the label for this category, examples are by no means confined to the realm of business regulation and moreover that not all instances of what is ostensibly business regulation would fall here. The Community Action Program of the War on Poverty provides a classic case. Potentially serious conflicts over the goals of the program were averted by creating community action boards with an ambiguous mandate to secure "maximum feasible participation" by all "relevant community groups." Thus it was left unclear exactly who was to participate, how much they were to participate, or precisely what they were empowered to do.[43] Likewise Frances Fox Piven and Richard Cloward have persuasively demonstrated that much of the more traditional social welfare policy can only be properly understood as regulative, not only because such programs as Aid to Families with Dependent Children (AFDC) have generally been designed to control the poor rather than to attain a more equitable distribution of income, but in my terms, because they involve the delegation of broad discretion to administrators. The logic underlying their enactment indeed parallels that leading to the regulatory policies just reviewed, as congressmen faced with a conflictual demand pattern have responded by delegating the responsibility for choice elsewhere. On the one hand the potential beneficiaries pose a threat of social disorder in demanding some action; on the other hand middle-class constituents must bear the burden of any programs enacted. Although at least some members of this latter constituency may sympathize with the plight of the poor at least some of the time, there will be virtual unanimity among the middle class in stressing the work ethic and opposing welfare "handouts" for the undeserving. Thus the creation of large welfare bureaucracies has served a twofold purpose for congressmen: avoiding choice between the conflicting groups in such a way as to make both sides think they have won, and defusing the issue by making it appear amenable, at least eventually, to bureaucratic expertise.[44]

Much of what passes for business regulation can also be better understood as self-regulatory. Clearly this is what Stigler had in mind in suggesting that oligopolistic industries will in fact seek regulation in an effort to fix prices and restrict entry while avoiding antitrust prosecution. The Civil Aeronautics Board, for example, was created largely in response to airline industry demands for protection and subsidization on "infant industry" grounds. Entry was severely restricted, and the rate board functioned until quite recently as little more than a rubber stamp for the airline cartel.[45] Perhaps the most clear-cut example, as noted by Salisbury and Heinz, is occupational licensure, whereby professions seek legislation that will establish and legitimize their autonomy from government interference. The consensual nature of the demand pattern in occupational licensing was verified empirically by Stigler in a cross-state study.[46]

The National Recovery Administration, with its emphasis on industrial self-government, provides a quintessential illustration of the self-regulatory arena. Incorporated into this legislation were at least three conflicting underlying conceptions in the form of elements designed to appeal to the antitrust tradition, to those who believed in centralized planning, and to those who favored some form of "business commonwealth." The natural antagonism of management to the collective bargaining provisions of the statute was effectively neutralized by the business elements' ready willingness to accept as a quid pro quo the power to fix prices and restrict output through trade association activity. Thus the act appeared to be all things to all men and easily passed with only a handful of dissenting votes. This contrived consensus quickly collapsed, however, as virtually all sides found something to which to object in the administration of the act. Renewal of the act in 1935 seemed highly unlikely even before the Supreme Court's Schecter decision, which overturned the act for its blatant delegation of legislative functions to business and labor groups under the guise of advisory boards.[47]

By contrast, in the redistributive arena Congress actually makes an explicit choice among contending groups. Whereas the distributive arena also involves the specific allocation of benefits, the distinction between these two issue arenas lies in the demand pattern that gives rise to the allocation. Whereas the stakes can be kept non-zero-sum in the distributive realm by drawing the spoils from inactive participants outside the legislative process, in the redistributive arena both the potential winners and losers are attentive and aware of the stakes, thus making the legislative conflict inherently zero-sum in form.

Instances of genuinely redistributive policy processes are extremely rare. As Lowi suggested, congressmen confronted with such conflicting interests typically seek to avoid the responsibility for choice through some form of legislative delegation. Thus, as noted, most welfare programs are better understood as regulatory. Public housing and urban renewal appear to be distributive because the participants in the legislative process—builders, lending institutions—all gain at the expense of the inactive poor who, though the ostensible beneficiaries, find themselves displaced and forced to resettle at higher rents in housing units frequently inferior to those they left.[48] Social security and Medicare are only marginally redistributive at best. Central to their enactment was the calculated narrowing of their applicability to the aged and the disguising of the true nature of the income transfer through the adoption of a highly regressive form of financing.[49] The Nixon Family Assistance Plan would have had profoundly redistributive consequences but was defeated.[50]

It must be clearly understood, however, that changes in the distribution of income are not confined to policies explicitly defined as redistributive, either here or in the original Lowi typology. In the distributive arena, for example, the redistributive effects are immediate and direct. Subsidies, tax loopholes, import quotas, price supports, and water projects—classic pork-barrel projects—all allocate tangible benefits and thus directly affect the distribution of income by transferring resources from certain groups in society to other groups, but the incidence of these transfers is concealed. It may be good politics to identify the gainers from such policies, but the victims must be kept unaware of the real stakes if the demand pattern is to be kept consensual. Even delegative outcomes ultimately produce some change in the distribution of income, although just what their effect will be is typically left unclear by design. Self-regulatory policies, like occupational licensing, operate to increase the profits going to the professions or industries obtaining legitimized autonomy; similarly business regulation often operates to redistribute income from consumers to clientele groups successful in capturing the agencies charged with regulating them.

The key to interest group success on such issues is to control the scope of conflict. The central role of deception cannot be overstated, as the manipulation of symbols to maintain political quiescence provides a special case of what Schattschneider has termed *privatization of conflict.* Schattschneider believed that government's proper role was to act as a counterbalance to the inequities inevitably generated by the private sphere.[51] While he recognized the incentives for the winners in the private sphere to avoid socializing conflict, he overlooked the equally important advantages such groups possessed in approaching government in seeking to expand or consolidate their gains. Recent evidence that all forms of political participation vary directly with income and education suggests in fact that the losers in the private sphere may well be the least likely to approach government.[52] Government may thus act not to counterbalance the inequities generated by the private sector but to widen them.

Ironically then, policies significantly modifying the existing distribution of income are most likely to occur almost exclusively outside the redistributive arena, and their impact is typically to reinforce the preexisting inequities rather than to rectify them. In sum, organized groups seeking governmental largesse in the distributive and self-regulatory arenas will strive to keep these conflicts privatized, often succeeding in keeping the "audience" unaware that a conflict even exists. At the same time, potentially redistributive policies will either be rather easily deflected into the regulatory arena where organized groups can dominate administration or be prevented from surfacing at all.

The final two arenas represent additions to the Lowi and Salisbury schemes because they recognize that the policy process may seemingly yield no outcome at all. Such an eventuality is not at all trivial, however, and in no way implies inactivity or that power has not been exercised. Peter Bachrach and Morton Baratz have identified a "second face of power," whereby entrenched elites suppress conflict and limit the agenda of actual decision making to "safe" issues.[53] Some fine case studies have pointed to the importance of such "nondecisions," most notably Matthew Crenson's *The Un-politics of Air Pollution,* and Bruce Oppenheimer's *Oil and the Congressional Process.*[54]

Bachrach and Baratz, it should be noted, identified two distinct barriers to the formal decision-making arena (and thus two distinctive forms of non-decision making): that of community values and that of institutions and processes.[55] There are thus two conceptually separable phenomena to be explained, although the classification of observed cases may prove problematic. On the one hand inaction may stem from an apparent value consensus in favor of some aspect of the status quo. I say "apparent" because an issue may fail to surface for a variety of reasons: a genuine satisfaction with existing conditions, a failure to perceive the existence of a problem, a sense of fear or futility that prevents those affected from raising the issue, and even the manipulation of dominant values and symbols to make demands for change seem illegitimate. In any event the issue has not reached the institutional agenda; there is no demand for action and none is forthcoming.

On the other hand legislative inaction may simply reflect a challenge to the existing order by groups too weak to force concessions. Here the issue has reached the institutional agenda but has been blocked by successful defensive lobbying. As both Truman and Dexter have observed, most lobbying is in fact defensive.[56] Issues must pass through multiple veto points as they move along the congressional obstacle course, so they may be defeated at any stage. In this regard Bachrach and Baratz have done little more than label a phenomenon long recognized by scholars of the legislative process. Reformers have long lamented the antimajoritarian implications of such institutions as the filibuster, the Rules Committee, the seniority system, and even the separation of powers, all of which they thought characteristically produced stalemate and inaction.[57] With the exception of Roosevelt's first one hundred days and Johnson's legislative successes in 1964 and 1965, deadlock does seem to be the norm, at least for the president's program. By and large, reformers have had slim and uncertain majorities at best. At worst, divided control of the White House and Congress have produced truncated majorities, making stalemate almost inevitable.[58]

Crenson's study of pollution policy provides a particularly striking example of an issue failing to overcome the first barrier to the formal decision-making arena. Some cities were inactive because they had no pollution problem. In other cities, pollution, although a serious problem, was odorless and colorless and thus not perceived. Where pollution *was* perceived, political parties had no incentive to raise the issue because it offered no opportunities for the dispensing of private favors. Interestingly, Crenson found little evidence of the overt suppression of conflict. Most often the issue was not raised at all as a result of what he termed *indirect influence:* Relevant actors perceived industrial groups as powerful, assumed they would be opposed, and thus regarded efforts to raise the issue as futile. Yet where the issue was raised at all, it tended to be raised successfully. Regulation would be imposed, and political parties would finally pick up the issue, offering relaxation of enforcement in return for political support.[59]

As described by Oppenheimer, the oil depletion allowance provides an equally striking instance of the manipulation of institutions and processes to block legislative action. Prior to 1969 the oil industry was able to kill all proposals to reduce the depletion allowance in the Ways and Means Committee. Indeed through the sympathetic intervention of the Speaker, Sam Rayburn, the industry had obtained a virtual veto over appointments to that committee. In 1969, when the House finally passed a bill cutting the depletion allowance from 27½ percent to 20 percent, the industry successfully appealed to the Senate Finance Committee to limit the cut to the 22 percent level. This maneuver, combined with a change in the price measure employed by the industry to compute gross income, rendered the impact of the cut minimal. At the same time, the industry used the cut in the depletion allowance as an issue in lobbying for the preservation of other tax shelters.[60]

The National Rifle Association has been consistently successful in invoking the constitutionally guaranteed right to bear arms to block periodic efforts at gun control, even in the wake of such dramatic focusing events as the assassinations of President Kennedy, Robert Kennedy, and Martin Luther King. Nadel has argued that recent consumer protection acts also provide instances of this second face of power because producers have successfully prevented any fundamental reforms, limiting their apparent legislative defeats to quintessentially symbolic delegations of authority to previously captured regulatory agencies. The 1962 drug amendments, for example, grew out of a Kefauver committee investigation into pharmaceutical industry profit levels. Industry opposition coupled with presidential indifference to the issue would have been sufficient to block legislative action altogether had it not been for the well-timed thalidomide scandal. Even so, the amendments as enacted were relatively mild, and the issue of administered pricing was never raised again.[61]

As McConnell, Lowi, and Nadel have all observed, public policymaking is by no means confined to formal public institutions. Binding public policy can also be made by ostensibly private organizations, as when farmers, acting autonomously, make decisions affecting price and output or when corporations make decisions regarding occupational safety or product availability.[62] In Nadel's terms, the nondecision arenas merely fail to produce formal legislative outcomes; instead, their outcomes constitute instances of what he would term purely private policymaking, whereas the distributive, regulatory, and self-regulatory arenas typically represent varying mixes of private and public authority.[63] Only in the redistributive arena do formal authorities make explicit choices between the indulged and the deprived, with examples of such pure public policymaking being few and far between. Thus Lowi's polemic in *The End of Liberalism* and *The Politics of Disorder* can be seen as a call for more formal redistributive processes because the distributive, regulative, self-regulative, and even the nondecision arenas all represent variants of interest group liberalism insofar as they all delegate public power to private groups.

It would be unwise to make too much of this, however, for it must be remembered that nondecisions may also represent defeats for organized interests—including corporations—seeking governmental largesse in the distributive and self-regulative arenas. For example, corporations left to their own devices are free to form cartels, set administered prices, and manipulate production, as Nadel argues. In the absence of government intervention all these actions will be contingent on the successful acquisition and maintenance of market power, without which potential competitors may be attracted by excess profits. Cartels sooner or later tend to collapse of their own accord, as each of the colluding parties has incentive to cheat on the agreement. Price fixing may be attacked under the antitrust laws.[64]

By contrast, in the self-regulatory arena, government creates and legitimates market power by granting autonomy to professions or industries, allowing them to restrict entry and to control prices and output. This autonomy is sought from government precisely because it is nonexistent or unstable without the coercive power of the state. Self-regulatory delegations thus need not reflect economic market power; they merely represent concessions to political market power. What such groups are too weak to secure privately, they may be strong and cohesive enough to obtain publicly.

In the same way, government in the distributive arena in effect subsidizes some activities at the expense of others. All too often there is no economic justification for these subsidies; they merely reflect the relative clout of some groups over others. Witness the Corps of Engineers and rivers and harbors legislation, or the domestic sugar industry's invocation of national defense needs as a rationale for production quotas and stiff restrictions on imports. An even more striking example is provided by the oil industry's similar manipulation of the national security rationale to obtain oil import quotas in the 1950s. Arguing the need for a thriving domestic industry in case of war, the industry thus obtained import restrictions that would have the effect of unnecessarily and prematurely depleting domestic supplies, thus rendering the country all the more dependent on foreign supplies in case of war. In the distributive arena as well, government intervention thus all too often involves the creation and institutionalization of economic privilege through the exercise of political market power.

In sum, the two nondecision arenas account for those instances in which no legislation is passed. Much has been made of the power of "elites" to suppress conflict by controlling access to the formal decision-making agenda; yet such nondecisions may also reflect the failure of such groups to obtain the devolution of power. Under such circumstances private power may still be exercised but without the strengthening and stabilizing support of the state. Autonomy as exercised in the nondecision arenas, although significant, is fundamentally different from that formally sanctioned by government. In the nondecision arenas groups exist in a Hobbesian world, forced to survive in an unstable and potentially hostile environment. In the distributive and self-regulatory arenas, groups can legitimately restrict entry and dominate policy subsystems. Often much the same thing is true in the regulatory arena as well, as groups can recoup their legislative losses by "capturing" agencies and dominating administration. It is in this sense that Lowi could assert that chaos is better than a bad law.

The typology just reviewed, although suggestive, can ultimately do no more than just suggest the appropriate directions for asking more fundamental questions. Like any other typology, it may aid in the categorization of legislative cases, thus helping to bring some order out of apparent chaos. Classification represents only a preliminary stage in theorizing, however; a typology is explanatory only when it is possible to predict accurately the eventual placement of a given case into one of the categories. Any typology that fails to provide a theory adequate to explain its underlying dimensions simply begs the more fundamental questions of interest to the researcher. What is needed is a theory of political markets and political market failure.

III

Exchange Theories
of Political Markets

The foundation for a theory of political markets has already been laid. In recent years a variety of scholars, mostly economists, have attempted to operationalize and test exchange theories that would explain departures from economic policy prescriptions in terms of pressure group activity. The seminal effort in this regard is Stigler's "economic theory" of business regulation.[1] Two other economists, Charles McPherson and Jonathan J. Pincus, have employed Stigler's theory with mixed success to explain tariff policy.[2] Most recently, two political scientists, Salamon and Siegfried, have attempted to measure corporate success in obtaining preferential tax treatment.[3]

Any theory of political markets must address both the demand for and the supply of public policies. In explaining demand pattern, all these theories begin with Olson's public goods theory of collective action, for Olson suggests that organization is far from automatic even for groups with common interests.[4] The crucial variable in his analysis is group size: small, concentrated groups will be far more likely than large, diffuse groups to organize and lobby. Salamon and Siegfried hypothesize in this same vein that industrial concentration will tend to be translated into both economic and political market power. These studies all fail, however, to make any distinction between consensual and conflictual demand patterns; yet only when this distinction is made explicit do their seemingly inconsistent findings take on a coherent pattern.

On the supply side, these exchange theories all assume that congressmen more or less passively deliver public policies to pressure groups in return for their electoral support. Insurmountable measurement problems preclude the operationalization of such fundamental variables as interest group intensities and strategies, the complexity of self-interest, and the latitude available to congressmen. As a result these studies treat the terms of the exchange between legislators and lobbyists as quite one-sided and thus fail to provide an adequate response to Bauer, Pool, and Dexter's call for a transactional conception of interest groups and Congress.

A transactional theory is incompatible with simplistic notions of corporate power. There has been a resurgence of interest in the extent of corporate power in recent years in both semipopular and scholarly writings. The view that corporate power is excessive has recently gained scholarly respectability in the writings of Nadel, Lindblom, and Salamon and Siegfried.[5] It is far more useful to strive for a broader, more comprehensive theory of political market failure. Such a theory must recognize that exchanges between legislators and lobbyists are mutually beneficial; and in so doing, it must go beyond Olson's theory of group formation and incorporate the exchange theories of Salisbury and Wilson.[6] Moreover, such a theory must go on to explain the exchange relationship between legislator and lobbyist as well as that between interest group entrepreneurs and their memberships.

GROUP SIZE AND THE FREE RIDER PROBLEM

Olson is concerned with the incentives for organization and collective activity facing groups with common interests. He focuses primarily on organization for the purpose of obtaining narrow, quantifiable economic benefits, such as tariffs and favorable regulatory legislation, although his theory may be extended to any other type of benefit that may be converted into economic units of measurement.[7] He demonstrates that even if every member of a group would benefit from collective action the individual members may well find it irrational to participate.

He begins by making a fundamental distinction between collective benefits (or public goods) and selective benefits (private goods). Once a collective benefit has been provided for a group, it cannot be withheld from any member of the group. Consumption of such a good is in no way tied to contributions toward its provision; a tariff or tax exemption obtained by a single firm inevitably benefits all other firms in the industry whether or not they participate in lobbying activity. Hence public goods are vulnerable to what he terms the *free rider problem*, creating an incentive for each member to withhold their contributions and hope someone else will provide the good. This problem is particularly acute for large and diffuse groups, where the analogy with a perfectly competitive market of price-taking firms is especially apt. Each individual's share of the collective benefit is quite small, and no single individual's contribution will by itself substantially affect the good's provision, so the incentive to be a free rider dominates all other considerations.

For small groups, however, the share of the collective benefit going to each member may be sufficient to outweigh their shares of the cost of providing the good. Even within large groups some individuals may stand to gain a great deal more than others from the provision of the good because they are larger and will consume more of it if provided or simply because they like it more. Such individuals may find it worthwhile to obtain the good for themselves and to tolerate the parasitic behavior of free riders. In both these cases at least some of the collective benefit will be provided, although the amount will be suboptimal and the burden-sharing inequitable.[8]

Finally, collective benefits may also be provided as a by-product activity of organizations already formed for the purpose of obtaining selective benefits, which can be withheld from noncontributors.[9] For example labor unions became effective according to Olson only with the advent of compulsory union membership, which meant that consumption of union benefits (higher wages, better working conditions) could be withheld from nonmembers. Thus unions initially focused on providing selective benefits to their memberships and only later undertook lobbying activity for collective benefits from government.[10]

In short, Olson persuasively demonstrates that some groups are much more likely than others to organize and obtain collective benefits. Only very small groups and "privileged groups"—those in which some members have an interest sufficient to induce them to provide the benefit for the entire group—will be able to overcome the free rider problem. Unless previously organized to provide selective benefits for members, large, diffuse groups will be acutely susceptible to this problem, and will be unlikely to organize at all.

Stigler has argued that it is more accurate to refer to a "cheap rider" problem, for no ride is ever entirely free. When a given group member chooses not to contribute toward the provision of a collective benefit, he runs the risk that it will not be provided at all or be provided in a form or an amount that he does not favor.[11] Thus in loosely oligopolistic industries constituting privileged groups, the few large firms can easily threaten potential cheap riders with the possibility that the provision of the collective good will not otherwise reflect their interests. In this way Stigler is able to account for the formation and survival of trade associations in a variety of industries that would otherwise appear too large and diffuse to overcome the free rider problem. Wilson has presented evidence that many trade associations attract a stable core of large members without ever successfully attracting all of the peripheral firms in the industry. In fact these smaller firms are much harder to recruit and exhibit a high degree of turnover, as the larger firms are better able to afford the membership dues.[12] Nevertheless these cheap riders contribute by their dispersion and often their very weakness to the lobbying success of such privileged groups.

ECONOMIC THEORIES OF POLITICAL MARKETS

Efforts to develop an exchange theory of lobbying have come primarily from economists, following Stigler's effort to develop an "economic theory" of business regulation. Previous theories had been unable to account for the frequently observed tendency for oligopolistic industries actively to seek regulation. The early public interest theory of regulation assumed that government action represented an efficient response to observed market failure; yet a closer inspection of the evidence reveals no consistent correlation between market failure and the enactment of regulatory legislation. Moreover when prior market structure is taken into account, it becomes apparent that price regulation seldom benefits consumers; rather, producer protection is the norm. Regulation of natural monopolies, such as public utilities, fails to bring about significant reductions in prices or in the exercise of price discrimination against consumers and in favor of large industrial customers. In oligopolistic industries (railroads and airlines, for example) regulation typically results in increased prices and all too often merely legitimates price discrimination in favor of organized customer or supplier groups.[13]

The traditional capture theory attempted to account for such behavior by positing a life cycle for regulatory agencies. In response to scandal, aroused public opinion, strong executive leadership, or activity by aggrieved groups, regulation would be thrust upon an industry. At first enforcement would be vigorous and in the consumer interest. Struggles would ensue over appropriations and subsequent legislation to amend the agency's powers or resources. In the courts the constitutionality of the agency's mandate would be challenged. Gradually, as public attention inevitably waned, the agency would be captured by those industry groups it ostensibly regulated. Samuel Huntington has documented the passing of Interstate Commerce Commission (ICC) through just such a cycle.[14]

Unfortunately this theory was powerless to explain numerous instances in which oligopolistic industries actively sought regulation and no such life cycle ensued. In these instances capture was immediate and apparently intended by the framers of the legislation; the Civil Aeronautics Board provides a classic example.[15] Stigler suggests that rational, self-interested firms will find it in their interest to cooperate in obtaining favorable regulatory legislation. In Olson's terms, regulation provides a number of collective benefits for such industries; by legalizing collusion, price fixing, and barriers to entry, it shores up otherwise unstable cartels.[16]

Stigler subjects this profit-maximizing theory of regulation to empirical test in a cross-state regression analysis of occupational licensing. The dependent variable, a measure of lobbying success, is the length of time it took each profession in his sample to obtain licensing authority. The two independent variables, which measure lobbying resources, are size of the occupation (and hence potential voting power) and concentration of the occupation in large cities, which should be directly related to lobbying success insofar as the costs of mobilizing support should be less for geographically concentrated occupations. In general the results are in the expected directions, although the regression coefficients are not consistently significant for all the occupations examined; the total variance explained for each of the occupations was, moreover, quite low, never exceeding .329.[17]

Stigler's theory was next applied to the tariff by McPherson, one of Stigler's doctoral students. Following Olson he assumed that very small groups and privileged groups would be more likely than large, diffuse groups to organize and lobby for tariff protection. To operationalize this group-size variable, he employed the concentration ratio, a concept developed in the field of industrial organization to measure market concentration. This ratio is simply the percentage of sales within an industry accounted for by the four largest sellers.[18] Not all scholars of industrial organization agree that this operationalization adequately measures the concept of oligopoly, but it does seem an ideal measure of Olson's group-size variable. Small and privileged groups should have very high concentration ratios, whereas large, diffuse industries should exhibit very low ones.

McPherson then hypothesized a direct relationship between this group-size variable, among others, and lobbying success as measured by the absolute level of tariff protection: Small and privileged groups would obtain high tariffs; large groups, hampered by the free rider problem, would receive little or no protection. Unfortunately this hypothesis is not borne out by his statistical analysis. Using data for 1954 and 1963 McPherson regresses the group-size variable against the nominal tariff rate in combination with a variety of additional measures of lobbying resources, such as number of firms in the industry (i.e., potential voting power), industry employment and labor intensity (measures of the size of the work force and hence of voting power), and geographic concentration of industry employment (as with Stigler, a measure of the relative difficulty of mobilizing support). The concentration ratio was not significantly related to tariff level by itself (the simple correlation for 1954 was .02 and for 1963, $-.01$), and it remained insignificant in all the regressions combining various independent variables. The remaining independent variables fared no better; by no measure did heavily protected industries show evidence of being politically more powerful than industries with low tariff levels. In all, the results could hardly have been more discouraging.[19]

By contrast, Pincus found considerable support for such a political exchange model when applied to the tariff of 1824—a very different period than that observed by McPherson. Regressing against nominal tariff level a variety of measures of group size, concentration, and resources comparable to those employed by McPherson, Pincus concluded:

> In 1824, the structure of the tariff was influenced by the willingness of proprietors to bring pressure, and by the responsiveness of Congressmen. Both pressure group activity and political bargaining were involved. . . . The strong pressure groups had few proprietors, in relatively easy distances for communication, and able to capture for themselves most of the quasi-rents from the tariffs. However, pressure was brought to bear within a political system of geographical representation. Evidently, although pressure came mainly from the relatively few larger establishments, the mere existence of numbers of smaller, dispersed firms helped lend weight in Congress, so industries with many establishments and with sales spread more evenly across states or with establishments in many states obtained higher duties.[20]

These results, although far from perfect, were quite impressive; the total variance explained by the variables in combination was over 60 percent.[21]

Salamon and Siegfried have made perhaps the most explicit argument that economic power translates into political power as well. They attempted to relate a variety of measures of market structure to lobbying success. Their dependent variable is each industry's tax avoidance rate, defined as the extent to which its average tax payment falls below the standard corporate tax rate. A variety of market-structure measures are employed as independent variables: size of the median firm (dollar assets), size of the industry (number of employees), four-firm concentration ratio, average profit rate, and geographic concentration.[22] Multiple regression analysis was employed, although the independent variables admittedly suffered from severe problems of multicollinearity.[23]

Median firm size was found to be significantly related to tax avoidance rate, suggesting that market power is in fact correlated with political clout. Profit rate is inversely related to tax avoidance rate, however, as is the four-firm concentration ratio, data the authors interpret to mean that such industries seek to maintain a low profile politically to avoid calling attention to their size and profit levels.[24] The remaining variables interact in a complex manner discussed more fully later. Unfortunately all five variables combined account for only 16 percent of the variation by industry in tax avoidance rate.[25]

These findings are reinforced by a more detailed examination of the petroleum refining industry's lobbying success. Breaking tax avoidance rate down by size of firm reveals that the largest firms tend to be the most successful in obtaining and taking advantage of loopholes. Moreover a cross-state regression analysis reveals that the industry tends to do best in those states where it is largest (measured in terms of value added to state income and of number of employees) and where it is dominated by large firms.[26] Thus Salamon and Siegfried conclude that corporate political power is clearly a function of economic market structure.

INTEGRATING THE FINDINGS

In light of the typology of policy processes developed in the previous chapter, it is clear that all these studies err in assuming that there is a single, typical legislative process to be explained. Not surprisingly the empirical evidence for these theories seems inconclusive at best, consisting of strong support in some cases, mixed or weak results in others. Once it is recognized that these studies have in fact focused on distinctively different legislative arenas, clearer patterns begin to emerge.

For example the two studies of tariff policy by Pincus and McPherson focus on two distinctively different historical periods. Prior to 1934 specific tariff levels were still set in Congress. As Schattschneider convincingly documented, the tariff issue in that period remained distributive in nature; overwhelming coalitions of industries sought protection, and potential conflict was accommodated through logrolling. With the passage of the Reciprocal Trade Agreements Act of 1934, however, Congress delegated the rate-setting responsibility to the Tariff Commission, permanently shifting the whole pattern of politics to the regulatory arena. Moreover, as Bauer, Pool, and Dexter observed, by the 1950s, when McPherson examined the issue, the arena was highly conflictual, with hundreds of groups active on both sides of the issue.[27]

This shift in demand pattern is by itself sufficient to account for the failure of McPherson's study. Any relationships tested—whether between lobbying success and group size, geographic concentration, or whatever—would apply equally to those groups active on *both* sides of the issue. Thus any straightforward correlation of tariff levels across industries with these various measures of organizational size and resources would ignore the fact that not all industries in the sample actually sought higher tariffs. Nominal tariff level is thus not a valid measure of lobbying success. Moreover, after the Smoot-Hawley tariff of 1930, almost every item had some positive duty, and most can be classified as heavily protected.[28] Beatrice Vaccara classified industries into five protection classes ranging from unprotected to heavily protected; approximately three-quarters of all those she classified fell into one of the two most heavily protected categories, showing that there is not a great deal of variation in the nominal tariff rate across industries.

More significantly, though nominal tariff level may have reflected group strength in 1930, it does not do so accurately now. Since the Reciprocal Trade Agreements Act of 1934 the tariff issue has revolved around proposed reductions in the basic 1930 levels. Thus even if McPherson were not misguided in attempting to correlate group size with lobbying success directly, he would have needed data on tariff *reductions*, rather than nominal tariff rates, to assess group strength for the years he examined. McPherson did not have these data, although he approximated them through the use of cross-time regression analyses—change in concentration ratio against change in tariff. Such an approximation is crude at best, as McPherson himself admitted.[29] In any event, the relationship to be expected should be between group strength at a given point in time (not the change in that strength, as he suggests) and the group's capacity to forestall large reductions in its tariff level. Thus a simple cross-time regression is misguided, and the insignificance of his results here tells us nothing whatsoever about the relationship between group size and size of tariff reductions.

In 1824, by contrast, the tariff issue remained distributive; virtually all groups active on the issue sought higher tariffs, and the relationship between the various independent variables and nominal tariff levels should thus be susceptible to straightforward measurement and analysis, accounting for the striking success of Pincus's study. Pincus explicitly recognized this, noting that:

> The Tariff Act of 1824 more faithfully reflected pressure group successes than do contemporary tariffs because today, besides tariffs and quotas, firms seek various subsidies, tax credits, military procurements, freeways, etc., some of which might be more easily secured or more attractive than import protection, even for import-competing industries. In other words, McPherson's dependent variable—nominal tariff rates—is only part of what his independent variables explain.[30]

The politics of special tax provisions is likewise distributive, which makes possible the relative success of Salamon and Siegfried's study as well. They mistakenly assert that the issue is redistributive, on the grounds that tax loopholes do undeniably redistribute resources. This is only one part of what makes an issue redistributive, as income redistribution just as clearly takes place in the distributive arena as well. In the latter arena, however, the demand pattern is kept consensual by excluding the potential victims from the process—by keeping what Schattschneider would term the "audience" unaware of the very existence of a conflict.[31] For the participants the stakes remain cooperative, as conflict can always be accommodated by logrolling at the expense of those inactive and inattentive on the issue. Seen in these terms the politics of tax avoidance is quintessentially distributive. As Surrey has shown, political activity on this issue bears a strong resemblance to that surrounding the tariff in

Schattschneider's era: reciprocal noninterference among groups seeking tax exemptions, logrolling, and the lack of effective opposition from organized groups.[32] Indeed Salamon and Siegfried's own data suggest that there is little active opposition to such loopholes. Those highly profitable firms that do not really need special tax treatment and who might be expected to be in opposition tend instead to maintain a low profile in order to avoid calling attention to themselves.[33] Thus, once again, the dependent variable chosen, tax avoidance rate, provides a valid measure of lobbying success, and the relationships between it and the various independent variables are therefore straightforward and readily observable.

Occupational licensing, as argued in the previous chapter, is self-regulatory in nature. Groups seek autonomy from outside interference and, more importantly, the power to restrict entry and thus to limit competition. Stigler's data suggest that the demand pattern here is typically consensual. Groups encountering no opposition or those with clientele large, diffuse, and thus vulnerable to the free rider problem tended to obtain licensing authority early and easily. Those with clearly defined and well-organized customer or employer groups generally encountered considerable difficulty and were licensed much later if at all.[34] In any event all the professions in Stigler's sample did in fact seek such authority; indeed, Stigler asserts that it can be taken as axiomatic that all groups strong enough to do so will.[35] Thus his dependent variable, the date at which licensing authority was obtained, provides a valid measure of lobbying success for these professions, accounting for the relative success of his study as well.

Once these studies are understood in terms of this typology of policy processes, it becomes possible to derive some tentative generalizations regarding each of the underlying dimensions. When the apparent failure of McPherson's study is properly attributed to his failure to take into account the conflictual demand pattern on the tariff issue in the 1950s, these studies, taken together, can be seen to lend considerable support to Olson's theory of collective action. In particular they point to the relative political appeal of privileged groups: those able to overcome the free rider problem and at the same time large and diffuse enough to have widespread political clout.

Sheer size by itself is a mixed blessing for any group. The larger and more diffuse the group, the more constituencies in which it can lay claim to political support. Kingdon has observed that congressmen are most responsive to interest groups that are constituency based; they view Washington-based lobbyists as less legitimate and as having fewer potential negative sanctions. Thus it is extremely important for groups to be dispersed, with members in a large number of congressional districts.[36] Yet such a group must somehow overcome the free rider problem in order to lobby at all. Highly concentrated industries, although ideally suited to overcome the free rider problem, tend through their very market power to be highly profitable in the absence of government action and thus have less incentive to seek benefits. For example highly concentrated industries find it easiest to overcome the free rider problem and approach government in quest of self-regulatory legislation; they also find it easiest to overcome the free rider problem to form and enforce entirely private collusive arrangements because their small numbers reduce the costs of negotiating and policing cartels. It is the loosely oligopolistic industries—the privileged groups—that find cartels most appealing, hardest to negotiate, and most unstable.[37] Moreover, highly concentrated groups, though readily mobilized, have political clout limited to a small number of constituencies. Finally, they may well choose to maintain a low profile, as Salamon and Siegfried observed; indeed, according to Bauer, Pool, and Dexter, DuPont and General Motors exercised corporate restraint on the tariff issue in the 1950s:[38]

G.M.'s reluctance to speak up for its views on foreign trade was at least in part a reflection of the marked sensitivity which certain giant corporations in America have developed over their public image. Large firms which have been the object of antitrust action or have been generally viewed as throwing their weight around may indeed sometimes use their economic strength to influence public policy or to take advantage of their business competitors. But, if they sometimes do so in fact, such industrial giants must take all the more pains to avoid the appearance of so doing. And, as many of them have learned by harsh experience, the best way to maintain the image of probity is to maintain its practice, too.[39]

Thus privileged groups can be seen to have the best of both worlds: a core of a few large members with a substantial stake in obtaining the collective benefits and therefore willing to bear the costs of lobbying, and a larger group of peripheral firms widely distributed to maximize political appeal. These cheap riders, in Stigler's terms, contribute through their dispersion and often through their very weakness to the political appeal of the industry. Indeed empirical analyses of the relationship of industrial characteristics to nominal tariff levels have consistently revealed the triumph of the weak over the strong; the most heavily protected industries tend to be relatively diffuse, labor intensive, import competing, inefficient, and declining. They are both more likely to seek tariff protection and to receive it than their more profitable and concentrated brethren.[40]

Although the variables employed varied from study to study, taken together they lend considerable support to this generalization on the particular appeal of privileged groups. Group size, however measured, was generally significant only in combination with geographic concentration, suggesting that the most successful groups were those with a relatively small core of larger establishments and a large number of widely dispersed smaller firms. Pincus's findings, as summarized earlier, are quite striking in this regard.[41] Stigler found much the same thing. Moreover he found that the larger occupations (privileged groups) typically generated correspondingly large and diffuse clientele; the larger their potential opposition, the less likely it was to overcome the free rider problem and lobby against licensing.[42] "Thus a small occupation employed by only one industry which has few employers will have difficulty getting licensure; whereas a large occupation serving everyone will encounter no organized opposition."[43] Similarly, in Salamon and Siegfried's study, median firm size was significantly related to tax avoidance rate, whereas the relationship of industrial concentration to tax avoidance rate, controlling for median firm size, was actually negative and significant.[44] Here the median firm size variable points to the importance of having a core of a few large members even as the inverse relationship between concentration and lobbying success suggests the virtues of an outer circle of cheap riders.

Salamon and Siegfried's more intensive examination of the tax avoidance rate for the petroleum industry reinforces this. They found that the very largest companies, in particular the integrated "majors," were most successful in taking advantage of special tax provisions.[45] What is important here, however, is that the oil industry constitutes a quintessential privileged group. As Oppenheimer has shown, these findings can be readily explained by the importance of the depletion allowance to the industry for the period examined and by the way that provision operated to the advantage of the majors at the expense of the much smaller and more numerous independents. Most of the independents were never able to take full advantage of the depletion allowance and were much more concerned with the tax treatment of intangible drilling costs. From 1969 on, the majors launched intensive lobbying campaigns to preserve the depletion allowance, often explicitly invoking its alleged importance to the independents.[46]

McPherson's study, despite its apparent failure to support the political exchange model, does not really contradict any of this. In view of his failure to take into account the conflictual nature of the demand pattern on the tariff issue in the 1950s, McPherson found just about what he should have expected. Although few generalizations can be drawn with confidence from his study, his analysis demonstrates clearly that the free rider problem and the relevance of various organizational incentives and lobbying resources apply equally to *all* groups potentially affected by an issue, not just those seeking governmental largesse.

The greatest weakness of the studies reviewed here is that, though relatively successful in identifying which variables contribute to lobbying organization and strength, none are very successful in ultimately explaining lobbying success, the variance explained for most of them being disappointingly low. The variance explained for McPherson's study is negligible; for Stigler's regressions, it never exceeded .329; and for Salamon and Siegfried's analysis, it was approximately 16 percent. Pincus's analysis is by far the most successful at better than 60 percent. This would typically suggest measurement problems or the omission of important explanatory variables; here the problem is a little of both.

Empirical tests of these exchange theories share a common and fatally flawed approach. Faced with the virtual impossibility of operationalizing the intervening variable of lobbying *activity* (strategy, skill, intensity of commitment, etc.), all these researchers have been forced to fall back on a straighforward correlation of measures of lobbying resources with measures of lobbying success. Such a formulation of necessity ignores entirely the considerable latitude available to congressmen that Bauer, Pool, and Dexter observed. Thus these exchange theories, at least as operationalized and tested, ultimately provide an extremely primitive view of the legislative process. Self-interest is assumed to be readily identifiable, and lobbying resources are thought to be easily translated into lobbying success. Most important, congressmen are viewed in the tradition of Latham as little more than passive referees of the group struggle; Congress is merely the arena in which the final outcome of that struggle is ratified.[47] This conception was articulated most clearly by Pincus, in many ways the most cautious of these writers:

> The model is as follows. Various groups organize to put pressure on Congress; how badly or well the groups reflect the interests of their members depends on things like numbers, homogeneity, and costs of organization. *The various pressures and forces on Senators and representatives then determine how successful the groups will be* (Emphasis added).[48]

In Pincus's case this in no way reflects naïvete. He merely made his underlying assumptions more explicit because he saw more clearly than the other authors the inevitable limitations imposed by the inability to measure lobbying activity. Only Pincus explicitly recognized the necessity of looking at lobbying activity and the obstacles to operationalizing measures of it.[49]

This simplistic pressure group model so convincingly refuted by Bauer, Pool, and Dexter has largely been abandoned by political scientists only to be superseded by an equally naïve view of the marginality of such groups. Salamon and Siegfried's study can thus be understood as a welcome albeit overstated corrective to this view. By contrast, the various economists reviewed here, not having read *American Business and Public Policy*, have not been affected by the new orthodoxy it helped to create. Neither, however, have they benefited from its insights, in particular from its call for a transactional view of interest groups in which power is viewed as reciprocal and legislators and lobbyists as interdependent.[50]

The exchange theories reviewed here, resting as they do on the notion of mutually beneficial transactions between congressmen and interest groups, should have much in common with such a view. But the shortcomings of these studies point up the inherent limitations of attempts at systematic empirical analysis of the relationship between lobbying resources and political outcomes: the obstacles to the measurement of crucial process variables, particularly lobbying activity, the complexity of self-interest, and the freedom of action available to even the most paranoid of reelection-minded congressmen. Thus these studies fall prey to the same fallacy that plagued the earlier power elite theorists: the equating of the potential for power with power itself.[51] This suggests at a minimum a continuing place for case study and anecdotal approaches in combination with efforts to overcome the measurement problems that hampered these seminal efforts at rigorous quantitative analysis. Above all it suggests the need for a serious response to Bauer, Pool, and Dexter's call for a transactional theory of interest groups and the legislative process. Properly understood, these exchange theories can provide a giant step toward such a theory.

TRANSCENDING EXCHANGE THEORIES OF CORPORATE POWER: TOWARD A THEORY OF IMPERFECT POLITICAL MARKETS

A transactional view of the legislative process requires a more complex and cautious formulation than that underlying the studies just reviewed. Naïve pressure group conceptions must be rejected along with misleading efforts to derive a theory of corporate power. More useful would be a transactional theory of political markets that recognized that such markets seldom operate ideally. All the exchange theories reviewed here treat legislatures as political markets and thus assume the provision of political benefits subject to laws of supply and demand analogous to those governing economic markets. The single most important implication of such a formulation, however, is that political markets, to function ideally, must meet all the same assumptions underlying the operation of ideal economic markets. Corporate power, to whatever extent it exists, constitutes evidence only for imperfect competition in the demand for public policies; yet perfect competition is only one of several prerequisites for an ideal market.[52]

In this regard the evolution of Lindblom's theories over the past quarter century provides perhaps the clearest illustration. In *Politics, Economics, and Welfare*, Lindblom (along with Robert Dahl) held out a vision of political markets as a potential remedy for the inevitable failures of economic markets;[53] political market solutions (the "science" of "muddling through") are made necessary by the impossibility of rational and comprehensive analysis in a world of value disagreements and imperfect information.[54] In his early writings, particularly *The Intelligence of Democracy*, Lindblom was quite explicit in developing and applying this market analogy to the political context.[55] He was unfailingly optimistic about the functioning of such political markets, extolling the virtues of "disjointed incrementalism" and "partisan mutual adjustment." At no time however did Lindblom systematically address the question of whether the conditions for an ideally functioning market were met in a political context. Insofar as he touched on these assumptions at all, he did so only to advance his case for political markets. He treated information cost, for example, essentially as a limitation of the rational-comprehensive ideal and thus as yet another argument for the superiority of and necessity for muddling through.[56] He asserted that "every important interest has its watchdog,"[57] and accepted without question the Bauer, Pool, and Dexter service bureau conception of interest groups.[58] More recently, in *Politics and Markets*, Lindblom has recognized some of the problems in his earlier formulations; but unfortunately, rather than systematically investigating the prerequisites underlying smoothly functioning political markets, he focuses solely on the existence of disproportionate corporate power, which he regards as incompatible with democratic theory.[59]

Wilson has disputed this assertion on classic pluralist grounds, accusing Lindblom of confusing the possession of substantial resources with power itself:

> The fallacy of the Lindblom view is well-known to every student of politics: one cannot *assume* that the disproportionate possession of certain resources (money, organization, status) leads to the disproportionate exercise of political power. Everything depends on whether a resource can be converted into power, and at what rate and at what price. That, in turn, can only be learned by finding out who wins and who loses.[60]

Wilson then points to a variety of issues (such as auto safety regulation and the imposition of occupational safety regulation) on which corporations have suffered serious setbacks. To this, Lindblom would reply in an inference reminiscent of C. Wright Mills that corporations often lose on such "secondary issues" but never on the "grand issue" of public versus private ownership and control.[61] Such a view equates corporate *survival* with disproportionate power. One need only point however to Lindblom's own earlier arguments on the prevalence of disjointed incrementalism to account for the failure of industrialized polyarchies to adopt centralized planning, particularly in view of the gradual but steady extension of the public sector in most Western democracies.

Clearly there is imperfect competition in the demand for public policies. The free rider problem leads to the underrepresentation of certain types of groups. As Salisbury has shown, this bias is most pronounced in hard times, when potential members can least afford the dues, and for groups for which the costs of membership work a particular hardship (such as small, declining firms and members of the lower classes).[62] This is by no means sufficient evidence however to establish the existence of disproportionate corporate power. Frequently corporations encounter stiff resistance from other corporations as well as from farm, labor, or other groups. Although corporations can at times make binding public policy in the absence of government action, this capacity is by no means confined to corporations. They may also exercise considerable influence when unopposed, as in the distributive and self-regulative arenas, but this is also true of a variety of organized groups operating with distributive subgovernments: agricultural groups, sugar producers, the Corps of Engineers, even the various gray lobbies. Similarly, a wide variety of professions—barbers and beauticians every bit as much as the American Medical Association—have been successful in obtaining autonomy through occupational licensure.

Whatever conclusions one draws on the implications of corporate power for pluralism, perfect competition in the demand for public policies is only one of several prerequisites for a smoothly functioning political market. Perfect competition is no more likely to occur on the supply side. Party competition in the United States is duopolistic at best and, according to Downs, unlikely to yield distinct policy alternatives because electoral incentives operate to produce party convergence to the center of the ideological spectrum.[63] On certain issues, moreover, congressional committee chairmen can exercise something approaching monopoly power, at least in blocking legislation; the roles of Wilbur Mills in delaying Medicare and of Russell Long in blocking President Nixon's Family Assistance Plan (FAP) and in modifying President Carter's energy proposals provide classic examples.[64] Finally, for many issues the group struggle will ultimately be resolved in the bureaucracy, where imperfect competition can be taken as axiomatic. At times the bureaucracy will exercise monopoly power over benefits vitally important to its clientele; Cloward and Piven have pointed to social workers in this regard.[65] Alternatively, regulatory capture may be the pattern, as the agency finds itself confronted with a single, cohesive, demanding group and no other source of legislative support.[66]

Factor immobility is also the norm in political markets; that is, resources once committed are very difficult to shift to more profitable opportunities. Concrete examples are provided both by the inertia of executive agencies that continue to survive and even thrive after they have either fulfilled their original missions or demonstrated their incapacity to do so,[67] and by the related tendency of congressmen when dealing with the budget to focus exclusively on incremental spending increases while ignoring each agency's base.[68] Indeed Lindblom argues that policymakers will focus exclusively on incremental options, disregarding any proposals differing fundamentally from the status quo.[69] Kingdon has observed in this regard that congressmen are often constrained by the need to appear consistent with their past voting records and thus make only incremental departures from their previous positions.[70] The fact that most effective lobbying campaigns require a tremendous amount of advance planning also contributes to maintenance of the status quo. Members must be motivated to write letters; constituent elements of the coalition must be mobilized at the appropriate time. Such cumbersome campaigns once initiated are quite difficult to maneuver with any precision. This reduces the flexibility available for tactical shifts and provides the congressional leadership with at least one important resource: its control over the timing of hearings, floor debates, and roll calls. This also helps to explain the efforts by lobbyists to obtain firm voting commitments from legislators, for such commitments once made are almost inviolate and thus represent limits on the tactical flexibility available to congressmen as circumstances change.[71]

In addition spillovers abound in political markets. In economic markets a spillover occurs whenever the benefits or costs of a given transaction are not confined to the contracting parties. Pollution provides a clear illustration; the costs of a smoking factory spill over onto third parties not engaged in either production or consumption of the offending good. In the same way, education increases the earning power of students, but at the same time the benefits of that education may spill over onto society at large in the form of a better educated work force, higher productivity, cultural or political advances, or perhaps a cure for cancer.[72]

Within political markets, spillovers provide the basis for the paradox of logrolling identified by William Riker and Steven Brams.[73] According to this paradox a variety of interest groups approaching Congress in quest of benefits will find it in their interests to trade votes. The logrolling observed on the tariff in Schattschneider's era provides a classic example. Each such trade will be rational for both parties to it; each firm gains more from having its own tariff enacted than it loses through the increased prices resulting from the enactment of the tariff on the other's good. When all such trading is completed, however, each firm must weigh the benefit of having its own tariff enacted against the sum of the spillover costs to it of having to pay higher prices for all the other goods receiving tariff protection as a result of the logrolling. This sum may well outweigh the benefits of a tariff for each firm, resulting in the paradox whereby it becomes collectively irrational to logroll. Even realizing this, each individual firm still has no choice but to logroll because they are all trapped in an n-person prisoner's dilemma:[74] Each knows that even if it abstains from logrolling it cannot prevent the remaining firms from doing so anyway. Thus if a firm does not logroll, it will in all likelihood bear the sum of these spillover costs without even the compensating benefit of obtaining a tariff for itself. Every firm faces this same calculation, and the paradox, like the original prisoner's dilemma, becomes inescapable. Though Schattschneider's tariff provides an especially striking case of this, because the tariff of 1930 helped to contribute both to the severity of the Depression and to the subsequent defeat of the Republicans at all levels in 1932, it is by no means unique. James Buchanan and Gordon Tullock convincingly argue that democratic legislatures will provide an excess of logrolling,[75] and Mayhew has provided empirical evidence that such particularized-benefit legislation is much more widespread than is commonly understood.[76]

Perhaps most significant of all is imperfect information in political markets. This problem has been addressed extensively in the literature on public choice, organization theory, and democratic theory. According to Herbert Simon, it forces decision makers to "satisfice" rather than maximize.[77] It provides, according to Lindblom, the basis for the superiority of disjointed incrementalism over the synoptic ideal. Moreover, imperfect information contributes to the complexity of self-interest identified by Bauer, Pool, and Dexter and with it the susceptibility of both mass publics and organized interests to obfuscation and symbolism, which has profound implications for the electoral accountability of policymakers. Indeed, as Downs has shown, were it not for the existence of imperfect information, elections would be no contest at all, with incumbents always losing.[78]

By the same token, congressmen must also be prisoners of their information; they can only represent what they know about. Imperfect information cuts both ways, and it offers certain advantages to organized interests. Because interest groups are rarely counterbalanced in Congress, demand patterns are frequently consensual.

Kingdon has found in this regard that unorganized inerests often are simply not perceived at all: "It appears, in short, that in order to be heard, one must organize and lobby."[79] Inevitably organized interest groups will possess substantial advantages over unorganized publics by virtue of their superior capacity to make their views known and to threaten electoral sanctions. The evidence suggests that organized interests will provide the only reliable constituency cues available to congressmen on many issues.

Measures of constituency opinion available to the average congressman tend to be unreliable at best, at worst, misleading. There simply are no polls taken on most of the issues facing Congress in any given session, and when such polls do exist they generally reflect national samples. When district or state polls do exist, questions are often worded so broadly that the responses offer little guidance on the complexities of the legislation congressmen must face. Attempts by congressmen to conduct their own polls are frequently hampered by tendentious question wording and biased sampling procedures. Congressmen tend to hear from an unrepresentative sample of their constituents, and they tend to poll those that they hear from.[80]

Thus Kingdon has found that, though constituency is the single most important variable affecting roll-call voting in the minds of most congressmen,[81] they often fail to distinguish clearly between constituency and interest group influences. Interest groups tend to be regarded seriously only when they are constituency based, that is, they must be perceived essentially as organized constituents.[82] For salient issues, constituency considerations are often overriding; yet salience is typically defined in terms of the extent of interest group activity.[83] Congressmen regard their mail as a crude measure of intensity because writing requires some expenditure of time and effort and thus weeds out the less intense. Yet the mail comes disproportionately from elites within the district.[84] Kingdon presents evidence that congressmen will almost always act to protect industries located within their districts.[85]

Surprisingly, imperfect information can operate to the advantage of unorganized or nascent groups. Interest groups may bargain by claiming to be able to deliver blocs of voters or campaign activists, claims that Schattschneider has persuasively argued are often exaggerated (though his argument assumes perfect information).[86] Wilson has shown that considerable uncertainty often does surround such claims:

Negroes, for example, may represent customers or voters to business-
men and politicians, but if Negro leaders cannot alter the buying hab-
its or switch the votes of their followers, the potential resources are
useless. At this point, deception may become important. To the extent
that Negro leaders are able to bargain at all, it is frequently a result of
ignorance (or at least imperfect information) on the part of those with
whom they are dealing.[87]

According to Wilson this uncertainty is greatest for previously
excluded groups like Negroes, whose separation from the rest of
society by great gaps in status or class tends to reduce the information each party has about the other. Well-established groups will
have had the credibility of their claims verified over time. The fact
that claims of previously excluded groups and protest organizations
remain to be tested provides them with at least one temporary
advantage.

In sum, then, what is needed is not so much a theory of corporate
power as a theory of political market failure. Corporations are not
alone in manipulating such markets to their advantage. Such markets
appear to favor organized groups of all sorts at the expense of unorganized groups and inattentive publics. The conditions for mutually
beneficial transactions frequently exist between reelection-minded
legislators and lobbyists, a pattern that frequently extends to the
administrative realm as well.

EXCHANGE THEORIES OF INTEREST GROUPS:
A SEARCH FOR THE TRANSACTIONAL ROOTS

The works reviewed here provide a solid foundation for the
development of a theory of political markets. A necessary first step
must be to make explicit the transactional underpinnings of these
exchange theories, recognizing the complexity of self-interest, the
mutually beneficial conditions for any exchange, and thus the inter-
dependence of all the participants in the legislative process. These
works all focus narrowly on economic benefits. On the demand side
they treat self-interest as self-evident and assume that only the free
rider problem stands in the way of organization. On the supply side
they view congressmen as largely passive, responding to a field of
interest group forces. A transactional theory of lobbying, by contrast,
must begin by recognizing that interest group organization is far from
automatic even for those groups with an incentive to overcome the

free rider problem. Such a theory must address the exchange relationship between interest group leaders and their memberships and assess its implications for the relationship between legislators and lobbyists.

In this regard Salisbury has criticized Olson's theory for its failure to explain the mechanics of how groups actually come into existence. In examining the formation of agricultural groups in the period after the Civil War, Salisbury failed to find evidence supporting any of the extant theories of interest group formation. Farm groups neither proliferated steadily nor formed in waves in response to threats or economic disruptions; paradoxically, membership rose in times of prosperity and fell in times of adversity. Salisbury could account for this only by suggesting that groups are initiated by entrepreneurs who offer a mix of benefits to members in exchange for dues. The benefits are not just material rewards but purposive and solidary benefits as well; members gain from the expression of broader public policy positions and from social interaction with their fellows. In good times, more potential members are able to afford the dues; in bad times, group memberships are among the first luxuries to be sacrificed. Thus such groups survive only as long as entrepreneurs manage to operate at a profit.[88]

Salisbury's exchange theory owes much to Peter Clark and James Q. Wilson's theory of organizational incentive systems; more recently Wilson has revised and expanded that analysis. Like Salisbury, Wilson believes that organizations are almost invariably initiated by entrepreneurs. He advances a similar typology of benefits that may be employed to attract and hold members: material, solidary, purposive, and collective solidary (essentially patronage, status, or "positional" goods). For entrepreneurs, self-interest will not be obvious. Their chief aim will be organizational survival; they will "satisfice" rather than maximize. For members, joining will be instrumental; they will seek the dominant rewards of the group, which may or may not have anything to do with the organization's avowed purposes.[89]

Wilson goes on to suggest that the demand for different incentives will be a function of the social structure, as members of different classes will respond to quite different motivations. For example members of the lower classes, however defined, will tend to disdain intangible, purposive benefits, preferring more immediate and concrete material rewards, whether because of shorter time horizons or because their lower incomes preclude contributions toward abstract, long-term ends. Members of the middle and upper classes will have longer time horizons and be better able to afford an interest in intangible or distant rewards.[90]

By the same reasoning, virtually all entrepreneurial activity will originate in the middle and upper classes. Material profit is clearly not the motivation in most instances, according to Wilson, for interest group leaders often persist for long periods in the face of substantial economic losses, hoping that sooner or later their visions will take hold. Thus Wilson's theory takes it as axiomatic that the motives of group leaders differ fundamentally from those of their followers. Leaders will of necessity have longer time horizons and be more concerned with purposive rewards.[91]

Salisbury has suggested that much lobbying activity is not geared toward membership preferences or organizational maintenance needs but reflects the discretionary activity of interest group leaders. This helps to explain the frequently observed tendency of lobbyists to take positions at odds with their memberships—for example, union support for strong civil rights legislation—or to represent broader constituencies, as with Greenstone's observation that labor has entered into a stable alliance with the Democratic party and come to represent consumer-class interests on a broad spectrum of legislation pertaining to consumer protection, the environment, and the aged.[92] Of course much lobbying is readily accounted for as instrumental in providing the mix of benefits offered in exchange for dues. Most of the attraction of a trade association may well lie in its potential for obtaining favorable tariff or regulatory legislation. Similarly much union lobbying is in fact directed at legislation directly affecting union members such as right-to-work laws, common-situs picketing, and occupational safety and health. Nonetheless, because of the vulnerability of such collective benefits to the free rider problem, groups, to survive, have to offer some mix of material and solidary benefits to members. Entrepreneurs who are particularly successful in this regard will receive "surplus profits," which they will be free to reinvest as they see fit, turn to their own personal consumption, or employ at their discretion in lobbying for their own causes. According to Salisbury, these surplus profits are thus analogous to the "free votes" available to legislators when, in V. O. Key's phrase, the constituency "simply isn't looking."[93] Wilson likewise attributes a good deal of lobbying activity to this phenomenon. Established organizations whose organizational maintenance problems have been solved may have to grant considerable discretion to staff members primarily concerned with purposive rewards.[94]

Unfortunately although Salisbury and Wilson have a great deal to say about interest group formation and maintenance, neither really provides a fully adequate exchange theory explaining the relationship between legislators and lobbyists. For any given issue, Salisbury cannot predict whether an entrepreneur will exercise discretion or follow the wishes of his membership; once some position is taken, Salisbury can only provide a post hoc rationalization. Nevertheless he has made a fundamental contribution in reminding us that interest group leaders, no less than legislators, must act as representatives of constituencies with complex self-interests and that they, like congressmen, will often retain considerable latitude.

Wilson does not attempt to develop a theory of lobbying per se, although his work is rich in implications for such a theory. Instead he focuses on the systemic level, suggesting, for example, that the supply of incentives available to organizations in a given political system will be a function of the political structure. In general, centralized political structures will tend to breed centralized, national groups, few in number, each tending to monopolize its own turf and thus to attract a high proportion of potential members. By contrast, decentralized political structures will typically generate a multiplicity of smaller organizations, competing for narrower and often overlapping constituencies.[95] Within legislatures, interest groups will be relatively weak whenever centralizing forces such as political parties are strong and cohesive. Under such circumstances, lobbying will be directed at the party leadership rather than the rank and file. When authority is dispersed, groups will be stronger, and lobbying will be directed at key individual legislators such as committee and subcommittee chairmen. Finally, he suggests that the nature and extent of organizational activity will be a function of the incidence of the benefits and costs for any given issue. He thus concludes by proposing a typology of policy stakes and suggesting appropriate strategies for organizations seeking to revise existing policies.[96]

It is necessary to build upon these exchange theories of group formation to explain the demand pattern dimension. The first requirement is a taxonomy of organizations. Though it is clear that organized groups possess certain advantages over unorganized publics, all forms of organization are not equally successful, nor do policymakers respond to all organizations in the same way. Different kinds of organizations will have different maintenance needs and enter into different types of exchanges with legislators. Wilson's typology of policy stakes can then form the basis for predictions as to activity by different kinds of organizations.

IV

Toward a Theory of Demand in Political Markets

The studies reviewed in the previous chapter all pointed to the importance of the demand pattern dimension. In particular, Olson's privileged groups were seen to possess considerable advantages, having a core of members with an interest sufficient to overcome the free rider problem and a periphery of cheap riders distributed throughout congressional districts to ensure widespread political support. Moreover it is clear the free rider problem applies equally to all groups affected by an issue, not just those seeking benefits from government. A theory of demand in political markets, building on Olson's theory, should be able to predict what groups will be active on any given issue by identifying those affected and examining their size, distribution, and incentives to overcome the free rider problem.

In so doing, it is first necessary to examine the stakes for that issue: Who is affected and in what ways? Lowi was quite correct in asserting that expectations about issues will serve to structure subsequent political activity, although his issue arenas failed to provide a sufficiently clear delineation of the forms that these expectations may take. In this regard, Wilson's typology of the incidence of costs and benefits flowing from public policies provides a valuable starting point. Though Wilson's theory helps to predict organizational activity on issues, it is also essential to examine critically the significance of formal organization, the advantages of which, although real and substantial, are in fact quite finite. Moreover, organizations vary considerably in resources, legitimacy, staff capabilities and commitments, and issue and institutional focus; and not all organizations are equally successful. It is possible to advance a taxonomy of organizational styles and examine the incentive systems, resources, and strategies associated with each. Returning to Wilson's typology of stakes it is then possible to predict what kinds of organizations will be activated for each combination of benefits and costs.

THE INCIDENCE OF COSTS AND BENEFITS

Wilson posits that the extent and nature of organizational activity for any given issue will be a function of the perceived incidence of costs and benefits. Costs of a given issue may be widely distributed, as with the general tax burden or rising crime rates, or narrowly concentrated, as when for example regulations are imposed on a single industry or a highway construction program destroys a particular community. Benefits too may be widely distributed (national defense, social security) or narrowly concentrated (a tariff on a particular product, or occupational licensing authority). Thus policy proposals may be classified on the basis of the incidence of their anticipated benefits and costs, falling into four broad categories: distributed benefits-distributed costs, distributed costs-concentrated benefits, distributed benefits-concentrated costs, and concentrated benefits-concentrated costs.[1]

Although Wilson is careful to point out that not all distributed benefits are public goods in Olson's terms (social security would provide an exception, for example),[2] it would seem reasonable to predict that concentrated benefits or costs would arouse smaller groups relatively likely to overcome the free rider problem, whereas widely distributed benefits or costs would tend to affect large, diffuse groups less likely to organize at all. Indeed something like this reasoning seems to underlie Wilson's discussion of these categories. In any event such an assumption seems a reasonable starting point for a theory of demand in political markets.

Wilson distinguished efforts to enact new policies from efforts to modify existing policies. Most important new policies, in his view, result from major changes in the climate of ideas, extraordinary executive leadership, the rise of new elites, or dramatic events that help to redefine and broaden the legitimate scope of government.[3] Although Wilson's criteria for distinguishing "important" new policies from unimportant ones are unclear, his analysis seems most accurate applied to those regulative and redistributive policies that challenge the established social order, particularly policies that impose concentrated costs on entrenched elites. By contrast, the analysis in Chapter Two suggests that it is much less difficult to initiate distributive and self-regulatory policies, which tend to spread costs thinly over a generally ignorant and inattentive public. It is relatively easy to place issues on the political agenda when no one else who matters very much is looking.

Wilson addresses efforts to modify existing policies at greater length, for such policies are in his judgment much more likely to activate organized interests. Established programs tend to become legitimate and routinized and to attract clientele-group support. Wilson assesses the extent to which policies will become entrenched and proposes appropriate strategies for political entrepreneurs seeking to alter them.[4]

Policies involving distributed benefits and costs can be problematic to enact. In the public finance literature, this sort of general benefit–general taxation case often involves public goods, but the free rider problem makes their provision unlikely in the absence of some coercive mechanism. Such policies once adopted will be readily institutionalized. Insofar as the benefits are perceived as universal, such programs are almost immune to criticism. Unless a sudden, dramatic increase in costs occurs at some point, threatening escalating budgets and providing fuel for taxpayers' revolts, there is little entrepreneurs can do beyond inveighing against waste.

Concentrated benefits combined with widely distributed costs will tend to produce distributive subgovernments characterized by strong clientele support and no permanent organized opposition. Opponents will face the free rider problem, as the benefits accruing to any individual from overturning the policy will be minimal. Supporters, with a large material stake in the issue, will possess the considerable advantages of organization and will cultivate ties with members of key congressional committees and executive agencies. Entrepreneurs will be forced to rely on purposive inducements, characterizing the benefits of established policies as going to "selfish" or "vested" interests. Such groups, as Salisbury observed, will be inherently unstable because potential competitors will find it relatively easy to enter the bidding, offering expressive benefits, so that members will sooner or later require tangible evidence of some accomplishment in return for dues.

Some policies will involve widely distributed benefits and narrowly concentrated costs. In this general benefit–specific taxation case, according to Buchanan and Tullock, the majority will impose its will on a minority, obtaining benefits for themselves up to the capacity of the minority to pay for them.[5] This is also the pattern Downs predicted, whereby political parties compete for votes of the masses by "soaking the rich," at least up to a point:

> Clearly, in a society where every citizen has one and only one vote, the best way to gain votes via redistribution is to deprive a few persons of income—thereby incurring their hostility—and make this available to many persons—thereby gaining their support. Since the pretax distribution of income in almost every society gives large incomes to a few persons and relatively small incomes to many persons, a redistribution tending toward equality accomplishes the very political end government desires.[6]

This process is tempered, but not reversed, by a number of factors, according to Downs. First, opposition to complete income equalization will be almost universal, as voters recognize the adverse effects of such a policy on work incentives and total output. Moreover, uncertainty allows many low-income citizens to believe that they may, in Horatio Alger fashion, acquire high incomes themselves. Perhaps most important, inequality of income tends to carry with it inequality of political influence, as the rich employ their financial advantages to consolidate or expand their gains.[7]

In Wilson's view, such policies—benefiting as they do large, diffuse groups—do not typically represent organizational triumphs. They tend instead to result from some combination of scandal, media coverage, and congressional or executive leadership. These policies seldom if ever destroy their victims. The targets of such legislation, having a substantial material stake in its implementation, generally devote their efforts to capturing the newly created agency as public attention wanes or shifts to other matters. Various auto safety and consumer protection acts provide illustrations. Regulated groups find little difficulty in organizing around material incentives. By contrast, beneficiaries have to rely primarily on purposive incentives to motivate organizational activity, as once again the material rewards going to each individual will be quite small. Although Paul Sabatier has demonstrated that regulatory agencies can successfully mobilize supporting constituencies, instances of this are quite rare and, in view of the analyses of both Salisbury and Wilson, likely to remain so.[8]

Finally, policies involving benefits and costs that are both concentrated will tend to produce continuing organized conflict, as between labor and management in the NLRB. The institutionalization of conflict by such agencies makes regulatory capture unlikely. Policy changes will tend to occur as a result of shifts in the balance of power among the participants stemming from turnover in relevant congressional committees or agency personnel. Affected organizations will obviously seek to influence such changes, although their efforts will be long-term propositions at best, subject to the vagueries of seniority and fixed terms.

Wilson's theory of incentive systems has a great deal to say about group formation and organizational maintenance, and his typology of stakes provides at least a beginning in identifying what kinds of groups will be active for different kinds of issues. Beyond this, however, he is not concerned with the exchange relationship between legislators and lobbyists. While he regards formal organization as an advantage, he clearly recognizes the considerable variation in the forms that organization may take. He does not really address the differences in legislative influence accruing to different kinds of groups beyond making the prediction that purposive groups will find organizational maintenance, and thus prolonged attention, more difficult than groups relying on material rewards.

THE SIGNIFICANCE OF FORMAL ORGANIZATION

Wilson is by no means alone in assuming that substantial advantages accompany formal organization. Indeed the significance of formal organization has by and large been taken as axiomatic by group theorists. While Truman conceded that unorganized "political groups" might also be politically significant under certain circumstances, he nevertheless stressed that formal organization carried with it at least a minimal degree of interaction and cohesion, certain expectations of permanence, an internal division of labor, and the formalization of values shared by the group.[9] By the same token, the significance of the free rider problem to Olson was that it precluded certain kinds of groups from attaining these benefits of formal organization. The writers reviewed in the previous chapter took it for granted that organized groups would be the most significant actors in legislative markets.

Indeed, the evidence of the last two chapters all points to the significance of formal organization. In political markets characterized by imperfect information, unorganized interests often go unperceived; to be heard, according to Kingdon, such groups simply must organize and lobby.[10] Issue salience and intensity, as perceived by congressmen, will typically be a function of organized group activity.[11] Often interest groups will provide the only source of constituency cues available to congressmen.

Edelman has suggested that organized interests will consistently triumph at the expense of the unorganized. He distinguishes between what he terms "Pattern A" and "Pattern B" groups. Pattern A groups are characterized by a high degree of formal organization, precise information, relatively small numbers, a strong sense of political efficacy, and an interest in tangible resources. Pattern B groups exhibit poor organization, imperfect and stereotypical information, relatively large numbers, anxieties and feelings of inefficacy, and a susceptibility to symbolic reassurances. Edelman argues that Pattern A groups will obtain tangible rewards at the expense of Pattern B groups by manipulating symbolic reassurances to maintain their political quiescence.[12] Thus he notes tangible benefits are frequently not distributed as promised in regulatory legislation, but the deprived seldom display any awareness of their deprivation. In fact the most intensive dissemination of symbols typically attends the enactment of that legislation having the least impact on the allocation of tangible resources.[13]

Edelman's argument is reinforced by the rational choice theories of Downs and Tullock among others. Because the expected benefits of voting are so low, most citizens will find it irrational to vote unless they can hold the costs of voting to an absolute minimum. Many of these costs being unavoidable (registration, time spent standing in line, etc.), the costs associated with obtaining and interpreting information become a prime target. Thus many voters remain almost entirely ignorant on most political issues, absorbing at best only that information available to them at negligible cost: nightly news broadcasts, propaganda from the candidates, or an occasional headline. The vast majority of voters will never advance beyond the casually informed stage, scanning headlines and reading an occasional political piece. Such voters will vary in what catches their interest: ethnic identifications, political scandals, or editorials reinforcing preexisting biases. At best they will remain completely ignorant on most issues and attain only a superficial understanding of some others.[14]

Members of the mass public will generally find it irrational to obtain the information necessary to identify their interests on any given issue and moreover will be ill-equipped to interpret any information they do obtain. By contrast, according to Tullock, pressure group (Pattern A) voters will have a clearer understanding of their stake in the issue, will more fully understand the consequences of congressmen's stands for their position, will remain attentive to potentially adverse effects of the administration of the law, and will be quite unforgiving in both their voting and their campaign activities in the next election. This argument is entirely compatible with recent empirical evidence on the nature and extent of issue voting. David RePass in particular has found that a substantial number of voters possess accurate information and vote instrumentally on a small number of issues (often only one or two) of immediate interest to them while remaining largely ignorant and apathetic on most others.[15] Rational congressmen concerned with reelection are likely to respond to pressure groups and unorganized masses of casually informed voters in radically different ways: providing Pattern B groups with symbolic reassurances and Pattern A groups with tangible rewards.[16]

These arguments, although persuasive, seem to overstate the advantages available to organized groups. On the one hand the evidence from the mass communications literature suggests that Pattern B groups may not be quite as malleable as Edelman suggests, if for no other reason than that the same incentives making it rational for most voters to remain largely ignorant on most political issues also operate to reduce the attention given to political symbols. Selective attention, perception, retention, and recall all serve to reduce the capacity of even the most skillful propagandists to manipulate audiences.[17] On the other hand Pattern A groups are by no means as rational or monolithic as Edelman would imply. They are better understood as open systems existing within an environment that is not always stable and may at times be threatening. They must be concerned first and foremost with organizational survival. Although they will be self-interested, as suggested in the previous chapter, there will be distinct limits to their rationality.[18]

Organizational goals will seldom be self-evident. The first priority will be organizational maintenance. Groups will search for a successful mix of incentives in an effort to attract and hold members. In this they face not only the free rider problem and the necessity for inducing contributions from members who may be ill-equipped to afford the dues but the threat of competition from other entrepreneurs for their constituencies. Beyond mere survival, self-interest becomes quite complex. The proximate environment of any interest group will offer a confusing mix of threats and opportunities. Political institutions such as Congress may provide sources of both potential benefits and threats. Interest groups will of necessity seek to influence key congressional committees, floor votes, executive departments and agencies, and the courts. In these efforts, other interest groups may provide opportunities for coalition building, potential sources of opposition, or competition for the group's constituency. Finally, potential auditors may be empowered to monitor the group's behavior and punish violations of previously defined rules of the game—for example, the Internal Revenue Service's (IRS's) authority to withdraw tax exempt status from public interest groups engaged in lobbying activity or the Justice Department's authority to bring antitrust suits against corporations that "throw their weight around."[19]

In adapting to this complex and uncertain environment, interest groups will be characterized by "bounded rationality."[20] All issues will not be equally salient; many issues will simply go unnoticed because of resource constraints. Problems that are perceived will generate a search for "satisficing" responses;[21] in this regard it must be recalled that most lobbying is defensive, in Dexter's terms, "putting out brushfires."[22] Berry has observed that most interest group positions in fact represent automatic responses rather than comprehensive searches for optimal solutions. In fact previous decisions regarding organizational goals, structure, resource commitments, and institutional focus severely constrain organizational flexibility. Sunk costs thus contribute to incrementalism in group decision making on most issues. Decisions to take up new issues are likewise a function of staff interests and capabilities, both of which are the product of prior decisions and resource commitments.[23]

TOWARD A TAXONOMY OF ORGANIZATIONS

Clearly, all organizations are not alike. Groups will vary considerably in the kinds of benefits they seek, the kinds of constituencies they seek to mobilize, and the formal resources they can bring to bear in approaching congressmen. A theory of demand in political markets must come to grips with the need to develop a useful taxonomy of organizations. If different kinds of organizations can be shown to wield different degrees of influence, then the demand pattern dimension must be considerably more complex than was assumed in the previous chapters. To specify the demand pattern for any given issue, it becomes necessary to identify the *kinds* of groups active on each side.

Previous taxonomies have focused on organizational structure, the nature of benefits sought, or the focus of organizational activity. As Scoble has observed, the most common structural distinctions examined have been those between unitary and federated forms and between peak associations and nonassociational forms; but empirical research has failed to demonstrate any important or enduring consequences stemming from either of these distinctions.[24] In this regard, for example, the obstacles to cohesion confronting federations (as outlined by Truman)[25] have not prevented the American Federation of Labor and Congress of Industrial Organizations (AFL-CIO) from successfully becoming a major element in the support coalition of the Democratic party.

Groups have also been classified according to the nature of the benefits they seek. The standard textbook distinctions drawn among business, labor, farm, and civil rights groups provides one such example. Others would include that drawn between economic and noneconomic benefits;[26] Edelman's between Pattern A groups with an interest in tangible, material rewards and Pattern B groups vulnerable to symbolic reassurances; and Olson's between collective and selective benefits. Unfortunately all these classifications erroneously assume that group goals are monolithic and readily identifiable, when in reality, as both Salisbury and Wilson have convincingly demonstrated, groups will typically be forced to offer a mix of benefits in order to survive. In some instances it may be possible to identify the dominant rewards offered by particular groups and thus to treat them for analytic convenience as if they were primarily interested in purposive, material, or solidary rewards; but more often such conventions are at best useful fictions and at worst dangerously misleading. Such classifications must be employed with extreme caution, particularly in view of Wilson's observation that group leaders and followers will frequently have sharply divergent motivations and thus require very different rewards.

Finally, groups have been classified according to the focus of their activity, for example, single- or multiple-issue focus; lobbying, litigation, or campaign activity; or institutional focus on Congress, the executive branch, or the courts.[27] As Berry has clearly shown, such considerations of strategy and tactics are typically subordinate, however, to prior decisions regarding group goals and resource commitments. If most issue positions reflect automatic responses in view of resource constraints and if the choice of new issues is determined by staff capabilities and interests, then strategies and tactics must be a function of organizational experience and competencies.[28]

All this suggests that the most useful basis for a taxonomy of organizations may well lie in those prior decisions organizations must make in seeking to adapt to an unstable and potentially threatening environment. According to David O'Brien, the first priorities of any nascent interest group must be to obtain a stable source of financial resources and to acquire legitimacy.[29] It follows that the most important distinguishing characteristics of any organization, nascent or mature, will reflect the degree to which and the manner in which it succeeds in responding to these organizational imperatives.

In deriving a taxonomy of organizations, then, the first defining dimension focuses on the group's resource base. Financial resources may be drawn primarily from member dues or from outside. In this regard, McFarland has contrasted what he terms "staff" and "membership" groups:

Public interest groups are either membership groups or staff groups. A membership group is one that has a large number of contributors from the general public and a board of directors elected by the members. A staff group, on the other hand, does not have such an elected board, and usually does not have a large number of contributors from the public. (Nader's Public Citizen has 100,000 contributors, however, but no elected board.)[30]

The relevance of this distinction, at least for public interest groups, has been verified empirically by Berry. He found that most public interest groups lack mass memberships;[31] moreover, few communicate with members in any ongoing way beyond the publication of newsletters or occasional alerts.[32] Of the groups he examined, 57 percent provided no means whatever for formal membership influence on group decision making, and more than two-thirds had no local chapter organizations.[33] Not surprisingly, the professional staff dominates the decision process for most (69%) of the groups Berry examined.[34] This staff domination is most pronounced among the consumer and environmental groups in his sample,[35] but the pattern is by no means confined to public interest groups. Other examples include the National Association for the Advancement of Colored

People (NAACP), the Urban League, the Congress of Racial Equality (CORE), the Student Nonviolent Coordinating Committee (SNCC), and at least in its early years, the National Welfare Rights Organization (NWRO). Mass membership organizations, by contrast, include Common Cause, Consumer's Union, the Audubon Society, the National Wildlife Federation, the Farm Bureau Federation, the National Association of Manufacturers (NAM), the Chamber of Commerce, and the major labor organizations.

Distinctions between peak and nonassociational or unitary and federated forms seem less fundamental here than the basic division between those groups that seek a membership base and those that do not. At one level, this organizational style reflects a decision regarding the group's resource base, as emphasized by O'Brien. Entrepreneurs may seek resources from members by offering benefits in exchange for dues. Alternatively they may seek some or all of their funds elsewhere, from foundations, churches, wealthy benefactors, or individual donations. The Alinsky organizations sought support from local community-based institutions.[36] The NWRO relied heavily on foundation grants, funds from the Inter-Religious Foundation for Community Organization, and donations by wealthy benefactors.[37] A wide variety of groups solicit small contributions from sympathetic individuals, who receive monthly newsletters and occasional fund-raising or issue-oriented alerts but who seldom if ever formally convene together as a body.[38]

This initial decision regarding the group's resource base has important implications for the kinds of benefits the group will seek. In mass membership groups, leaders and followers will differ greatly in motivations, social status, and time horizons. Leaders will tend to be drawn from the middle and upper classes, to have distant time horizons, and to be interested predominantly in purposive rewards. To survive, however, they will be forced to attract and hold members likely to require more immediate and tangible gratifications, so a mix of incentives will have to be offered.[39] By contrast, leaders of staff organizations will be freer to pursue purposive benefits almost exclusively. Berry found that most public interest groups provided few selective benefits beyond subscriptions to group newsletters and virtually no solidary rewards, for few of them ever held chapter meetings.[40]

A group's choice of resource base will also affect the strategy and tactics available to it. Scoble has drawn a distinction between groups whose power base derives from money and those whose base derives from sheer numbers, or voting power.[41] As Kingdon has observed, groups with a strong constituency base will have more electoral clout with congressmen than Washington-based staff organizations.[42] In addition, as noted earlier, staff groups are severely constrained in their use of financial resources by legal prohibitions against using tax-exempt funds for lobbying. Groups relying on contributions from foundations or wealthy contributors may be tax exempt under section 501(c) of the Internal Revenue Code. This exemption applies to individual contributors as well, making contributions to such organizations relatively attractive insofar as they are tax deductible. If the 501(c) status is forfeited, the group's resource base is correspondingly reduced.[43] Thus staff groups will tend to eschew lobbying in favor of other avenues such as litigation, social protest, or publicity. Mass membership groups on the other hand will possess the resources to make lobbying relatively effective: money for campaign contributions and numbers for voting power, campaign activity, and effective lobbying.

A few staff groups do in fact engage in such activities. The National Committee for an Effective Congress, for example, focuses almost exclusively on electoral activity; and ideological groups, such as the Americans for Democratic Action (ADA) and the American Conservative Union (ACU), publicize voting records. These exceptions are rare, however, as most such groups seek to protect their tax-exempt status and in any event lack electoral clout within congressional constituencies.[44] Selective enforcement by the IRS has tended to operate to moderate group demands, as various administrations have employed tax audits to harass potential opponents. The Nixon administration's investigation of the relationship between the NWRO and the Inter-Religious Foundation provides one example.[45]

This points to the importance of legitimacy for any nascent group. Whether a group's demands are perceived as legitimate, and whether the group expects its petitions to receive serious attention, can affect both the kinds of tactics the group will find it rational to employ and the ways in which legislators are likely to respond. William Gamson has distinguished between what he terms *alienated*, *neutral*, and *confident groups*. Alienated groups feel that policymakers or the rules of the game are biased against them and do not expect their demands to be favorably received. Such groups frequently lack bargaining resources and may find it rational to engage in social protest activities to manufacture some leverage in dealing with authorities. Confident groups consider the system biased in their favor and consequently find it necessary merely to employ persuasion in dealing with authorities. Neutral groups do not consider the system biased one way or the other and find it rational to offer policymakers inducements (campaign contributions, political support, etc.) in return for favorable political outcomes.[46]

In Gamson's view, these group orientations toward authorities are not necessarily related to the age of the group. Furthermore, any group may be alienated for some issues and confident on others. The evidence suggests that groups do however move through a life cycle of sorts and that nascent groups and established groups will behave in very different ways. By their very nature nascent groups tend to lack legitimacy. According to O'Brien, such groups will remain quite vulnerable for a time, as hostile groups and rivals for their constituencies often seek to discredit their demands.[47] This problem will be especially pronounced for groups seeking radical changes in the existing order and for groups drawn largely from or seeking benefits for the lower classes or racially excluded groups.

Ironically, as Wilson has observed, their very exclusion may give such groups short-lived bargaining advantages for as long as the ability of group leaders to deliver on threats and promises remains untested. Policymakers may well elect to play it safe until the leadership has been tested.[48] The group's illegitimacy may also open up certain avenues for precipitating crises and getting attention (violence, social protest, etc.) that would not otherwise be available; yet the evidence suggests that this lack of legitimacy typically precludes such groups from capitalizing on the unrest they generate. Third parties—the media, moderate groups with established bargaining relationships with political leaders, or sympathetic civic leaders or politicians—must be activated if lasting gains are to be made.[49]

Established groups, by contrast, will possess the access to policymakers necessary for effective lobbying; and they will be careful to preserve that access, eschewing actions that might be branded illegitimate or regarded as unwarranted pressure and performing instead as service bureaus for sympathetic congressmen. Thus Gamson's assertion that alienated groups will tend to employ sanctions in dealing with authorities whereas confident groups are much more likely to employ persuasion seems to apply with some accuracy to groups in different stages of their life cycles as well.

Moreover, whether a group's formal resources can be translated into effective influence will also be a function of its perceived legitimacy. Congressmen will judge whether the group is a reasonably permanent element in their environments, one with which they will have to reach some sort of accommodation sooner or later; if not, perhaps it can safely be ignored, co-opted, or branded illegitimate. The group's influence will also depend on its prestige and professional reputation. Prestige will be a function of the group's status and perceived expertise: whether its lobbyists genuinely seem to speak for their constituencies, whether they seem to know what they are talking about, whether their distinctive competence is in short supply, and whether their pronouncements capture the attention of the media or of other publics monitoring a given issue area. A group's professional reputation goes beyond its perceived clout within congressional constituencies, although, as Kingdon has shown and the evidence from the previous chapter reaffirms, this is a crucial component. Every bit as important will be the group's cohesiveness, seriousness, and competence. Does the group seem sure of what it wants? What it will settle for? Does it send clear and consistent signals? Does it apply resources in the right places at the right times? Are its lobbyists tenacious? Do they keep calling back? Are they credible? Do they deliver on threats and promises?[50]

In sum, at least two definitional dimensions seem to hold promise in deriving a tentative taxonomy of organizations. The distinction between staff and membership groups is quite clear-cut, and a considerable degree of empirical evidence points to its relevance. The second dimension, not so well-defined, seems to suggest a continuum of organizations ranging from previously excluded groups usually lacking in legitimacy and often alienated from the existing political system, to mature, established groups confident that the system is biased in their favor. Mature organizations will of course vary considerably in prestige and professional reputation but on the whole will be likely to possess considerable advantages in these respects over nascent groups. Nor of course will all nascent groups lack legitimacy or feel that the system is inherently biased against them. Consumer groups, for example, did not possess either of these characteristics in their incipiency. But on the whole, these tendencies seem to be associated with identifiable stages in the life cycle of organizations. In any case, these two dimensions may be combined to yield four more-or-less distinctive organizational forms with their own maintenance needs and resources and with corresponding implications for the kinds of political benefits they will seek and the methods they are likely to employ.

Nascent Staff Organizations
Some entrepreneurs in nascent staff organizations may reject the

system altogether and seek a radical transformation in society, focusing almost exclusively on long-term purposive rewards. Such groups may remain staff rather than membership organizations less by design than by virtue of their failure to overcome the free rider problem and to offer a mix of benefits attractive to potential members. O'Brien has criticized the Students for a Democratic Society (SDS) strategies of neighborhood organization on these grounds, for naïvely appealing to ideology or altruism without facing up to the need to provide attractive incentives to residents that should be regarded as rational, self-interested actors.[51] Similarly Greenstone has noted that the Knights of Labor completely ignored problems of organizational maintenance in distinct contrast with the early AFL. The Knights pursued broadly expressive rewards, quintessentially vulnerable to the free rider problem, and even welcomed members from all walks of life, including bankers and stockbrokers. More important, they naïvely rejected any collective strategies such as strikes insofar as they seemed to imply an acceptance of the wage system.[52] As McConnell has shown, much the same could be said for the National Farmers' Union in contrast with the early Farm Bureau Federation.[53] In Wilson's terms, such broadly expressive groups would be classified as ideological in their focus on broad social transformations.[54] Other excluded staff groups may reject political action altogether, stressing instead the transformation of individual group members. These Wilson terms *redemptive associations*; anarchists, the SDS, and SNCC provide examples.[55]

Other nascent staff groups may seek access to the existing system but lack resources and legitimacy. Some, like CORE, will respond to these problems by employing social protest to manufacture bargaining resources or to activate third parties, with the limitations just discussed. Others will simply choose the path of least resistance, adopting those tactics best suited to legitimating their demands. The NAACP, for example, began as a threat-oriented organization, often focusing on those abuses, like lynching, that could in no way be reconciled with prevailing beliefs and values.[56] Its focus on litigation reflected not only its lack of lobbying resources (money and votes) but the fact that the Constitution, with its due process and equal protection guarantees, offered the most immediate potential legitimacy to Negro grievances. Similarly the Urban League sought legitimacy by attracting wealthy, white contributors.[57] Such groups may lack mass memberships chiefly because of the difficulties inherent in attracting and holding members of the lower classes, who can ill

afford the luxury of paying dues to predominantly purposive organizations.

Public interest lobbies, by contrast, typically face a much more
tractable problem of legitimacy. Most of these organizations
represent predominantly middle- or upper-class groups previously
excluded only by virtue of the difficulties facing such large, diffuse
groups in overcoming the free rider problem. They tend to accept the
basic legitimacy of the political system, seeking by their activity only
to plug in to the pluralist process and to remedy its imbalances.
McFarland has observed that most public interest groups hold to
what he terms a "civic balance" system of beliefs.[58]

Despite their lack of mass constituencies, at least some of these
public interest groups do attempt to lobby, their purpose inevitably
being to make a name for themselves in order to attract members or
contributions.[59] Insofar as they offer broadly expressive rewards in
exchange for mass individual contributions, these groups will search,
in Mayhew's terms, for opportunities for "plausible credit-claiming."[60] "Position-taking" is the norm, for winning is less important
than visibility.[61] Thus, as Nadel has shown, in the 1960s consumer
groups and sympathetic congressmen eschewed lobbying and coalition building in favor of personal publicity and credit claiming.
Because of the position-taking nature of these issues for such groups,
access is therefore relatively unimportant.[62] It is not surprising therefore that both McFarland and Berry found public interest groups
quite willing to approach and even to antagonize legislative opponents. Lacking both money and mass memberships, such groups find
adverse publicity one of their few effective weapons in influencing
congressmen.[63]

Established Staff Groups

Older staff groups will have solved their maintenance problems of
obtaining legitimacy and stable financial resources. Entrepreneurs
will have considerable discretion to seek purposive rewards and will
employ "surplus profits" to these ends. Whereas the Nader groups in
their early years tended to flit from scandal to scandal in search
of publicity, in recent years they have invested in significantly
expanded backup facilities. Research organizations now constantly
monitor policy areas that previously received only sporadic attention. The provision of technical information to policymakers has
tended to supplant the earlier emphasis on publicizing bureaucratic
or corporate abuses. Increasingly, public interest law firms have

sought permanent remedies through litigation.[64] Access has become increasingly important as symbiotic relationships are cultivated with sympathetic legislators, administrators, and reporters.[65] Indeed the creation of the Environmental Protection Agency and the Council on Environmental Quality has helped to institutionalize environmental subgovernments; the ongoing push for a consumer cabinet department represents a similar effort to institutionalize access for consumer interests. In short, as organizational maintenance considerations fade, winning becomes more important to entrepreneurs seeking purposive rewards. This helps to account for Berry's recent finding (in distinct contrast with Nadel's earlier study) of the great significance most public interest groups now attach (or at least claim to attach) to coalition formation.[66]

Nascent Mass Membership Groups

In nascent membership groups entrepreneurs will rely on membership dues for their chief source of funds, so they will be obliged to offer a mix of benefits to attract and hold members. In Olson's terms, they will have to overcome the free rider problem by offering some combination of collective and selective benefits. Sooner or later, if they are to survive and exercise effective influence, they will be forced to face up to the problem of acquiring legitimacy. Legitimacy will be necessary both to enter into productive bargaining relationships with established actors and to attract members. Nascent groups face the threat of competition for their constituencies from other enterprising entrepreneurs, and in this competition a reputation for success—in particular, perceived access—can make a group more attractive to potential members.

The evidence is unclear as to what mix of benefits nascent groups will find most profitable to offer. Salisbury suggests that entrepreneurs will begin by offering primarily material rewards because solidary benefits alone are difficult to sell and expressive benefits are highly vulnerable to the free rider problem. Expressive groups may well abound nevertheless, he suggests, because position taking is relatively inexpensive, thus requiring a negligible initial outlay. Such groups will be inherently unstable, however, as they will inevitably face competition from rivals claiming to be the true defenders of the faith. Thus most groups will be forced to settle sooner or later upon some mix of expressive, material, and solidary benefits; and those groups initially offering material benefits will be the most likely to survive.[67]

By contrast, Wilson stresses the divergent motivations of group leaders and followers. Entrepreneurs will almost surely have distant time horizons and an interest in purposive rewards; thus he predicts many groups will begin by stressing such purposive incentives, the entrepreneurs often persisting for long periods in the face of increasing losses, waiting for their reforms or ideological visions to catch hold.[68] At some point, reality will set in, and expectations will be altered. For the group to survive, entrepreneurs must come to grips with the problem of organizational maintenance. The point will come for most groups when they are forced to provide material rewards in order to satisfy member desires for more immediate, concrete gratifications.[69]

Once again Mayhew's analysis is suggestive. Just as in staff organizations, entrepreneurs of mass membership groups will require opportunities for plausible credit-claiming. In particular, group leaders must deliver to members particularized benefits. Whether they be material, solidary, purposive, or positional counts less than whether they are clearly perceived as benefiting the group directly and—equally important—as stemming from the readily identifiable actions of group leaders. Both of these elements are vital to plausible credit-claiming. Thus, as Olson suggested, many organizations will provide selective benefits for precisely this reason, and collective benefits must be confined as narrowly as possible to the group itself.

The failure of the Knights of Labor to stake out a clearly defined constituency and to narrow benefits accordingly is instructive in this regard. Their strategy provides a distinct contrast to that of the more successful AFL. From the beginning, Gompers stressed organizational maintenance considerations and recognized the need for particularizable benefits. Nonworkers were excluded, and organization focused on skilled trades from single or allied crafts. A system of high dues and selective benefits was established to give members a strong material stake in their organization, and the national organization was granted supremacy over locals to prevent ill-conceived strikes and to aid the leadership in shifting resources from strong locals to weaker ones under attack.[70] Moreover Gompers's early stress on voluntarism saw government intervention in the economy as a threat to union organization:

> AFL officials were particularly opposed to programs that might have allowed the government to compete for their members' loyalties such as protection for collective bargaining, medical insurance, minimum-

wage, and maximum hour laws (at least for privately-employed adult males), and unemployment insurance. This last program, for example, threatened to make union activities like collective bargaining seem less vital.[71]

Nascent membership groups, because they must compete for constituencies, will also engage in position taking. As Salisbury observed, it is relatively costless to offer a mix of expressive benefits in an effort to differentiate the group from competitors; group rhetoric will often be quite militant, particularly where aimed at potential rivals. Despite the AFL's early emphasis on voluntarism, as Greenstone has observed, Gompers undercut the Knights wherever possible and expressed a militant hostility toward capitalism that frequently took on socialistic overtones.[72] The early civil rights groups exhibited similar behavior, reflecting the intense conflict between the followers of Booker T. Washington and W. E. B. DuBois. *The Crisis*, the journal of the early NAACP, provided a vehicle for DuBois's attacks on Washington and other black leaders. By 1917 *The Crisis* had attained a circulation more than four times the dues paying membership of the NAACP and provided for many blacks the public image of the organization.[73] Walker also found considerable mutual hostility and distrust expressed by black-moderate and social-protest group leaders in Atlanta, much of this rhetoric aimed at each group's internal constituency to undercut the appeal of rival strategies.[74]

To the extent that nascent membership groups approach government at all, it seems likely that they will mobilize seriously only in pursuit of particularized benefits. For such benefits, as Mayhew observed, plausible credit-claiming hinges on success. Groups may also take positions on a broad range of issues in order to offer expressive benefits to members. On such expressive issues, however, winning will be much less important than being clearly perceived as being on the "right side" of the issue. Scarce resources will not be committed to lobbying on such issues, and there will be few incentives for bargaining or coalition formation. Once again the early AFL provides a clear illustration, as Derek Bok and John Dunlop have observed:

Although stray planks of the Federation platform might favor government ownership of the telegraph industry, advocate free school textbooks, or even disarmament, little or no effort was expended to achieve these objectives. Reforms of this kind were too radical to command strong support among the highly skilled, better-paid craftsmen who made up the bulk of AFL membership. And in the hostile climate which confronted the federation, serious efforts for such measures would have aroused wide antagonism from the public, with little hope of achieving practical results. Thus, the radical planks inserted in the AFL program were largely token gestures to satisfy political activists in the Federation conventions.[75]

As observed earlier, such groups will be characterized by bounded rationality. They will engage in a lengthy search for a successful mix of incentives, and not all will survive. Some will fail to deliver benefits or to obtain enough dues; others will succeed too fully and face the problem of modifying the group's goals and incentive system. As Mayer Zald and Roberta Ash have observed, too much success can be fatal to any group; the ideal situation is to be perceived as steadily progressing toward a goal without ever quite attaining it.[76]

Nor are group boundaries and issue focus by any means givens. Entrepreneurs must choose whether to adopt a single- or a multiple-issue focus, a choice with profound implications for the size and homogeneity of the group's constituency. George Wiley faced such a choice in forming the NWRO. He began by attempting to involve welfare recipients in demonstrations by offering the prospect of immediate material rewards in the form of special welfare grants from state governments. Such a strategy required a relatively small commitment by group members and provided an avenue for establishing the sense of political efficacy so notoriously lacking among lower income groups. For much the same reason Wiley employed what Wilson would term *collective solidary rewards*, providing a variety of leadership positions to create a sense of involvement and a stake in the organization's success for at least the more enterprising and articulate members. In time, however, elected officials developed effective counterstrategies. In many states the special grants were simply abolished. With the elimination of these readily attainable material rewards, participation in demonstrations became harder to induce.

Moreover, from the beginning Wiley sought to acquire legitimacy for the group and to plug in to conventional political channels. Social protest was merely a stage in the development of a mass-based poor people's lobby. As Wiley sought to expand the group's base beyond Aid to Families with Dependent Children (AFDC) recipients to include the working poor and recipients of other forms of welfare, he encountered internal resistance. Some organizers, like Piven and Cloward, feared co-optation by established elites and thus rejected any efforts to work within a system they regarded, in Marxian terms, as inherently exploitative. More significant, however, was the opposition by group leaders, many of whom had never occupied any positions of significance before and saw any expansion of the group's constituency as a threat to their own leadership positions. Ultimately Wiley was forced to resign from NWRO; he was attempting to create such a broader coalition through a new organization, the Movement for Economic Justice, at the time of his death in 1973.[77]

A variety of writers have suggested that the need of nascent groups for respectability will produce moderating tendencies, and even goal displacement, in social movements. For example, Lowi posits an iron law of decadence whereby social movements gradually acquire a stake in preserving the fruits of their success.[78] Similarly, Hans Toch has observed that

> if and when a social movement becomes dominant in a society, its victory makes it vulnerable to two forms of self-destruction. If the movement persists in playing a protest role, the inappropriateness of this stance invites loss of membership. If, as is more usual, the movement proceeds to consolidate its new power, it risks becoming absorbed in the effort. The life cycle we have described may thus be renewed. The movement may lose its original identity and become blind to developing needs. In due time, it may have to suppress the manifestations of discontent of new underprivileged groups.[79]

Perhaps the classic explanation for this phenomenon is that of Robert Michels, who advances an iron law of oligarchy whereby all groups must of necessity delegate power to administrators. With the development of a leadership class, groups become increasingly conservative as the interests of group leaders diverge from those of the masses. Organizational maintenance becomes a primary consideration, and group leaders develop a vested interest in preserving their own positions.[80] Thus trade unions, "whose primary aim is to gain the greatest possible number of new members," will discard ideology and principles, stressing instead personal accusations and criticisms of rivals—obviously "the means vulgarly employed by competitors who wish to steal one another's customers."[81]

There is considerable consensus on the inevitability of bureaucratization and staff discretion within interest groups. Such groups may be founded by entrepreneurs, but all must face sooner or later the

death or retirement of their founders. Although routinization of charisma does typically require considerable bureaucratization, the
implications of this for group conservatism are not entirely clear.
Zald and Ash suggest that the loss of a charismatic leader will engen-
der a succession struggle between professionalized elites seeking to
consolidate power and radical splinter groups concerned with preserving or restoring the group's original vision. The outcome of this
struggle is by no means foreordained, and the potential for increased
radicalism also exists. Moreover, as the group evolves and rank-and-
file intensity and interest gradually wane, greater leadership discretion will result; and it may produce either organizational conservatism, as predicted by Lowi, Toch, and Michels, or increased
radicalism.[82]

Greenstone found support for this in his study of labor in American politics. Bureaucratization merely enabled union officials to
exercise discretion; it in no way determined the way in which it
would be exercised. Particularly in the CIO unions, staff discretion
tended to produce reformist impulses.[83] Wilson has suggested in this
regard that pressures for reform may be most likely in older, established organizations. Only in such organizations, where maintenance
problems are largely solved, will "slack resources" or "surplus profits" exist sufficient to permit the discretion necessary to attract and
hold professionalized staff members interested in purposive rewards.[84] Moreover, only such groups will possess the combination of
resources, prestige, and professional reputation necessary for effective influence on behalf of reformist objectives.

Established Membership Groups
It thus seems misguided to posit any iron laws regarding interest
group evolution and conservatism. As Wilson has observed, increasing conservatism is less inevitable than an increasing concern with
organizational maintenance. As organizations become bureaucratized, however, the insights of modern organization theory become
increasingly relevant. In particular, the evidence suggests strongly
that successful (i.e., surviving) membership groups will at some point
seek to negotiate with their environments in order to reduce uncertainty. At the individual level they will enter into service bureau
relationships with congressmen and bureaucrats. As observed by
Bauer, Pool, and Dexter, such groups will seek to preserve effective
access and will thus temper their behavior accordingly. Access not
only provides an avenue for effective bargaining relationships but

helps to contribute to the group's reputation for success and thus helps to attract and retain members. Recall Zald and Ash's observation that too much success can be fatal—or at the very least create considerable uncertainty—and that steady progress is preferable to either clear-cut failure or success. In Mayhew's terms, winning is less important than being clearly perceived as relevant; access is a clear manifestation of relevance. In this regard the relationship between politicians and lobbyists is clearly transactional. Groups providing assistance to legislators will be rewarded by being taken into their councils, whereas groups that pressure or antagonize policymakers may forfeit access and thus lose the symbolic benefits of being consulted and the opportunities for credit-claiming that go with it.

At a broader level, such groups may seek to institutionalize access by entering into alliances with political parties. Greenstone has pointed to the substantial interpenetration of labor and the Democratic party. Labor—particularly the AFL-CIO—has come to perform a variety of aggregative functions normally associated with political parties. At the same time the alliance has tempered labor's pursuit of its own pluralist goals, expanding the range of issues on which it takes positions, and at times forcing it to subordinate narrow group pursuits to broader party interests.[85]

For example Greenstone found that AFL-CIO lobbyists were persuaded to postpone efforts to repeal section 14(b) of the Taft-Hartley Act and to focus instead on the Johnson administration's broader legislative program in the Eighty-eigth and Eighty-ninth Congresses, including such nonlabor issues as Medicare, civil rights, and reapportionment. As labor acquired an interest in electing liberal Democrats to advance its own program, it gradually entered into a transactional relationship of mutual dependence with the party. As with so many other legislative functions, reciprocity became the norm. Labor's range of position-taking issues was gradually expanded until it came to represent, at least according to Greenstone, a force for broad, consumer-class interests.[86]

In fact the considerable mobilization on such issues suggests that they constitute something more than purely position-taking issues in Mayhew's terms. Although winning on such issues might not matter greatly to union members, failure to mobilize would be clearly perceived as a breach of the labor-party alliance. Labor activity on a broad range of liberal causes can therefore be understood as a form of logrolling to gain Democratic support for labor issues as much as it is an outgrowth of professional staff members pursuing idiosyncratic purposive rewards.

Wilson has suggested that such partisan alliances are increasingly common, thus helping to account for the broad range of positions routinely taken by a variety of seemingly heterogeneous groups such as NAM, the Chamber of Commerce, and the Farm Bureau Federation. Bauer, Pool, and Dexter suggested that such groups would require quasi-unanimity as a precondition for lobbying activity.[87] By contrast, Wilson suggests that, because such groups will lack a single-issue focus, staff members will be relatively free to take a broad range of issue positions and to enter into long-term alliances with political parties or with individual policymakers so long as their actions are not inconsistent with the organization's incentive system.[88]

Established membership groups will thus behave differently than either social movements or staff organizations. Their maintenance needs will by and large have been solved. They will have acquired a stable membership base and with it a steady flow of funds, perhaps even by employing coercive mechanisms to ensure participation (e.g., union shops, dues checkoffs, etc.). They will also have institutionalized access through alliances with key policymakers or political parties. They may or may not be conservative, but their reformist impulses—whatever their needs to appease ideological staff members—will be tempered by their acquired stake in the established order. Such groups will in a real sense be establishment groups. No longer radical, and not necessarily co-opted, they will become orderly, restrained reformers.

These groups will have successfully buffered their environments. They will no longer have a stake in large social changes, which threaten to increase uncertainty. Established alliances and institutionalized access create the potential for steady progress toward goals that are never fully achieved. The group struggle of classic pluralist theory can thus be seen to be non-zero-sum in form, as groups share an interest in obtaining particularized benefits and find little conflict in position taking on a wide range of expressive issues. As Dexter has shown, such groups will at least go through the motions in attempting to obtain private favors for members,[89] and they will mobilize for benefits that can be narrowly confined to their constituencies—for example, labor's all out effort to repeal 14(b), as observed by Greenstone, or more recently, to enact common-situs picketing. Moreover such groups will be quite successful at defensive lobbying, as illustrated by the oil industry's success in protecting the depletion allowance.

The nature of position taking will be somewhat different for established organizations as well. Whereas nascent groups, often faced with competition for their constituencies, will engage in militant rhetoric, attempting to outbid their competitors in expressive benefits, groups with established memberships will have overcome their maintenance problems, so their militant rhetoric eases. Competitors have either died out or ceased to pose viable threats, as with the AFL and the Knights of Labor, or with the Farm Bureau and the Farmers' Alliance, the Farmers' Union, the Grange, and the Non-Partisan League. In some instances a division of labor may have evolved whereby formerly competing groups develop distinctive areas of competence, as within the civil rights movement or more recently the environmental movement.[90]

Militance may recur periodically in response to threats from the organization's internal or external environments. For example leadership challenges may once again provoke militant posturing by group leaders. Similar posturing may accompany efforts to integrate members in response to external conflicts. For example Albert Blum has argued that collective bargaining negotiations typically evoke such symbolic posturing on the part of both labor and management. Often the final terms of settlement are more or less understood by both parties at the outset; but because group leaders must sell the inevitable compromise to their respective constituencies, the settlement must appear the result of hard-fought negotiations. Opponents must therefore be portrayed as hostile or unreasonable, and negotiations must be protracted in order to heighten the dramaturgic aspects of the symbolic conflict.[91] An increase in legislative position taking may accompany such circumstances. Ironically the evidence suggests that such behavior may well be most pronounced for the most formally democratic unions. In unions like the International Typographical Union, where competition for leadership positions is institutionalized, incumbents find it rational to tailor union policies so as to provide as little ammunition as possible for potential opponents.[92]

Finally, implementation of lobbying strategies can become increasingly problematic for established, bureaucratized organizations. Established membership groups may face severe problems of interorganizational coordination, as a division of labor often exists between lobbying and political campaign organizations. Normal bureaucratic problems of coordination between these two arms may at times be exacerbated by disagreements over values or priorities. Within the AFL-CIO, for example, political action at the district level is assigned to local Committee on Political Education (COPE) organizations, while lobbying remains the responsibility of a separate legislative department. Labor lobbyists must of necessity be prepared to bargain to obtain the best legislation possible, whereas the COPE organizers are frequently much more militantly concerned with broader welfare state issues, which reflects their needs for expressive rewards to recruit voters and campaign workers in order to win elections.[93]

The evidence suggests, however, that such problems are not exclusively confined to fully bureaucratized organizations. Walker has identified a similar, albeit informal, working arrangement between moderate Negro groups and militant protest organizations in Atlanta. The social protest organizations are able to precipitate crises precisely because of their illegitimate status; yet they lack the ties to established political leaders necessary to capitalize on them. The moderate groups, with their respectability and links to establishment groups, are able to nail down concessions but find themselves unable to initiate action. Although these two groups voice considerable mutual hostility and distrust, the evidence strongly suggests that they need each other.

THE CONFIGURATION OF DEMAND

It should be apparent that the exchange theories reviewed in the previous chapter rested on an inadequate conception of demand in legislative markets. The demand for public policies was viewed almost exclusively in terms of organized group demands. Such groups were regarded as rational and self-interested, and the exchange relationship between legislators and lobbyists was seen as quite one-sided. Groups were seen as monolithic and ruthlessly efficient, whereas congressmen were viewed as little more than Latham's passive referees ratifying the outcome of the group struggle. The configuration of demand—just who would be active on which sides—could presumably be predicted from Olson's theory of collective action. Large, diffuse groups would possess enormous potential voting power but would find it almost impossible to overcome the free rider problem. Small groups would be much more likely to organize and lobby for collective benefits. Privileged groups, it was seen, often had the best of both worlds.

Too often, unfortunately, these theorists tended to overlook the fact that Olson's theory applies equally to all groups affected by a given issue, not just those seeking benefits from government. In this regard Wilson's typology of stakes offered a distinct advance, recognizing as it did that organizational activity would be affected by the incidence of both the potential benefits and the potential costs of proposed legislation. Thus Wilson's theory in combination with Olson's might be employed to salvage an economic theory of demand in political markets. Widely distributed benefits or costs would tend to affect large, diffuse groups vulnerable to the free rider problem, whereas concentrated benefits and costs would be more likely to generate activity by organized groups.

Such an economic theory of demand would still regard pressure groups as the fundamental actors in the legislative process. In this vein, Downs, Tullock, Edelman, and Buchanan and Tullock among others have attributed great influence to highly organized, well-informed pressure groups at the expense of apathetic, largely ignorant mass publics susceptible to symbolic reassurances. These efforts provide a plausible explanation for the failure of much regulatory legislation to protect consumers, for example.

Such theories, for all their insight and appeal, ultimately prove too simplistic. An aroused public opinion can produce significant policy changes, which Charles O. Jones terms "public satisfying speculative augmentation."[94] Admittedly the attention span for such publics is typically quite limited, and the constraints imposed by aroused publics are not terribly confining with regard to the precise content of the required legislative response. Still, the evidence suggests that mass publics may well be much less manipulable than Edelman implies. At the same time, organized interests will be far from rational and monolithic. They can best be understood as open systems seeking to adapt to threatening and unstable environments. They will be self-interested but subject to bounded rationality. Beyond mere organizational survival, organizational goals will be quite ambiguous.

Moreover groups will search for an effective organizational style, and the choices they make in this regard will affect the resources, strategies, and tactics available to them. Staff groups will be relatively free to pursue purposive rewards but will lack many of the prerequisites for lobbying clout. Social protest groups will be able to force issues but will lack the legitimacy necessary to obtain lasting gains. Nascent membership groups will be primarily concerned with organizational survival, in particular with acquiring legitimacy and a stable source of financial resources. Older, institutionalized groups will be relatively free to pursue purposive rewards and will possess the resources necessary for effective lobbying influence; yet they will most likely have developed a stake in the existing order and in maintaining relationships with established policymakers and political parties. They will also face the problems of bureaucratic inertia and coordination common to large organizations.

Clearly it is necessary to specify the precise configuration of demand, not merely which sides are most likely to organize but the kinds of organizations most likely to be active on each side. Wilson's typology can help in this regard. In general, concentrated costs or benefits will be more likely to affect small or privileged groups and hence to generate organizational activity. Under such circumstances, in Olson's terms, each individual's share will more likely be sufficient to induce participation, and reliance on material rewards will be feasible. By contrast, distributed costs or benefits will be less likely to produce mass membership organizations. Each individual's share will of necessity be quite small, making it necessary to rely primarily on purposive incentives. Expressive benefits are notoriously vulnerable to competition from rivals and so provide little potential for plausible credit-claiming. Thus large, diffuse groups will typically be represented, if at all, by staff organizations relying on purposive incentives. Such groups will lack lobbying clout but will not feel as constrained to preserve access; hence they will be much more likely to rely on the provision of technical information, the manipulation of publicity, or litigation.

These generalizations must be qualified, however. The free rider problem makes the organization of small groups far from automatic even as large, diffuse groups may well succeed in overcoming it, either as a by-product of previous organization for other purposes or as the result of government efforts to facilitate their organization. In this regard it is worth recalling the government's role in fostering the organization of trade associations, labor unions, the Farm Bureau, and most recently, the National Council of Senior Citizens.[95] Groups seeking to block reforms will be more likely to act, other things being equal, than groups seeking change. The lobbying advantages to defensive groups provided by the multiple veto points existing within the American political system have long been recognized. Wilson has suggested, however, that such groups will also be more likely to organize and act because the incentives facing defensive groups will be more favorable than those confronting groups seeking changes. Costs, particularly concentrated costs, will be clearly perceived as threatening and thus lend themselves quite readily to organizational activity. By contrast, even the most concentrated benefits will upset existing arrangements and thus carry with them considerable uncertainty.[96] To a group that has struggled long and hard to buffer its environment, stability, however unsatisfactory, can be preferable to the risks associated with radical social transformations.

Groups seeking major social changes must face problems of legitimacy and uncertain revenues. Thus concentrated benefits may well fail to generate activity by mass membership organizations, as potential members find they cannot afford the luxury of paying the necessary dues or as group leaders seek long-term purposive rewards that fail to attract a stable membership base. It will be particularly difficult to organize lower class groups, characterized by low incomes and short time horizons, and previously excluded groups, whose members may lack the sense of political efficacy necessary for sustained participation. Such groups will typically be represented if at all by staff organizations. Like all staff organizations they will tend to lack lobbying clout, a problem made all the more severe by their lack of legitimacy. Failure to face up to this problem almost guarantees that such groups will lack effective political influence; at best they will be able to activate sympathetic third parties. Efforts to attain legitimacy, as George Wiley found out, risk not only co-optation and goal displacement but the loss of membership support.

Finally, interest groups are by no means the sole components of demand pattern. Mass publics—Edelman's Pattern B groups—will exert influence under certain circumstances. Moreover sympathetic third parties may act on behalf of otherwise unrepresented interests. Presidential leadership, political parties, and congressional entrepreneurship may all act to counterbalance interest group activity, although, as Crenson has shown, the electoral incentives facing these actors provide little cause for optimism. Distributed costs or benefits offer politicians few opportunities for private favors or plausible credit-claiming, so rational, reelection-minded politicians will not find such issues attractive.[97] This points once again to the considerable latitude available to legislators, as observed by Bauer, Pool, and Dexter.

V

Toward a Theory of Supply in Legislative Markets

Any attempt to derive a theory of supply in legislative markets must begin, as Downs observed, by rejecting naïve formulations resting on the underlying assumption that policymakers will automatically act as public interest maximizers. Politicians, no less than firms and consumers, must be understood as self-interested actors.[1] Thus I build upon the pathbreaking works of Mayhew and Fiorina, who have persuasively demonstrated the potential for rational choice explanations of congressional voting behavior based on the powerful assumption that the primary goal of most congressmen is to achieve reelection.[2] At the same time, however, such a theory must be transactional. It must recognize the costs of information, the complexity of self-interest, and the considerable latitude available to congressmen in dealing with lobbyists.

In examining the interrelationship between demand and supply pattern and exploring the incentives facing congressmen confronted with different environments, it is clear that for the most part congressmen will find it rational to allocate resources directly when faced with a consensual demand pattern and to avoid choice through legislative delegation when confronting a conflictual constituency. The distributive and regulative categories, by this reasoning, should be by far the most common empirically, although circumstances contribute to other policies processes as well.

The dimensions of both the demand and supply patterns are much more complex than previously assumed. For example, what is most important about demand pattern is not merely whether groups encounter opposition but, as shown in the previous chapter, the crucial *configuration* of demand: what kinds of groups are active and on which sides. The supply pattern dimension is equally complex. Within the regulatory arena in particular, different configurations of conflictual demands can yield quite different delegative outcomes.

CONGRESSMEN, CONSTITUENCIES, AND INFORMATION COSTS

A theory of supply in legislative markets must begin by explaining legislative decision making. Mayhew has argued that much congressional behavior is designed primarily to minimize conflict among the members. Because all congressmen share the goal of reelection, they will find it rational to search for ways to cooperate in securing that common goal. They will find little conflict inherent in position taking, and they will share an interest in logrolling to provide pork-barrel legislation, which Mayhew termed *particularized benefits*. This fundamental insight, that congressmen share a common interest in securing reelection, suggests that the legislative stakes are seldom zero-sum in form, at least for congressmen.[3]

Once this is understood, Fiorina's more elaborate theory can be seen to provide an excellent foundation for the development of a theory of supply in legislative markets, both for what it tells us regarding congressional roll-call voting strategies and for what it fails to explain. Fiorina identifies a dominant electoral strategy for congressmen facing consensual demand patterns, but he fails to find any corresponding solution for those confronting polarized constituencies. There is in fact a way out for congressmen facing conflictual demand patterns; such congressmen can play off counterbalanced interests, as Bauer, Pool, and Dexter observed. This is made possible by the complexity of self-interest and the potential for obfuscation it creates. In short, Fiorina's analysis can be salvaged only by introducing the notion of information costs.

Fiorina begins by assuming that congressmen are rational actors casting votes to enhance their chances of achieving reelection. In this effort, he distinguishes between two alternative strategies. One is simply to maximize the subjective probability of reelection; congressmen adopting this Downsian goal are termed *maximizers*. The alternative goal, in the tradition of Simon, is to maintain some aspiration level, or satisfactory subjective probability of reelection; congressmen adopting such a goal are termed *maintainers*. Clearly maintainers will be much freer than maximizers. Whereas maximizers are obsessively concerned with reelection and thus face a determinate optimal strategy in most instances, maintainers can exercise a bit more independence and choose at least some of the time to vote so as to make good public policy or gain prestige within the assembly.[4]

Fiorina explicitly assumes what he terms an "ungrateful electorate"; that is, representatives believe that votes in accordance with group preferences will gain them relatively less credit than a vote against group preferences will lose them. In short, voters are more likely to punish their enemies than to reward their friends.[5] A mounting body of evidence from survey research reinforces this assumption. For example John Mueller has found that increases in the unemployment rate cost presidents popularity that can never be regained. As presidents make decisions they must over time alienate more and more of their supporters, thus accounting for the gradual downward trends in the popularity of virtually all presidents over their terms. Mueller terms this effect the *coalition of minorities*.[6] Fiorina expects congressmen faced with conflictual demand patterns to experience an analogous decline in popularity over time.

The environment facing the congressmen from a consensual constituency is a comforting one. The optimal strategy is obvious, particularly for vote maximizers; where an issue affects all the active groups in the same way, the maximizing representative will vote with these groups regardless of how salient the issue. Maintainers, although somewhat freer, will be forced to vote with their constituents more often than not, especially if the issue is highly salient. All in all, however, a consensual environment is highly desirable because in it the intelligent representative can make his seat safe and keep it that way.[7]

The environment is more threatening when the congressman faces a conflictual constituency because however he votes, he must of necessity offend someone. A maintaining strategy may not exist at all, and maximizing will consist at best of minimizing losses. When the conflicting groups are unevenly matched in resources, organization, or intensity of preference, and hence in their capacity to affect the representative's reelection, the optimal strategy will resemble that for the consensual constituency; maximizers will always support the stronger group, and maintainers will do so more often than not. The congressman can only minimize his losses. When the contending groups are evenly matched, his dilemma is even more acute, for he cannot even trade off the support of a relatively weak group for that of a strong one. There are simply no good options for such a representative; over time he must inevitably forfeit the support of a majority of his constituents and be defeated.[8]

Fiorina examines abstention as a way for such congressmen to avoid choosing among conflicting groups. Ultimately this provides no solution for, however much individual congressmen may try to avoid choosing among groups on an issue, Congress as a body cannot. Whether the bill is passed or defeated, some groups must triumph at the expense of others. The losing groups will almost surely hold the abstaining representative responsible for failing to support their cause, while the victors will owe him no corresponding debt of gratitude. It would appear, then, that there is no way out for the congressman from a conflictual constituency.[9]

In a more recent work Fiorina has returned to this dilemma, suggesting that the solution may lie in casework. By this reasoning, congressmen divert the attention of demanding groups by intervening in the bureaucratic process to obtain private favors for constituents.[10] Thus the bureaucracy provides not only a convenient whipping boy for policy failures but an abundant source of Mayhew's particularized benefits as well. It should be clear, though, that casework cannot by itself resolve the no-win situation faced by congressmen from conflictual constituencies. Given Fiorina's assumption of an ungrateful electorate, the coalition-of-minorities effect will sooner or later operate to overcome the effects of even the most diligent casework. By this assumption, groups once alienated are lost forever; no amount of casework can bring them back. Nor can any amount of casework prevent the alienation of groups when the congressman votes, as sooner or later he must, against their interests.

Because neither abstention nor casework can effectively shift the responsibility for choice from individual congressmen, any solution to this dilemma must somehow allow congressmen to avoid a clear-cut choice among contending groups while at the same time permitting them to at least appear to take a clear stand on the bill. In short, some way must be found to make both sides simultaneously think they have won. The opportunity to do so is afforded by the costs associated with acquiring and interpreting information, for whenever some or all of the publics active on an issue possess imperfect information, the potential for political deception exists.

The key lies in Congress, as a body, avoiding choice among the conflicting groups. The way out here does not lie in passing no bill at all, because such an outcome could not avoid benefiting some groups and hurting others. The solution is to pass a bill that appears to be a victory to both sides. As suggested in Chapter Two, this can be accomplished through legislation that delegates the real responsibility for choice among the competing groups to an administrative agency or the courts, which is the essence of Lowi's policy-without-law:

> The politician's contribution to society is in his skill in resolving conflict. However, direct conflicts are sought only by the zealous ideologues and "outsiders." The typical American politician displaces and defers and delegates conflict where possible; he squarely faces conflict only where he must.[11]

Fiorina failed to recognize this solution because his analysis rested on the unrealistic assumption of perfect information. Indeed the notion of an ungrateful electorate implicitly treats constituents as vigilantly monitoring the behavior of congressmen and never forgiving or forgetting past transgressions. Such a conception is clearly at odds with the bulk of both the empirical and the theoretical evidence. As suggested by Edelman and Tullock among others, groups will vary considerably in the extent to which they will find it rational to acquire information on any given issue and in their corresponding vulnerability to symbolic reassurances.[12] Once it is recognized that some or all of the groups affected by an issue will possess severely limited information, the potential for obfuscation through legislative delegation becomes readily apparent. Casework, rather than being the solution to the dilemma of a polarized constituency, is a source of benefits made possible by the growth of legislative delegation. Ambiguous legislative mandates provide congressmen both with a mechanism for avoiding hard choices among contending groups in the short run and with a fruitful source of particularized benefits later on.

In sum, congressmen facing consensual demand patterns will find it relatively simple to maintain themselves in office by allocating resources directly in response to group demands. The rational response to conflictual demand patterns will be to avoid a clear-cut choice among contending groups through legislative delegation. In practice, however, the pattern is not quite this simple. Indeed Fiorina suggested that the solution to the conflictual case would in fact vary depending on the nature of the contending groups; he thus distinguished between conflicts involving relatively equal groups and those involving unequal groups. Unfortunately he failed to examine the factors contributing to a group's relative capacity to affect a congressman's perceived probability of reelection.[13]

Here the distinctions among organizational styles become relevant. Different organizations, characterized by different resources and capabilities, tend to adopt quite different strategies and tactics. Membership groups will tend to possess electoral clout within districts and will be more likely to rely on traditional lobbying and campaign techniques. Staff groups will be forced to rely on different strategies such as publicity, the provision of technical information, or litigation. Nascent groups will face serious problems of legitimacy and resources. Established groups—at least those that have survived—will have overcome these problems but at the same time will have acquired a certain stake in the established order. These different kinds of organizations will vary, among other things, in their relative emphasis on position taking and particularized benefits, on the extent to which they challenge the established order, and on their relative dependence on access to policymakers.

THE CALCULUS OF LEGISLATIVE DECISION MAKING

Thus the demand pattern dimension can now be seen to be considerably more complex than previously argued. Consensual and conflictual demand patterns may well take on a wide variety of forms. What matters is not just the presence or absence of conflict but the configuration of demand: the kinds of groups active on a given issue and on what sides. As already observed, Wilson's typology of stakes provides the beginnings of an explanation for this dimension but no more. Distributed benefits or costs are more likely to affect relatively large groups vulnerable to the free rider problem and thus to fail to generate organizational activity. It is necessary to go beyond Olson's theory and to treat the demand pattern dimension in its full complexity.

The consensual case is fairly straightforward, most commonly resulting from policies involving concentrated benefits and widely distributed costs. Conflictual demands may take on a variety of forms. The most clear-cut case is that of concentrated benefits and costs, which typically but not always generates a struggle among established membership groups. The case of distributed benefits and concentrated costs typically finds staff organizations or social protest groups challenging entrenched membership groups. A variation here involves either policy entrepreneurship by congressmen or vigorous presidential leadership. A final case, that of distributed benefits and costs, is particularly volatile because it typically involves no established membership groups at all. Under such circumstances, policymakers will possess a great deal of latitude in manipulating symbolic reassurances to gain electoral support, and they will find the temptation to do so almost irresistible. Ironically, in the absence of involvement by established membership groups, such strategies can be quite risky, producing very uncertain results.

In general, allocation is the rational response to consensual demands, although there are exceptions that must be addressed. As expected, legislative delegation is by far the most common outcome in the conflictual cases. The form of the legislative delegation, that is, the ground rules for the subsequent administrative policy struggle, will vary in significant respects depending on the configuration of the legislative conflict that gives rise to it.

Concentrated Benefits–Distributed Costs

The distributive and self-regulatory arenas typically involve concentrated benefits and widely distributed costs because often the only groups finding it rational to overcome the free rider problem on such issues are those seeking governmental largesse. Consequently it is possible to keep the legislative stakes non-zero-sum, with material rewards for the participants drawn almost entirely from the inattentive in the form of higher taxes or higher prices. The transactions are consensual because losers are outside the legislative process, perhaps even unaware that they are threatened by the legislation.

Congress will allocate freely under such circumstances. In the absence of attentive opposition groups, there are no significant electoral costs associated with explicit allocation. Not surprisingly Fiorina found voting with such a consensual constituency to be the dominant strategy for both maximizers and maintainers. Moreover significant electoral benefits may be reaped from such an allocation if the benefits can be tailored to clearly identify the congressman as their source. Thus policy outcomes in the consensual case will generally take the form of particularized benefits; and distributive outcomes should be much more common empirically than self-regulatory outcomes. To allocate directly under such circumstances is to create a long-term dependency on the part of the beneficiaries, who know the source of the benefits and have to keep returning for them year after year. To delegate under such circumstances is to forfeit these electoral advantages needlessly, for legitimizing a group's autonomy is by its very nature a one-shot affair unconducive to protracted dependency and electoral gratitude.

Still, the occasional occurrence of self-regulatory policies, like occupational licensing or the National Industrial Recovery Act in the 1930s, demonstrates that delegation retains some appeal in the consensual case.[14] Clearly there is incentive for groups to seek such benefits; Stigler suggested that all groups strong enough to do so would seek to erect barriers to market entry.[15] Legitimized autonomy also provides a powerful hold over members otherwise subject to the free rider problem or the attractions of rival groups. In addition self-regulatory policies often possess intrinsic symbolic appeal and thus can be more easily disguised than outright subsidies. Few people question the American Medical Association's (AMA's) authority to accredit medical schools, for example, or associate its market power with rising physicians' costs.

It follows that the incentives facing congressmen to delegate under such circumstances must not be electoral in origin. Rather, they consist of the classically invoked justifications for delegation: the costs of time and information. Legislatures have neither the time nor the expertise to perform as licensing bureaus for the professions. Similarly Congress shows little interest in the day-to-day administration of the price-support program, although it will jealously guard its prerogative to appropriate the funds for the subsidies. Explicit allocation will be the dominant strategy for congressmen from consensual constituencies whenever the potential victims are inattentive or whenever their attention can be deflected by symbolic justifications for the benefits, as with veterans' benefits or the concept of parity in agricultural price-support legislation.[16] Persistent demands for autonomy will ordinarily be accommodated only in conjunction with an ongoing appropriations process in order to assure that the beneficiaries will be forced to return periodically for ritual renegotiations of mutually acceptable transactions with policymakers. Lowi points to the example of the autonomy possessed by farmers in administering the price-support program;[17] the farm program thus combines distributive and self-regulatory elements. This autonomy possesses considerable symbolic appeal, as McConnell has observed, both through the myth of the yeoman dirt farmer close to the soil and through the notion that land grant colleges have somehow succeeded in making agriculture scientific and thus presumably no longer political.[18]

The foregoing analysis clearly rests on the assumption that widely distributed costs will tend to affect large, diffuse groups incapable of overcoming the free rider problem. Though this assumption is generally valid, exceptions do occur involving groups most likely to be represented, if at all, by purposively oriented staff organizations. Such organizations, though unable plausibly to claim control of their ostensible constituencies, possess other lobbying advantages; not being dependent on access to attract membership support, they can freely approach and even antagonize opposition congressmen. Indeed publicity is both an effective lobbying weapon and a relatively inexpensive source of plausible credit-claiming for the group's leadership. Illegitimacy can be a blessing, for lack of ties to established leaders may serve to make such groups all the more attractive to dissatisfied contributors seeking broadly expressive rewards.

The demise of the Sugar Act provides an instructive example.[19] Early in 1974 the House Agriculture Committee routinely reported the bill to the floor, and extension of the act seemed assured. The Department of Agriculture sought some modifications aimed at moving the industry toward a freer market. These amendments were rejected in committee, but the department still gave the bill its broad support. Events intervened, however, in the form of skyrocketing sugar prices. Substantial shortages of sugar resulted as domestic producers found more profitable uses for their acreage. Efforts to meet the shortage by purchasing on the world market met with uncharacteristically high world prices because speculators had recently acquired the bulk of the world supply. As a result U.S. sugar prices soared, calling widespread public attention to the Sugar Act for the first time in decades. Sugar producers and refiners responded by disingenuously asserting that the Sugar Act was responsible for keeping U.S. prices below the world market level. It is ironic that an aroused public should have finally become aware of the act at a time when this quintessentially protectionist measure happened to have quite inadvertently produced a higher world price. Nevertheless escalating domestic prices necessitated some form of "public satisfying," in Jones's terms,[20] and the activity of a variety of consumer groups led to the bill's defeat on the floor. The demand pattern had become conflictual, and the issue moved out of the distributive arena. The result was a nondecision (Barrier 2, see Table 3, in Chap. 2). Although the staff organizations lobbying against the bill lacked the electoral clout of broadly based membership organizations, the combination of an aroused public opinion, adverse publicity, and perhaps most important, the defensive advantage were sufficient to defeat the sugar subgovernment on the issue.

It is worth recalling here that nondecisions need not necessarily represent victories for entrenched elites seeking to suppress conflict; they may well constitute defeats for organized interests seeking governmentally contrived and legitimized economic power in the distributive and self-regulatory arenas. Nondecisions will not typically dismantle such groups; indeed these groups often retain considerable private power, as Nadel has observed and as the evidence suggests in the case of the sugar producers and refiners in the wake of the demise of the Sugar Act.[21] In the absence of governmental action, this private power will at least lack the supportive and stabilizing sanction of the state.

Distributed Benefits–Concentrated Costs

According to Fiorina any conflictual demand pattern places a congressman in a no-win situation in which any clear-cut choice must offend someone and thus carry with it adverse electoral consequences. Abstention and casework are dubious ways of minimizing losses. The way out, I have argued, lies in legislative delegation. To turn this bleak situation to their collective electoral advantage, congressmen must cooperate in an exercise in duplicity by passing a bill that can be interpreted as a victory by both sides.

Not all delegations of discretionary authority are alike, however. Some do not resolve the legislative struggle at all, creating instead a zero-sum administrative game for which the outcome remains indeterminate. Such a pattern of interest group liberalism, as Lowi observed, is most likely to result from a legislative conflict involving attentive and organized groups;[22] and such a struggle will most often occur over policies involving concentrated costs and benefits. By contrast, some delegations produce an administrative process almost certain to be dominated by organized interests at the expense of the unorganized. The latter outcome is particularly likely to occur whenever policies promise to impose widely distributed benefits and narrowly concentrated costs.

Under such circumstances the dispersion of the benefits makes reliance on material incentives unprofitable for entrepreneurs; and as Crenson has shown, political parties will for much the same reasons have little incentive to take up such issues.[23] Such large and diffuse interests will tend to be represented if at all by purposively oriented staff organizations. Even in the absence of such group activity, however, policymakers may still respond to the demands of an aroused and intense public opinion. Alternatively, indirect representation may occur through the entrepreneurial activity of legislative or executive policymakers. Jack Walker has suggested that such an entrepreneurial role will appeal to legislators whenever a serious problem affecting large numbers of people has been widely perceived. Such a problem will be more likely to reach the discretionary agenda if a readily understandable solution to the problem has been identified. Once a given issue attains the agenda in this way, a variety of related issues may quickly follow. Walker provides an example of one such issue cycle, beginning with the breakthrough on auto safety legislation in 1966 and continuing with the subsequent enactment of the Coal Mine Health and Safety Act in 1969 and the Occupational Safety and Health Act of 1970.[24]

The evolution of the pollution issue illustrates a combination of all these factors. As Crenson demonstrated, because of the incidence of benefits and costs it imposed, pollution was often ignored at the local level. Congressional activity on the issue through the 1960s followed classic incremental patterns, as Jones has shown.[25] Indeed even this gradual extension of federal powers would not have been forthcoming except for the entrepreneurial role of the Muskie subcommittee on air and water pollution.[26] Between 1965 and 1970, however, public awareness of the issue increased dramatically, and the number of environmental interest groups more than doubled from 1965 to 1973.[27] These developments rendered it unnecessary to engage in the normal processes of mutual adjustment and majority building, for the obvious need was to respond dramatically in order to satisfy an aroused public. The congressional reaction in the face of these unprecedented demands can according to Jones best be characterized as "public satisfying speculative augmentation," that is, nonincremental policy changes beyond the existing technological capacities of the affected actors, requiring for example that auto emissions be reduced by 90 percent within five years when no emissions systems then existed capable of meeting those deadlines.[28] Predictably, most of the ensuing legislation was regulatory, delegating broad discretion to administrators to determine the "best feasible technology," to relax deadlines, and so on. The Council on Environmental Quality and the Environmental Protection Agency, which emerged from the attempts of Senator Jackson and President Nixon to capitalize on the issue, were granted broad and ambiguous mandates to advise the president and to issue regulations, respectively.

Frequently, as Edelman has observed, consumers will receive symbolic reassurances that such newly created regulatory agencies have been charged to act "in the public interest," but the consumers themselves will not receive any permanently institutionalized role in the administrative process. They will be left instead to depend for real protection of their interests on their own continued, self-motivated attentiveness to the results of the administrative process. In time, with the inevitable lapse of public attention abetted by the impression that the issue has been favorably resolved, the administrative process will become non-zero-sum in form. Because this new game involves only the regulated groups and the regulators, it is hardly surprising when accommodations are worked out at the expense of the inattentive general public.

These non-zero-sum administrative processes provide the bulk of the evidence both for the traditional capture theory of business regulation and for Stigler's more recent economic theory. Both these explanations predict the eventual domination of administrative agencies by clientele groups; they differ only regarding which groups will initiate the demand for some form of regulation. Where Stigler sees industries as actively seeking regulation in an effort to shore up cartels, the capture theory predicts that demands for regulation will originate with an aroused mass public or a broad social movement, so that industries will have regulation thrust on them. There is evidence to support each theory, which suggests that neither is fully general. There is no compelling theoretical reason, however, to expect the demand for regulation to begin consistently with any single source.

What is vastly more significant is the evidence that the capture of these agencies has generally been intended in the originating legislation,[29] for only in this way could congressmen minimize the disturbance to the attentive groups important to their reelection while appearing concerned with the broader public interest. The time lag that sometimes occurs between enactment and capture seems merely to reflect a period of tentative public attentiveness to the regulatory process during which there is cosmetic regulation in the consumer interest designed to provide symbolic reassurances that the intent of the statute is indeed being carried out. Lowi is not entirely correct, then, in asserting that the real danger of policy-without-law lies in the refusal of Congress to choose among conflicting groups. In a very real sense when it creates these non-zero-sum administrative processes, Congress does choose insofar as the ultimate outcome is foreordained. Under such circumstances the real effect of delegation is not so much to avoid choice as to disguise it.

The implementation of the pollution legislation just described constitutes an exception that proves the rule. The pattern of enforcement, and the outcomes of subsequent legislative struggles over amendments to the original legislation, can best be characterized as a standoff between industrial and environmental groups. For example, recent amendments to the Clean Water Act "are so complex that environmentalists cannot even agree among themselves whether the alterations are good or bad."[30] This is chiefly attributable to the continued vigilance of the environmental groups in monitoring the administrative and judicial processes. This counterbalanced group activity has made for a zero-sum administrative process, and neither the capture theory nor the economic theory can provide any predictions as to the pattern of regulation in such an instance.[31] Zero-sum administrative processes more commonly result from policies involving concentrated benefits and costs (examined in some detail below).

A caveat is in order before proceeding, however. The foregoing examples have portrayed congressmen as essentially reactive, employing delegation to avoid the responsibility for choice in a conflict thrust upon them; but congressmen often find it useful to contrive such conflicts, making a scapegoat of an organized interest in an effort to create a favorable image among the mass of casually informed and ignorant voters. John Kenneth Galbraith has suggested that corporations employ advertising to contrive synthetic consumer wants for otherwise unnecessary items.[32] Although his argument remains controversial among economists, it seems to have considerable applicability for politicians seeking reelection. Tullock in particular has observed that politicians will find it rational to innovate for appearance's sake.[33] By this reasoning, the commonly perceived function of legislators is to legislate, whether new laws are needed or not. By all accounts there are few electoral rewards associated with diligent oversight activity, so politicians will seek to contrive synthetic preferences for some package of legislation they can claim as their own. Given that most voters never pass beyond the casually informed stage, it becomes possible to mount symbolic attacks on "vested interests" in such a way as to deceive the mass of voters without necessarily offending the organized groups essential to the congressman's reelection.

A classic instance is provided by the emergence of consumer protection as an issue in Congress in the early 1960s. The 1962 pure food and drug amendments, the 1968 truth-in-lending legislation, and the more recent automobile safety legislation were all passed ostensibly to benefit consumers, even though consumers did not provide the primary impetus for enactment. A quintessential instance of a large and diffuse group, they failed to overcome the free rider problem to lobby for such benefits. As predicted by Olson's theory, most consumer lobbying has instead been instituted as a by-product activity of previously organized groups, particularly labor unions.[34]

The more recent emergence of a variety of staff organizations in no way belies this, as such groups tend to behave in different ways and to lack the electoral clout of mass-based organizations. The focus of Ralph Nader's lobbying activities, for example, was not on the traditional techniques of bargaining, logrolling, or persuasion but on publicity—focusing public attention on previously unperceived abuses. Until quite recently the Nader group could not give prolonged attention to any single issue; lacking any ongoing consumer organization, Nader was forced to flit from one issue to another in quest of fresh scandals. The eventual restoration of quiescence on each issue was inevitable as Nader moved on to new ones.[35] In a very real sense, then, Nader survived, at least in the early years of the public interest movement, by dispensing largely symbolic rewards. In Salisbury's terms, he was forced by the sheer breadth of the consumer interest to deal almost exclusively in broadly expressive rewards.

The real pressure for consumer protection legislation has originated elsewhere, in the efforts of elected officials to manufacture an issue with positive electoral payoffs. President Kennedy made the first major presidential statement on consumer affairs since the New Deal, elucidating a series of consumer rights and pledging his administration to consumer protection. His commitment was evidently more symbolic than real, for his only intervention in consumer legislation was an attempt to weaken some sections of Senator Kefauver's original drug amendments.[36] The Johnson administration's legislative record on the issue was much stronger, but its commitment appears to have been no less symbolic. President Johnson's interest stemmed chiefly from his need for a relatively inexpensive new domestic issue in the wake of the Great Society. With consumer protection, no new bureaucracies would have to be created, and the costs of the programs would be absorbed by consumers and industry and thus not be reflected in the federal budget. Moreover it offered the administration a consensus issue inasmuch as opposition to the broad goal of consumer protection would be politically untenable.[37]

The electoral rewards associated with this issue were not confined to the presidency; throughout the period, much of the legislation originated in Congress. A variety of congressmen cultivated images as consumer activists. For Senator Magnuson of Washington, according to Nadel, identification with consumer protection served to counteract his prevailing image as a captive of Boeing Aircraft.[38] Potential industry opposition was mitigated, albeit not entirely eliminated, by the quintessentially symbolic nature of much of the legislation.

In the final analysis, consumer protection constitutes a classic example of a position-taking issue, in Mayhew's terms. Such legislation will be tailored to suit the electoral interests of its framers and will therefore most profitably be symbolic. Symbolic reassurances will suffice to establish a positive image on the issue while minimizing the electoral costs associated with potential industry opposition. Moreover consumer activists will care less that they win on a given issue than that they be clearly perceived as champions of the consumer cause. It should not be surprising, then, that Nadel found no stable consumer coalition in Congress and little overall coordination. Rather, the emphasis was on position taking, committee specialization, and personal publicity, to the point of occasional instances of outright rivalry among members active on the same issue.[39] Indeed the position-taking nature of the issue, with its attendant emphasis on publicity over substance, made for a symbiotic relationship among Nader, the press, and the consumer activists in Congress, a relationship in which all cooperated in dispensing symbolic reassurances to unorganized consumers.[40]

According to Nadel, the politics of consumer protection has remained for the most part within the realm of nondecision; fundamental changes in the relationships between buyers and sellers have been kept off the policy agenda entirely. Proposals that do reach the agenda are quickly emasculated, and the legislation that has been passed has been almost entirely confined to the regulative arena. Enforcement of product standards is generally delegated to an existing regulatory agency sympathetic to the industry position, and penalties for violations are mild or nonexistent. The costs of improved performance standards, where they are enforced, are imposed across the entire industry and thus in no way threaten the existing relations among competing firms. The associated costs to the industry are not excessive and can in any event largely be shifted to consumers in the form of higher prices. Thus consumer protection provides a classic instance of Bachrach and Baratz's "second face of power" even as it offers politicians the opportunity to appear vigilant in their protection of the public interest.[41]

Concentrated Benefits–Concentrated Costs

Whenever a conflict involves contending organizations, the congressman's dilemma will be more acute, for the stakes will more likely be zero-sum and recognized as such by all involved. There is thus no possibility for side payments drawn from unwitting spectators outside the legislative game because affected groups are attentive and active on both sides of the issue. As before, there is no choice but to delegate, for only by supporting a bill that seems like a victory for both sides can the congressman escape the electoral wrath of at least one of the blocs. Because both sides are well-organized and likely to remain attentive even after the legislative struggle is over, both must be granted institutionalized roles in the administrative process. To do otherwise would result in an ill-concealed defeat for one of the sides and inevitably in undesirable electoral repercussions.

Because the delegation is designed to avoid choice among the conflicting groups and because this ambiguity is reinforced by institutionalizing the representation of each of the groups in the administrative process, the eventual outcome of the implementation struggle will be indeterminate. The winners and losers are left unclear by design; usually they will vary from one round to the next. It is certain only that such instances will constitute exceptions to the capture and economic theories of regulation. When conflict has been built in by the assignment of permanent roles to the competing groups in the administrative process, regulators can more easily play the groups off against one another and thus avoid at least the appearance of capture.

The National Labor Relations Board provides a striking example here. Labor and management are both well organized, and both are guaranteed representation in the administrative process. Consequently "most analysts would agree that this is how regulation ought to operate,"[42] and Lowi finds in the NLRB an exception to the otherwise pervasive trend toward policy-without-law.[43] The relative success of the NLRB is attributable to the zero-sum nature of the stakes involved and to the conscious decision of the regulators to act as referees rather than as a conflict-resolving body.[44] Of course, not all regulation of conflicting groups has received comparable accolades. What frequently takes place instead is a more complex and less recognizable form of capture by a coalition of regulated groups at the expense of unorganized consumers, as in public utility and common carrier regulations benefiting coalitions between producer and customer groups and in airline regulation benefiting both airlines and supplier groups.[45]

Examples of policies involving concentrated benefits and costs are by no means confined to the realm of business regulation. The struggle over federal aid to education provides yet another contemporary example of a conflict among well-organized, established membership groups. In the 1950s the issue remained stalled by Republican opposition to federal involvement and by Democratic divisions over the issue of aid to segregated schools, as epitomized by the Powell amendment. With the election of 1960 the threat of an Eisenhower veto was removed, only to be replaced by the controversy over federal aid to private schools. President Kennedy felt constrained by his own Catholicism to oppose any assistance to parochial schools, thus assuring three more years of stalemate, as a deadlock had developed among contending groups. The National Catholic Welfare Conference steadfastly opposed any program of federal aid that did not include parochial schools, while the National Education Association (NEA) and the National Council of Churches just as steadfastly opposed any plan that would include such institutions.[46]

The legislative logjam was broken on this issue, as with so many others, by the Johnson landslide of 1964, which produced extraordinary Democratic majorities in Congress, altered the ratios and composition of key committees, and made possible rules changes facilitating legislative action. Moreover the passage of the 1964 Civil Rights Act, with its provisions affecting federal aid to segregated institutions, rendered moot the controversy over the Powell amendment. As the passage of some form of education bill began to appear inevitable, each of the three contending interests came to fear that continued intransigence might only produce a bill that failed to protect its interests. To retain some leverage over events, each group softened its position. The Council of Churches conceded that it could accept a bill providing for some aid to parochial schools even as the Catholic Conference withdrew its objections to any bill administering aid to parochial schools through a public agency.[47]

The shift in position of the NEA is particularly instructive for the example it provides of a group facing competition for its constituency. NEA leaders feared a loss of access to the Office of Education as a result of their intransigence in resisting any compromise with Catholic groups. Thus the seeming inevitability of passage of some kind of bill in 1965 posed a particularly serious threat that the eventual compromise would override the NEA's increasingly unwelcome objections. At the same time, however, the NEA also faced competition from the newer and more militant American Federation of Teachers (AFT), which was not similarly opposed to aid to parochial schools and which vigorously criticized NEA for its failure to deliver some form of federal aid bill. Thus some form of compromise with the church groups became imperative for NEA to retain its access to established policymakers and be able plausibly to claim at least some credit for whatever bill emerged.[48]

With the mellowing of these key groups, the way was at last opened for enactment of a compromise bill. Even so, as Eugene Eidenberg and Roy Morey report, the issue remained controversial, and the Democratic membership of the House Education Committee called on the Johnson administration to formulate a compromise acceptable to all groups.

> The explanation for this peculiar "surrender" of congressional autonomy over a vital phase in the decision making on the education bill is deceptively simple. The Congress, and particularly the members of the committee who had experienced education fights before, feared they would have to resolve the church-state issue on Capitol Hill. The political consequences of taking sides on the "religious issue" was the greatest concern of most members. One Democratic member of the committee put it this way: "We were all sensitive to the start of another holy war. Politically, not many of us can afford a religious war—at least those of us from two-religion districts."[49]

Not surprisingly, the formula finally adopted involved legislative delegation—a broad grant of discretionary authority to the Office of Education. Aid would ostensibly be given to students rather than institutions, and amounts would be tied to the number of poor children within each district as well as to the district's existing fiscal effort. In practice, however, the criteria for approving and funding aid requests remained quite vague. The final result was characterized as yet another categorical aid program but one with extraordinarily broad categories:[50]

Congress deliberately left the church-state question vague, and the agencies responsible for its administration are unable to clear the ambiguities. The state education agencies argue that they are merely middlemen used to channel the funds to local schools and, therefore, are in no position to resolve the controversy. The Office of Education claims that it cannot make a final determination of the issue either. At a news conference in November 1966, Commissioner Howe said that the courts will have to clarify the question, and until this is done his office and the state education agencies will continue to have trouble.[51]

The protracted struggle over Medicare, pitting the AMA against the AFL-CIO, provides yet another example of a classic group struggle. The AMA was joined in opposition to Medicare by a variety of threatened provider groups (the American Hospital Association, the Life Insurance Association of America, and the National Association of Blue Shield Plans, for example) as well as by such traditional Republican allies as the Chamber of Commerce, the NAM, and the Farm Bureau Federation. The AFL-CIO headed a loose coalition of groups in support of Medicare, including such traditionally Democratic groups as the National Farmers Union.[52] There was some activity by the so-called gray lobbies, but the brunt of the lobbying effort on behalf of the bill was borne by organized labor.[53] According to Greenstone, labor's involvement grew primarily out of staff discretion and a desire to expand the effective political constituency of the Democratic party.[54] For labor, then, Medicare was essentially a position-taking issue, whereas for the AMA and its allies, the issue posed a real material threat. Possessing the defensive advantage as well as established links to key committee chairmen, and aided by eight years of threatened Eisenhower vetoes, the AMA succeeded in keeping the issue in the realm of nondecision from 1949 to 1964. Like the case of aid to education, the stalemate was broken by the Democratic victories in the 1964 elections.

The result was a bill that was mildly redistributive at best. Medicare was linked to the long-established and popular social security system, which meant reliance on a highly regressive payroll tax in order to disguise the redistributive potential of the bill by portraying benefits as "entitlements."[55] Moreover, early on the bill was narrowed in scope to the aged, so that what had begun as a proposal for national health insurance eventually emerged as a program of carefully circumscribed assistance to the aged. "Everyone also knew that the aged—like children and the disabled—commanded public sympathy. They were one of the few population groupings about whom one could not say the members should take care of their financial-medical problems by earning and saving more money."[56]

More significantly, the bill predictably enough passed much of the group struggle along to the bureaucracy unresolved. Responding to the AMA's threats of noncooperation in implementing Medicare, Congress avoided prescribing a fixed fee schedule for physicians, allowing instead for the charging of "usual and customary" fees without defining "reasonable" levels. The eventual result was inflation in charges for physicians' services.[57] "The most striking development was the extent to which Medicare benefited those who opposed it most," according to Theodore Marmor,[58] who described the implementation of the bill in classic capture theory terms:

> Once Medicare was enacted, its publicity value dropped sharply. The press no longer had the drama of committee clashes or heated congressional debates to report to their audiences. The broad alignment of opposing economic interests that had marked the earlier Medicare debate fell apart as the issue turned from whether the government would insure the aged against health expenses to how it would do so. Groups in the medical care industry remained active, but their activities were consultative and relatively unpublicized, not those of diehard ideological adversaries. Administrative lobbyists representing hospitals, physicians, nurses, and nursing homes continually pressed their claims on the Social Security Administration and through their trade journals kept members aware of the actual workings of the Medicare program. In the process, the voice of the consumer became less distinct.[59]

Surprisingly, the Older Americans Act, also passed in 1965, provides a distinct contrast here insofar as it generated much more activity by senior citizen organizations than did the Medicare debate. Although the National Council of Senior Citizens was vocal on the issue, it was modestly influential at best; and the largest of the gray lobbies, the American Association of Retired Persons, took no action beyond the presentation of committee testimony. The National Council on the Aging was reluctant to become involved in the issue. "In the case of the struggle over the Older Americans Act, on the other hand, the AMA, AFL-CIO, and other political giants on Capitol Hill took no direct role, whereas the aging organizations were actively interested."[60]

This striking difference in attention to the two issues is readily explained in terms of the benefits each potentially offered to group leaders. Unlike Medicare, the Older Americans Act established a new, presumably clientele-oriented agency, the Administration on Aging, that promised to provide a mouthpiece for senior citizen concerns within the executive branch.[61] This constituted institutionalized access, thus opening up permanent avenues for plausible credit-claiming. Medicare, by contrast, offered tangible rewards to the aged but few particularizable benefits to gray lobby leaders. At best, credit would have to be shared with the AFL-CIO and the Democratic administration. As Gamson has insightfully observed:

> Interest groups face two simultaneous problems and must consider their actions in light of both. On the one hand, they are concerned with influencing authorities and producing favorable policies. On the other hand, they must maintain, or in many cases, create the support of a constituency. In this latter objective, they are in some respects competing with authorities for the support of a constituency. If trust is sufficiently high, interest groups may appear to be unnecessary mediators of solidary group interests. Why put time, energy, and money into an organization aimed at influencing authorities if these men can already be counted on to be responsive to the group's needs? A loss in trust in authorities may have the consequence of increasing the resources of interest groups by making the necessity of using them to influence authorities more apparent to solidary group members.[62]

The Older Americans Act seen in this light is a very different kind of issue than Medicare. Whereas Medicare concentrated costs on physicians, hospitals, and insurors (or at least threatened to), the Older Americans Act involved concentrated benefits and distributed costs. Not surprisingly the pattern here bears a striking resemblance to that surrounding the enactment of the various distributive and self-regulatory policies discussed earlier. Groups approach government seeking a devolution of power. Congress responds by channeling these demands, so far as possible, into the distributive arena, thereby creating a protracted dependency on the part of the beneficiaries and thus assuring a mutually beneficial transaction. As evidence of such dependency Pratt has identified no less than three distinct old-age policy subgovernments—centering around social security, in-kind services, and manpower programs—in which the various gray lobbies are now routine participants.[63] This partnership provides payoffs to all involved. Elected officials gain electoral support, a source of legitimation for their entrepreneurial efforts, and technical information on the problems of the aging. Gray lobby leaders obtain particularized benefits for their constituencies and, equally important, gain the symbolic rewards associated with perceived access: the conferrence of legitimacy, the visibility associated with being consulted, and thus credibility in their credit-claiming.

> Such involvement among other things serves to confer status and legitimacy on nongovernmental actors . . . senior citizen leaders, by identifying with public authority, are enabled better to regularize the internal affairs of their associations and reduce what is from their standpoint potentially disruptive factionalism.[64]

Indeed the evolution of the gray lobbies provides an instructive example of the life cycle of nascent membership organizations. The development of full-fledged membership organizations is a relatively recent phenomenon. The Townsend movement of the 1930s was never successfully institutionalized; and despite the breadth of its appeal, there is no evidence that it contributed significantly to the passage of the Social Security Act. That legislation actually reflected lobbying by early staff organizations (the American Association for Old Age Security and the American Association for Labor Legislation) and the political entrepreneurship of Edwin Witte within the Roosevelt administration.[65] A variety of social and economic disruptions combined to stimulate the development of senior citizen organizations in the 1950s and 1960s, partly through the efforts of such interest group entrepreneurs as Ethel Percy Andrus, founder of the American Association of Retired Persons, and partly as a result of such government efforts to reach the aged as the National Conference on Aging in 1950, the formation of senior citizens' centers in many communities, and the Democratic party's Senior Citizens for Kennedy group in the 1960 election, which eventually grew into the National Council of Senior Citizens.[66]

The aged, because they were widely perceived as deserving, did not face the problem of acquiring legitimacy that typically plagues nascent groups. Senior citizens groups were not immune to the problem of acquiring a stable resource base, however. None of these groups has been content to rely solely on member dues. The National Council of Senior Citizens, for example, has received substantial contributions from organized labor. The National Council on Aging has been successful in obtaining foundation grants. The American

Association of Retired Persons offers a variety of selective benefits, including life insurance coverage for members. The National Association of Retired Federal Employees similarly provides selective benefits through life insurance policies and casework investigations of members' grievances regarding federal retirement policies.[67]

These groups have also had to overcome the death or retirement of their founders. All have been successfully institutionalized with power transferred to the staff and workable bureaucratic standards and performance criteria evolved.[68] Predictably, these organizations in their formative years all engaged in competition in expressive benefits. The 1971 White House Conference on Aging was noteworthy for militant position taking. According to Pratt, the mood of social protest and rebelliousness was broken only by the extraordinary efforts at mediation by conference chairman Arthur S. Flemming. Ultimately the conference proved extremely productive, contributing to an increased consciousness of the problems of the aging, generating a large number of policy proposals subsequently accepted by the White House and enacted into law, establishing channels of communication with sympathetic congressmen, and increasing the sense of political efficacy of the gray lobbies.[69] In the wake of the conference, militant rhetoric faded; many of the groups moved to increase their staff resources; and efforts were made to formalize coalitions—a marked departure from the rivalries of their formative years. Subsequently the gray lobbies have consolidated their influence, attaining full partnership in the various aging-policy subgovernments described earlier.[70]

The evolution of civil rights policy provides an instance of a policy area involving both concentrated benefits and costs that was, until quite recently, characterized by relatively low levels of interest group involvement. Nevertheless the demand pattern has been consistently conflictual, and the legislative struggle has centered predictably enough around the ground rules governing the delegation of real authority to the executive branch. Legislative initiatives have tended to stem from entrepreneurial activity in Congress and the executive branch. In 1957, for example, Attorney General Brownell and other liberals in the Eisenhower administration sought to turn the issue to Republican advantage by exploiting Democratic divisions on the issue, while non-Southern Democrats fought to keep the issue bipartisan. Opposition by Southern Democrats was intense, however, and the skillful brokerage of then–Majority Leader Lyndon Johnson was instrumental in avoiding a filibuster in the Senate.

The 1957 and 1960 acts provide classic examples of legislative delegation in the creation of the Civil Rights Commission, which was granted extremely weak powers to enforce voting-rights provisions. The potentially redistributive Part III of the original 1957 bill, which authorized the attorney general to initiate desegregation suits, was eliminated from both bills.[71]

By 1964 the conflict had been "socialized," in Schattschneider's terms, by the social protest activity of the civil rights movement. Lacking lobbying resources, civil rights leaders stressed nonviolent demonstrations in an effort to add legitimacy to their demands. The widespread media coverage of the brutal response to these actions precluded Southern whites from "privatizing the conflict" once again. Interest group activity on the pending legislation was quite one-sided, with virtually no organized opposition to the bill.[72] At the same time the bill had the vigorous support of the Johnson administration and the Leadership Conference on Civil Rights, an umbrella organization of seventy-nine groups headed by the NAACP, the AFL-CIO, and the National Council of Churches. By all accounts, the activity of the church groups was pivotal,[73] and the AFL-CIO took an even stronger stand than the administration in favor of a fair employment provision and an end to the poll tax. Greenstone attributes this to labor's desire to strengthen the constituency of the Democratic party; certainly the lack of rank-and-file support for the measure suggests that such activity represented discretionary behavior by group leaders.[74]

The resulting Civil Rights Act of 1964 was in every respect a stronger bill than the 1957 and 1960 acts. Taken at face value, the act seems unambiguous, unequivocally outlawing discrimination in public accommodations and employment, expanding the powers of the Civil Rights Commission, and authorizing the attorney general to initiate desegregation suits. The act explicitly prohibited preferential treatment of any groups, expressly forbidding numerical quotas in section 703(j) of Title VII:

> 703(j) Nothing contained in this title shall be interpreted to require any employer . . . to grant preferential treatment to any individual or any group because of the race, color, religion, sex, or national origin of such individual or group on account of an imbalance which may exist with respect to the total number or percentage of persons of any race, color, religion, sex, or national origin employed by any employer.[75]

Moreover, statements made during the legislative debate to establish the legislative history and congressional intent were unequivocal on the issue of preferential treatment, as Nathan Glazer has shown:

> The Civil Rights Act's floor managers in the Senate, Senator Joseph Clark of Pennsylvania and Senator Clifford Case of New Jersey, stated that " ... It must be emphasized that discrimination is prohibited as to any individual ... The question in each case is whether that individual was discriminated against." [110 Cong. Rec. 7213] Senator Clark responded to the objection that "the bill would require employers to establish quotas for non-whites" with the flat statement "Quotas are themselves discriminatory." [110 Cong. Rec. 7218] Senator Humphrey, the majority whip, noted that "The proponents of the bill have carefully stated on numerous occasions that Title VII does not require an employer to achieve any sort of racial balance in his work force by giving preferential treatment to any individual or group." [110 Cong. Rec. 12723] Senator Williams, explaining Sec. 703(j), stated that it would "specifically prohibit the Attorney General, or any agency of the government, from requiring employment to be on the basis of racial or religious quotas. Under [this provision] an employer with only white employees could continue to have only the best qualified persons even if they were all white." [110 Cong. Rec. 14331][76]

Nevertheless, as Glazer goes on to show, by 1970 the staff of the Equal Employment Opportunity Commission regarded this provision as "a big zero, a nothing, a nullity."[77] The recent controversy over the Weber case suggests that this paradox persists. Justice Burger argued that preferential treatment of minorities was in no way required by the 1964 act, and Justice Rehnquist observed that nothing in the legislative history of the act could be construed to support it. At the same time, however, the majority opinion asserted that the plan in question was consistent with the *spirit* of the act.[78]

Such divergent opinions are reconcilable only when the 1964 act is properly understood as a quintessential instance of policy-without-law. In the final analysis the seemingly unequivocal provisions outlawing discrimination in any form left key terms undefined and thus left the fundamental conflict to be resolved in administration. Unfortunately, as the attempts to implement the law clearly demonstrate, the meaning of discrimination is not as clear as it would first appear. When no satisfactory definition of merit can be agreed upon, some other way must be found to determine whether or not discrimination has occurred. Seen in this light, the evolution of guidelines for compliance, culminating the demise of section 703(j), can be understood as a classic instance of incrementalism, as described by both Lindblom and Aaron Wildavsky, characterized by disagreement over values and over the very nature of the problem, by complexity, by trial-and-error, by incremental changes, and by reliance on aids to calculation and rules of thumb.[79] The seeming perversion of what appeared to be an unusually clear legislative intent in fact became inevitable when the fundamental conflict over definitions—which is to say, at least in this instance, over policy—was passed on to the executive branch.

Section 703(h) of Title VII authorized the use of ability tests in hiring decisions but placed the burden of proof on employers to demonstrate the validity of such tests. Validation of such tests is an expensive proposition in its own right, and it in no way guarantees that the courts will not rule a given test discriminatory nevertheless, in which case employers are subject both to fines and damage suits.[80]

In May 1968 the Department of Labor issued guidelines requiring employers to evaluate their utilization of minorities and to take affirmative action to rectify imbalances. At this point underutilization was not defined; employers were to set their own goals and timetables for compliance.[81] When these guidelines failed to produce satisfactory progress, employers were further required in February 1970 "to apply every good faith" to meet their own goals and timetables, although predictably, just what constituted a good faith effort was left unspecified.[82] By 1971 a random distribution assumption had been introduced, and underutilization was defined as "having fewer minorities or women in a particular job classification than would be reasonably expected by their availability."[83] "A substantial underrepresentation of women or minorities manifestly cannot be attributed to their lack of skill. Absent discrimination, one would expect a nearly random distribution of women and minorities in all jobs."[84]

The gradual erosion of section 703(j) was complete; the process of trial-and-error and incremental change was made inevitable by inherent ambiguities in the legislative mandate. The random distribution assumption constituted an attractive rule-of-thumb because no other criteria could be agreed upon by which to identify the occurrence of discrimination or to measure underutilization. Predictably, Congress had succeeded in straddling the issue, on the one hand condemning discrimination, on the other hand refusing to define it. It is not at all clear that a bill incorporating the random distribution assumption, or something like it, would have had majority support in Congress, and it is almost impossible to argue that it could have passed both houses. In any event, had the issue been framed in those terms, a conflict comparable to the "holy war" legislators sought to avoid on the issue of aid to parochial schools would surely have ensued. In the final analysis, the spirit of the law was to condemn discrimination symbolically while avoiding the electoral repercussions of really coming to grips with it.

The 1965 Voting Rights Act provides a similar example of "public satisfying," in Jones's terms. The extraordinary violence in response to Martin Luther King's march from Selma to Montgomery, Alabama, provoked widespread outrage; and the result was a genuinely redistributive bill that abolished literacy tests and provided for the federal registration of voters. The act constituted an extreme instance of concentrated costs, however, singling out as it did, seven Southern states where literacy tests were employed and where half the voting-age population voted. This suggests the tentative hypothesis that allocation may well be a rational response to a conflictual demand pattern when the costs of the policy outcome can be concentrated on a narrow and discredited minority.[85]

The 1968 open-housing law marked a return to the normal regulative pattern, however. Indeed this was the first of the civil rights acts to arouse significant activity by organized groups. It was also the first to apply nationwide and the first to lack the support of a majority of Northern whites.[86] The active opposition of the National Association of Real Estate Boards was instrumental in killing the legislation in 1966 and in nearly defeating it again in 1968.[87] The church delegations, so vital to the outcome in 1964 and 1965, were largely inactive on the fair-housing issue,[88] and public opinion played a very different role:

> The Leadership Conference on Civil Rights deplored the absence of mail on behalf of equal housing opportunity. Negro demonstrations, too, had a different impact. When Martin Luther King, Jr., led a band of Negroes into a white residential area of Chicago and engaged a white mob, he stirred up indignation in the North not unlike that aroused by Birmingham and Selma—but this time directed against, not for, his cause. "I have never seen such hatred—not in Mississippi or Alabama," said King.[89]

In spite of these otherwise unpromising circumstances, the activity of the Leadership Conference on Civil Rights, and in particular of its chief lobbyist, Clarence Mitchell of the NAACP, was pivotal.[90] Just as in the group struggle surrounding aid to education, the legislative response to this intensely conflictual demand pattern was to delegate. Moreover in view of the imbalance in lobbying resources and electoral clout he was up against, Mitchell did extremely well just to get some kind of bill passed; not surprisingly, the ground rules governing the administrative struggle did not favor minorities. The law banned discrimination in the sale or rental of almost 80 percent of the nation's housing and placed the responsibility for enforcement in the Department of Housing and Urban Development's Office of Fair Housing and Employment Opportunity,[91] but the agency was given a miniscule budget ($17.4 million in 1978) and little real power. It was authorized to investigate complaints of discrimination but not to initiate action. It has the authority to mediate between parties but no power to enforce agreements, and it can go to court only where a general pattern of discrimination has been found.[92] Thus the outcome of the administrative struggle was foreordained, and more than a decade later, the act has had little real impact on housing discrimination. The civil rights movement has failed to generate broadly based membership organizations; and Harold Wolman and Norman Thomas have shown that civil rights groups lack effective access to the policy-making elite within the education and housing agencies.[93] It should not be surprising, then, that the treatment of this issue should resemble the instances of regulatory capture discussed earlier.

Distributed Costs–Distributed Benefits

The most difficult demand pattern to deal with is that of distributed costs and distributed benefits because it is the least likely to generate organizational activity. The widely distributed nature of both benefits and costs renders both sides vulnerable to the free rider problem, at least with regard to material incentives. At most, purposively oriented staff organizations may be active on one or both sides of such an issue. Elected officials may also be attracted to the issue if it appears to offer attractive opportunities for position taking.

When no voters have passed beyond the casually informed stage on a given issue, the opportunities for political deception, particularly in the form of strategies of symbolic innovation as discussed earlier, would appear almost unbounded. Indeed this may account for the widely recognized ability of leaders to manipulate foreign crises to bolster their popular standing at home, inasmuch as foreign policy is noteworthy for its lack of organized interest group activity.[94] Similarly, in the domestic realm there is evidence, for example, that the War on Poverty had its origins in President Johnson's quest for a theme around which to build his 1964 reelection campaign.[95]

Surprisingly these innovative strategies are not devoid of risk. Although mass publics may well be vulnerable to symbolic appeals, it appears that their very lack of sophistication makes them particularly resistant to fine tuning for electoral purposes. Successful innovative strategies are in fact often made possible by the presence of some well-organized and attentive groups that can be made the symbolic victims of the legislative drama. Such groups are counted on to discount the accompanying political rhetoric even as it is accepted, more or less, by the target publics. When none of the affected publics have advanced beyond the casually informed stage, this sophistication can no longer be assumed, and there remains the very real possibility that the symbolic posturings will be believed by the ostensible victims without correspondingly deceiving the target groups.

A few examples suffice to illustrate the volatility of this demand pattern. Few generalizations can be drawn with any real confidence from these cases, and the remarks that follow are necessarily speculative. For example the supply pattern in such cases may well be delegative, as one would expect with a conflictual demand pattern, but it need not be. The Johnson administration's efforts to respond to the growing public concern with rising crime rates provides an instance of such a delegative response. Even as the issue was gaining increasing public attention, it failed to generate significant activity by organized interests. The demand pattern on the issue was conflictual nonetheless. As Thomas Cronin has shown, there was no consensus on the root causes of crime, and there was heated disagreement on how to deal with it. Within the administration, at least two distinct schools emerged. The "Get Tough" camp, which regarded criminals as rational actors calculating costs and benefits of illegal activity, called for more efficient law enforcement, stiffer sentences, and a reversal of recent Supreme Court rulings allegedly "handcuffing" the police. The "Social Justice" camp, which sought the causes of crime in environmental forces and regarded appeals for "law and order" as implicitly racist, called for strategies to reform the inequities in the criminal justice system, rehabilitate criminals, and open up blocked opportunities for the poor to advance.[96]

Predictably enough, these conflicts were left unresolved in the administration's proposals:

The Law Enforcement Assistance Act of 1965 was an attempt by the Johnson administration to show concern for the crime problem while awaiting more elaborate recommendations from its Crime Commission. It was in many ways the first major piece of legislation to engage the federal government overtly in local law enforcement. It authorized the attorney general to perform studies, to "collect, evaluate, publish, and disseminate information," and to make direct grants to states and communities for educating and training personnel who had any relation to criminal justice.[97]

The Office of Law Enforcement Assistance was created to administer the act. Given the uncontroversial nature of its mandate, the legislation aroused little controversy in Congress.[98]

The 1967–1968 struggle over the administration's response to the crime commission's report provides a distinct contrast. The "Get Tough" forces gained strength in Congress, as Republicans made significant gains in the 1966 elections and a conservative backlash set in against the administration of a variety of Great Society programs, particularly those imposing unpopular federal guidelines. Hostility to Supreme Court rulings and to Attorney General Ramsey Clark increased. The final legislative product was bound to involve some symbolic victories for the "Get Tough" group: amendments on wiretapping, more flexible propolice rules on criminal proceedings, and special funds for riot control. The most significant defeat for the administration came however with Congress's rejection of categorical assistance proposals in favor of block grants. By removing virtually all strings on federal assistance, the legislation not only bypassed an unpopular attorney general but reduced the discretion of the Office of Law Enforcement Assistance in disbursing federal revenues.[99] The end result represented not so much an explicit choice among the contending groups as a delegation of the real responsibility for choice to the states and localities. According to Cronin,

> there was unusual difficulty in the policy implementation stage, involving multiple and competing bureaucracies and interests. The absence of clear federal objectives invited competing bureaucratic interpretations. The LEAA habit was one of servicing state and local criminal justice systems, not regulating, leading, shaping, hassling, or in many cases even monitoring their use of federal monies. This was especially true because of the long-standing fears of a developing national police force or the centralization of these localized responsibilities.

The presidential and congressional intents were often at odds, and the injection of diverse and divergent local views about what was needed further intensified the conflict. These confusions, disagreements, and rivalries were evident from the policy initiation through the policy implementation stages, and they served to sap the will and capacity of the national government to shape crime policy decisively.[100]

The War on Poverty provides yet another instance of a delegative response. The absence of organized group activity on this issue has been well documented;[101] yet the demand pattern was at least potentially conflictual, as Daniel Moynihan has convincingly demonstrated. Potential conflicts failed to surface during the formulation of the bill, according to Moynihan, only because key terms were left undefined, particularly terms pertaining to the composition and mandate of the Community Action boards; the bill called, for example, for the maximum *feasible* participation of all *relevant* community groups.[102] Policymakers with widely divergent conceptions of poverty were able to see in the bill a victory for their viewpoint. This contrived consensus inevitably broke down in the process of administration. By 1966 the program had fallen under attack from a variety of sources: Republicans, who charged that the Community Action boards did not guarantee sufficient representation for the poor; urban mayors, who feared any program that bypassed them and threatened to subsidize the existence of community organizations that would, in turn, demand more benefits from urban governments; and Southern Democrats, who feared the participation of blacks and civil rights activists in the program.[103] With the escalation of the war in Vietnam, the act fell on budgetary hard times with the single exception of the Head Start program, which remained popular with congressmen as a source of particularized benefits for their districts in spite of adverse scholarly evaluations.[104]

In view of the ultimate bankruptcy of this symbolic strategy, the question arises as to why the administration embarked on it at all, particularly given the lack of group pressure on the issue. Piven and Cloward have portrayed the War on Poverty as a deliberate political strategy of the Kennedy and Johnson administrations aimed at solidifying the growing black vote in the central cities; both John C. Donovan and Moynihan have provided corroborative evidence in this regard.[105] By 1960, 90 percent of all northern blacks were concentrated in just ten of the most populous northern states, thus making them a pivotal electoral group. Their importance to the Democratic coalition was heightened by the decline of Democratic strength in the once-solid South, beginning with the defection of Strom Thurmond and the Dixiecrats in 1948 and continuing through two Eisenhower victories. By 1960, blacks were a key element in what remained of the Democratic coalition. This led Democratic administrations from 1961 to 1964 to seek new legislation explicitly aimed at problems of the inner cities: juvenile delinquency, mental health, community action, and model cities.[106]

In any event the strategy ultimately backfired, leaving the Democrats with the worst of both worlds. It is arguable that blacks had begun to recognize the predominantly symbolic nature of the War on Poverty by the late 1960s, as evidenced by the fact that rioting in major cities took on crisis proportions only after the enactment of these programs. At the same time, survey evidence suggests that whites did not recognize the symbolic nature of the recent black gains. What whites perceived instead was a pattern of successive black victories in the legislative arena followed by what appeared to be an increased militance in the form of social disorder and black power movements. By the fall of 1968 this backlash had become a major factor contributing to the size of the Wallace vote.[107]

The apparent failure of the "services strategy" of the War on Poverty prompted the Nixon administration to adopt "income strategy" that bypassed the burgeoning welfare bureaucracy. Such a strategy appealed to the president's instinctive distrust of the bureaucracy inasmuch as it rested on the widely held assumption that a service-oriented welfare strategy transferred income less to lower class welfare recipients than to middle-class welfare professionals. The Family Assistance Plan (FAP) proposed a form of guaranteed income, albeit one that rewarded work; as such, it would have had profoundly redistributive consequences, allocating tangible benefits directly to the poor.

Ironically this proposal in turn necessitated a distinct symbolic strategy of its own. The chief beneficiaries of the plan, particularly blacks, had voted against the president in large numbers in 1968 and could not be expected to support him under any foreseeable circumstances. At the same time, the plan involved a very serious risk of alienating the conservative core of the president's electoral coalition. Consequently the administration set out to reassure its natural constituency that the plan was not really designed to establish the principle of income by right but rather to reinforce work incentives and family stability. According to Moynihan, who participated in the policy debate within the administration, "Symbolic rewards were devised for 'Middle America' while legislative proposals were drafted for the 'other America.'"[108]

Nixon's symbolic strategy ultimately proved no more successful than Johnson's. It rested on the underlying assumption that the poor, left to their own devices, would recognize their own self-interest in what amounted to a form of guaranteed income even as the president's middle-class constituency was being deceived as to the real nature of the program. This assumption proved ill-founded, however, as conservatives very quickly recognized the plan as a guaranteed income and opposed it on these grounds, while the poor, and their traditional liberal allies, accepted the administration's rhetoric at face value. Attorney General Mitchell's attempt to make the administration's symbolic strategy explicit, by telling a group of black representatives to "watch what we do, rather than what we say," fell on deaf ears.[109] In the end, FAP came under attack from both the left and the right and was defeated.

By its very nature the proposal threatened to concentrate costs on at least two identifiable organized groups and thus constituted a very different kind of issue than community action. The National Alliance of Social Workers quickly perceived in the income strategy a threat to their jobs.[110] More significantly, the National Welfare Rights Organization adamantly opposed the plan. NWRO was composed almost entirely of Aid to Families with Dependent Children recipients, and its membership was heavily concentrated in the Northeast; the administration's plan actually threatened to reduce benefit levels for much of the group's constituency.[111] More significant, according to Moynihan, was the lack of incentive for the group's leaders to support the bill. It is worth recalling Gamson's observation that interest group leaders constantly face the threat of competition from authorities for the loyalties of their constituencies; a decline in the level of trust in policymakers can have the effect of contributing to the perceived relevance of group membership.[112] By such reasoning, NWRO leaders had little stake in any reforms for which they could not claim credit:

> To expect black "leaders," of whom few save the officials of the NAACP had any solid organizational base in black communities, to trade benefits that redounded largely to persons such as themselves, that is to say, the symbolic benefits of being consulted, being invited,

being included, for substantive benefits such as money in the pockets or food in the stomachs of Alabama dirt farmers was to expect what is rarely if ever encountered in public affairs. Symbolic rewards are immediate; program rewards in the best of circumstances are long delayed and often never do come to pass.[113]

In the final analysis, Nixon, like Johnson, ultimately had the worst of both worlds. Faced with an environment of counterbalanced mass publics, each sought to contrive a positive electoral image through a strategy of symbolic reassurances. Ironically, although the targets of the symbolism differed in the two administrations, in both instances the targets of the symbolic appeals saw through the strategy while the real beneficiaries of the legislation mistook the symbols for reality.

CONCLUSION

The theory of supply in legislative markets developed here is rooted in the assumption that politicians can be best understood as self-interested actors operating in an environment of considerable complexity and uncertainty. By and large congressmen retain considerable latitude in such a world by engaging in mutually beneficial exchanges in the consensual arenas and playing on imperfect information and the complexity of self-interest to avoid hard choices in the conflictual arenas. Yet interest groups are considerably more important than has been assumed in recent years. The refutation of the naïve pressure group model in no way implies the irrelevance of organized groups. Indeed this was never Bauer, Pool, and Dexter's argument; they called instead for a more sophisticated view of the relationship between lobbyists and legislators.

At the same time, the characterization of the policy process as a group struggle is both naïve and misleading. Often there is no conflict, as groups seeking benefits from government encounter no opposition. Even in the conflictual arenas, however, the stakes are seldom zero-sum for legislators, as Mayhew clearly showed. Much the same can be said for interest groups as well, particularly once the distinction is recognized between group leaders and followers. Interest group leaders represent constituencies, just as congressmen do, and many of the same considerations apply to the representational needs of both. They share a need for plausible credit-claiming and thus a stress on particularized benefits and visible position taking. Groups do, however, vary in organizational style and maintenance needs, so the rational response of reelection-minded congressmen will be a function of the configuration of demand and will result in a complex supply pattern.

VI

Political Market Failures

Economists have long stressed the virtues of markets as mechanisms for the most efficient production, pricing, and allocation of goods and services. By this reasoning, government intervention is warranted only when the assumptions underlying the efficient operation of such markets are not met through such phenomenon as spillovers, public goods, imperfect information, or imperfect competition. Naïve early formulations tended to view politicians as altruistic and efficient public interest maximizers. The abundance of empirical evidence to the contrary stimulated more recent efforts to develop exchange theories of political behavior that regarded political institutions as political markets characterized by their own laws of supply and demand. Interest groups were the central political actors in these formulations, and policymakers were treated as rational and self-interested in responding to pressure group demands. These theories, though insightful, ultimately proved simplistic and unsatisfying. The foregoing transactional theory of legislative markets recognized the importance of interest groups even as it stressed the latitude available to policymakers, making it possible to derive some tentative implications for the functioning of political markets.

At a minimum it should be quite clear that political markets, if they are to operate ideally, must satisfy all the same conditions as economic markets. Thus economic market failure is by itself insufficient to establish the superiority of governmental solutions; indeed government intervention may well serve to consolidate or reinforce private power or to make market failures worse. There is in fact little correlation between the occurrence of economic market failure and government intervention. All that can be said with confidence about political markets is that they, as much or more than economic markets, will seldom operate ideally. This failure of political markets is especially troublesome inasmuch as they constitute the last resort available against the inequities and inefficiencies generated by the private sector. No higher authority exists with the power to intervene to remedy political market failures. Pessimistic conclusions appear warranted regarding the size and composition of the public sector and the distribution of income to be expected in such an imperfect market situation. There is also little cause for optimism when one examines the prospects for issue movement to assess the potential for long-term changes in these conditions.

IMPLICATIONS FOR THE SIZE AND COMPOSITION OF THE PUBLIC SECTOR

In the literature on public finance and political economy at least two seemingly contradictory views can be identified regarding the size of the public sector. Some scholars point to the free rider problem and infer that the public sector will inevitably be too small in a democracy. Others focus on the paradox of logrolling and argue that the public sector will typically be too large. In light of the transactional theory advanced here, both these views can be seen to be partially correct once the existence of several quite distinct policy processes is recognized.

Olson quite clearly stresses the vulnerability of collective benefits to the free rider problem.[1] There is thus no guarantee that such benefits will be provided at all; and if some collective benefits are provided, the amount and burden sharing will almost surely be suboptimal. This logic applies both to broad benefits like national security that affect society as a whole and to benefits that affect narrower population groupings. Insofar as some groups with common interests fail to overcome the free rider problem, the full range of demands will not be adequately reflected in the pluralist equilibrium, and at least some desirable policies will fail to be enacted. Galbraith has advanced a similar argument in *The Affluent Society*, pointing to what he sees as public squalor in the midst of private affluence.[2]

Downs arrives at much the same conclusion by somewhat different reasoning, stressing the effects of imperfect information on political support for public outlays.[3] In the private sphere, transactions take place on a quid pro quo basis in which both benefits and costs associated with the transactions are clearly recognized by the parties involved, but no such direct link between benefits and costs exists in the public sector:

> Taxes are not allocated to individuals on the basis of government benefits received but on some other basis, usually ability to pay. Thus receipt of a given benefit may have no connection whatever with payment for it. And when a man pays his income tax or the sales tax on his new car, he cannot link these acts of sacrifice to specific benefits received. This divorce of benefits from payment for them makes it difficult to weight the costs and benefits of a given act and decide whether or not it is worthwhile, as can be done regarding almost every private transaction.[4]

This problem is made worse by the incentives facing most voters to limit the costs of acquiring and interpreting information. For the most part citizens find it rational to remain largely ignorant of the composition of the budget. Such voters will unavoidably possess by way of their tax burdens at least some information regarding the costs of public policies, whereas the benefits of public policies will typically be remote or hidden. Successful government efforts to deter foreign aggressors or to regulate product safety or water quality will be taken for granted; the more successful the programs, the less they will seem to have been necessary at all. To make matters worse, every voter will be able to find at least some programs in the budget he does not favor. Hence, each citizen will believe the government could be operated more efficiently through the elimination of projects from which he derives no benefit.[5]

These factors in combination with the free rider problem produce a tendency for most voters to undervalue the benefits accruing from public policies. As an inevitable consequence, according to Downs, the budget will be too small in a democracy, as vote-maximizing political parties respond to voters' desires rather than to their best interests.

> For the government is primarily interested in people's votes, not their welfare, and will not increase their welfare if doing so would cost it votes. And it would lose votes if it increased taxes or inflation—which people are aware of—in order to produce benefits which people are not aware of.[6]

Ironically, the more perfect the competition between the parties, the more pronounced will be the tendency for government to cater to public opinion and thus to acquiesce in this undervaluation of public policies.[7]

Other scholars have argued convincingly that the public sector will ordinarily be too large in a democracy. Buchanan and Tullock, for example, point to the incentives to logroll in the specific benefit-general taxation case. Similarly, Riker and Brams suggest that narrow interests will find it rational to trade votes beyond the limit at which the sum of the external costs of the various trades will exceed any benefits derived, thus producing a paradox of logrolling. Mayhew stresses the appeal of particularized benefits to legislators and presents empirical evidence that such logrolling is much more common than had previously been thought.[8]

In fact Downs also recognized this tendency and fully expected it to partially offset what he saw as the dominant tendency for voters to undervalue the benefits of public policies. Such logrolling will be most pronounced, according to Downs, when citizens are ignorant of all components of the budget except those benefits flowing directly to them. This state of "preponderant ignorance" is unlikely in that voters will typically be aware of their tax burdens and therefore will not require information on the content of new policies not affecting them directly in order to oppose any increases in their own tax burdens. Thus excessive spending through logrolling will occur only insofar as the true costs of programs can be concealed. Because voters will possess plentiful information regarding their tax burdens and the inflation rate, Downs believes it will be difficult to obscure the true costs of public policies, so this tendency toward overspending will be inherently limited.[9]

In this regard, however, Buchanan and Richard Wagner have recently pointed to the role of inflation as a hidden tax.[10] In particular they fault Keynesian economic theory for its misguided reliance on politicians to act as public interest maximizers in manipulating fiscal policy to maintain full employment. Prior to the 1964 tax cut, politicians were constrained by public opinion in holding to the precept that the budget ought to be in balance. Although this precept was violated more often than not, it nevertheless served to limit the logrolling tendencies of politicians, for budget deficits were popularly regarded as undesirable and justifiable as only temporary expedients. With the evident success of the 1964 tax cut, the myth that the budget had to be balanced was effectively shattered. Whatever its economic merits, the balanced budget myth did operate as a constraint on the behavior of politicians. The demise of this constraint significantly weakened the already tenuous link between revenues and expenditures.

Reelection-minded congressmen now had the best of both worlds: the ability to deliver more and more particularized benefits without increasing taxes. Inevitably the resulting deficits were financed either by printing money, and thus inflating the currency, or by borrowing, and thus driving up interest rates; and in neither case were congressmen held accountable. The true costs of spending increases were concealed, leaving the blame for mishandling the economy—and the electoral costs associated with cooling it down once again—to fall largely on the president.[11] In the long run the legacy of Keynesian theory was to turn fiscal policy into a distributive issue in which potentially competing interest group demands for shares of the budgetary pie could be logrolled at the expense of the inattentive and largely ignorant mass public.

This tendency is exacerbated by the incremental nature of the budgetary process whereby an agency's base seldom receives thorough scrutiny, the debate is limited to how large an increase should be granted, and the best predictor of an agency's allocation is what it received the year before.[12] Incremental budgetary increases compounding an ever-larger base produce a slow but steady increase in the size of the public sector, as the rate of growth of public outlays outstrips the normal growth rate of the economy. Sooner or later, the paradox of logrolling reasserts itself. As Richard Rose and Guy Peters have observed:

> Can government continue on a business-as-usual basis if the economy no longer produces the goods as in the past? The answer of this book is no. The reason is simple: past commitments to future spending threaten to overload government, requiring it to spend more money than can be provided by the fruits of economic growth. As and when this happens, politicians will be faced with the full force of the aphorism, "There is no such thing as a free lunch." Government must then put the brakes on public spending or else cut the take-home pay of its citizens. If it decides to cut rather than protect take-home pay, it faces the prospect of political bankruptcy.[13]

Two such divergent conclusions regarding the size of the public sector seem almost impossible to reconcile. Indeed Richard Musgrave and Peggy Musgrave have inferred from the intensity of this controversy that the truth must be somewhere in between and that the size of the public sector must be about right.[14] It is mistaken, however, to focus on the misleading issue of the aggregate *size* of the budget while ignoring its *composition*. Once this is recognized, both schools of thought can seem to be partially correct inasmuch as their generalizations apply to quite different policy processes.

On the one hand there is no reason to doubt the validity of Olson's conclusion that the supply of public goods will inevitably be suboptimal as a consequence of the free rider problem. Broadly distributed benefits or costs will be less likely to generate organizational activity. Political parties will show little interest in such issues. At best, purposively oriented staff organizations, lacking resources and lobbying clout, will represent such interests. The more remote and uncertain the potential benefits of a public policy, the more difficult the organizational task of political entrepreneurs.

On the other hand there will probably be an excess of policies involving concentrated benefits and widely distributed costs. Under such circumstances, demand patterns will most often be consensual, and electoral incentives will dictate the accommodation of group demands. Distributive and self-regulatory policies will abound, as legislators engage in mutually beneficial transactions with interest group leaders. Moreover conflictual demand patterns will tend to produce delegative outcomes, as policy-without-law operates to the advantage of both congressmen and group leaders.

Thus it becomes possible to point to an abundance of distributive legislation, the continuing devolution of power to private groups, and the rise of the modern regulatory state while at the same time lamenting the undersupply of public goods. In Jones's terms, many public problems are ignored by government even as many essentially private problems are acted upon as if they were legitimately public.[15] Even in the public sector, Galbraith might properly observe, public squalor would seem to exist in the midst of private affluence. The only real difference is that in the private sector consumers get only what they pay for and pay for what they get, whereas in the public sector the link between benefits and costs is broken, thus making it possible to shift the costs of one's consumption onto inattentive third parties.

IMPLICATIONS FOR INCOME DISTRIBUTION

It should now be quite clear why, as I have argued, policies significantly modifying the distribution of income will usually occur outside the redistributive arena, and their impact will often be to reinforce the preexisting inequities rather than to rectify them.[16] Struggles between haves and have-nots are intensely conflictual, and the electoral incentives stemming from conflictual demand patterns all point, at most, to legislative delegation, if not to nondecision.

Clearly, previously excluded groups will be at a tremendous disadvantage in challenging the existing order, lacking, as they do, legitimacy, resources, and ties to key committee chairmen. Established groups possess all these plus the defensive advantage. Challenging groups may be forced to rely on social protest but by their very nature are ill-equipped to capitalize on the events they force. Their demands may be branded as radical and thus easily deflected into the realm of nondecision. Concessions granted to quell unrest in the short run may be withdrawn, thus cutting off a source of particularized benefits available to insurgent leaders. Most important, the leaders, to survive, must sooner or later confront the problems of organizational maintenance. Faced with the need for plausible credit-claiming, they become extremely vulnerable to co-optation, as Piven and Cloward have observed:

> Organizers not only failed to seize the opportunity presented by the rise of unrest, they typically acted in ways that blunted or curbed the disruptive force which lower-class people were sometimes able to mobilize. In small part, this resulted from the doctrinal commitment to the development of mass-based, permanent organization, for organization-building activities tended to draw people away from the streets and into the meeting rooms. In part it resulted from the preoccupation with internal leadership prerogatives that organization-building seems to induce. But in the largest part organizers tended to work against disruption because, in their search for resources to maintain their organizations, they were driven inexorably to elites, and to the tangible and symbolic supports that elites could provide. Elites conferred these resources because they understood that it was organization-building, not disruption, that organizers were about.[17]

Thus, as Walker suggested, such groups will often be dependent on the indirect representation of moderate groups or the policy entrepreneurship of elected politicians.[18] Roger Cobb and Charles Elder argued for this reason that new issues must of necessity be framed in the broadest possible terms in order to attract wide support, for "the more ambiguously an issue is defined, the greater the likelihood that it will reach an expanded public."[19] This very ambiguity, however, facilitates the deflection of new issues into the regulatory arena. Publics aroused by such an issue will be particularly vulnerable to symbolic reassurances that it has been favorably resolved. Issues couched in ambiguous terms invite ambiguous legislative responses that render a hard-headed assessment of the stakes almost impossible. For congressional entrepreneurs, it may be recalled, such broadly defined issues offer avenues for electorally profitable position taking; the more ambiguous and symbolic the issue, the greater its potential. It should therefore come as no surprise when public attention wanes and agency capture by clientele groups ensues.

Often those policies that seem at first glance to fall within the redistributive arena prove on closer inspection to be something quite different. AFDC and public assistance, according to Piven and Cloward, are better understood as regulatory insofar as they involve the delegation of broad discretion to welfare administrators.[20] Public housing and urban renewal are quintessentially distributive, often benefiting builders and lending institutions at the expense of the unorganized poor. Community Action provides a classic instance of policy-without-law. Medicare is only mildly redistributive at best, focusing solely on the aged, relying on a highly regressive form of financing, and delegating considerable discretion to administrators with the predictable result that physicians have been among the primary beneficiaries.

Income redistribution is by no means confined to the redistributive arena. Distributive policies transfer resources directly, with losers excluded from the process and the demand pattern kept consensual through logrolling. In the regulatory and self-regulatory arenas the redistributive effects are, by design, indirect and ambiguous but no less real. Often this redistribution occurs up the income ladder, as regulated industries operate as governmentally sanctioned cartels. Capture, though a common result, is by no means inevitable. As Sabatier observed, effective regulation can occur when agencies succeed in mobilizing a supportive constituency.[21] This is a difficult task at best because the benefits are often widely distributed, necessitating a reliance on purposive incentives; yet the implementation of recent air and water pollution legislation suggests it can be achieved.

In the regulatory arena, redistribution may occur down the income ladder as well, albeit less often. Leaders of challenging groups will be highly vulnerable to co-optation as organizational maintenance needs make institutionalized access to legislative and administrative policy processes highly attractive. For this reason, as Gamson observed, authorities will manipulate access as a mechanism of social control.[22] Ideally, access could be limited to those groups most susceptible to control; but co-optation by its very nature represents a concession to groups threatening enough to force some form of highly visible response. Thus co-optation always carries with it certain risks for authorities:

> In other words, cooptation does not operate simply as a control device—it is also likely to involve yielding ground. For this reason, there are likely to be parallel fears on the part of authorities. They may worry that the act of cooptation represents the "nose of the camel" and be fearful of their ability to keep the rest of the camel out of the tent. Far from manipulation, some authorities may regard it as an act of undue yielding to pressure and the rewarding of "irresponsible behavior."[23]

One example of such redistribution within the regulatory arena is provided by the gains to blacks stemming from the 1964 and 1965 Civil Rights Acts. Although both these acts involved the delegation of considerable discretion to administrators, both have yielded at least incremental gains to blacks. For example the 1964 provisions on equal employment opportunity, as we have seen, have been interpreted and enforced much more vigorously by the bureaucracy and the courts than would have been anticipated from a reading of the substance and legislative history of the act. This suggests that entrepreneurship may yield minimal gains initially and yet place an issue on the periodic agenda, eventually producing substantial expansions of authority and resources as a result of incrementalism.

An even more striking example is provided by the gradual accretion of power to organized labor. According to O'Brien, nascent groups must engage in a lengthy searching process in an effort to reach an accommodation with their environments.[24] In so doing they must obtain legitimacy and a stable source of financial resources. The quest for legitimacy risks co-optation and goal displacement; yet in the absence of legitimacy such groups cannot plug into the pluralist process and obtain the particularizable benefits necessary to survival. Labor was successful in obtaining legitimacy and then expanding its influence:

> For example, since the thirties, American labor unions have gradually assumed stronger ties with other groups in the "respectable" community. However, labor was able to make this transformation from a

group outside the "respectable community" to a group very much part of the "establishment" only because it first gained *legitimacy* through the Wagner Act. Alternatively, other groups, such as the various third-party movements, have not been able to gain recognition as legitimate interest groups and thus, after the issues which they raised have been resolved, other persons and groups are not forced to bargain with them.[25]

Labor has not only won legislative victories securing basic rights in collective bargaining but come to represent broader, consumer-class interests, according to Greenstone.[26] Clearly co-optation of challenging groups is by no means the inevitable result of delegative outcomes; as Wilson observed, such groups may eventually become institutionalized vehicles for reformist impulses. Only in mature, bureaucratized organizations will slack resources and staff discretion combine to permit sustained and effective pressures for social change.[27] Reformism is, however, no more inevitable than conservatism in such mature, bureaucratized organizations.

ISSUE MOVEMENT

These pessimistic conclusions regarding income distribution and the size and composition of the public sector would be less disturbing if there were some long-term prospects for issue movement. Recall Lowi's suggestion that all issues would sooner or later progress from the distributive through the regulative to the redistributive arenas as they inevitably became increasingly conflictual.[28] If Lowi is correct, grounds for optimism would seem to exist regarding long-term trends toward a more equitable distribution of income and away from policy-without-law and the devolution of power.

Similarly, in attempting to build upon Edelman's analysis, Oppenheimer identified three issue categories: nondecision, symbolic, and material politics. It should be apparent that these three arenas are analogous to the nondecision, regulative, and redistributive categories in my own typology, as Oppenheimer focused solely on cases of defensive lobbying by the oil industry, ignoring the three consensual arenas entirely. Based on the water pollution and oil depletion cases he examined, Oppenheimer proposed a general pattern of issue movement over time, beginning with the politics of nondecision, in which established groups suppress efforts at change on the part of the unorganized. In time, these challenging groups gain strength, forcing the established groups to make at least symbolic concessions. Eventually, in the phase of material politics, the reform-ing groups win out, and the previously entrenched groups in turn seek symbolic reassurances that their status will be eroded no fur-ther.[29] This would imply a temporal issue movement down the right-hand side of my typology (Table 3 in Chap. 2).

Although this scenario clearly holds for the water pollution and depletion allowance cases Oppenheimer examined, it is not general. Obviously Oppenheimer can make no statements whatsoever regarding the self-regulatory and distributive spheres. Moreover, even when the concern is limited to defensive lobbying, there is no reason to assume that all issues will inevitably move all the way through the three issue types. Depending on the relative success of contending group strategies, any given issue can cease to move at any point.

In this regard, Edelman suggested that the tenacity of unorganized group demands will depend on securing some initial success. Thus satisfaction of an initial demand for material benefits will merely whet the appetite of a group, encouraging it to escalate its demands still further; whereas defeat will result in the restoration of quies-cence, especially if the defeat is accompanied by symbolic reassur-ances that the group's interests are recognized as legitimate.[30] While Edelman's hypothesis certainly permits issue movement in the direc-tion identified by Oppenheimer, it also recognizes that this move-ment might stop, subject to the relative success of established groups in blocking demands for material concessions. I have shown how demands of previously excluded groups for a redistribution of income or status rewards are particularly vulnerable to deflection into the nondecision or regulatory arenas.

Ripley and Franklin suggest that redistributive issues will often be redefined as distributive in the course of the legislative process. "The redefinition of redistributive issues may occur as the price for allow-ing any redistribution to emerge at all. Reaching accord is easier if the participants in a redistributive debate choose to emphasize the distributive aspects and mute the redistributive aspects."[31] This rede-finition may also take place through subsequent amendments to established legislation that gradually erode the initial redistributive emphasis.

The typology advanced here does not lend itself to any single pre-diction regarding the general form of issue movement. A given issue falls within one of the process categories only by virtue of its demand and supply pattern. These two dimensions are interrelated by virtue of the electoral cost-benefit calculus congressmen must employ in choosing their response to a given demand pattern. Issue movement, a shift of a policy from one issue arena to another, will thus occur only when there are significant changes in the costs and benefits associated with the various options facing congressmen, for example in the relative significance of potential opposition groups.

There would seem, for example, to be distinct limits to innovative policies. An established group, faced with a challenge by previously excluded groups, will attempt to suppress conflict, thus keeping the issue in the realm of nondecision. Lower class groups and broadly distributed interests will often be forced to rely primarily on purposive incentives and to frame issues ambiguously to attract broad support. By Edelman's reasoning, the defeat of a challenging group's initial material demands may restore quiescence; there is thus no guarantee that an issue will ever leave the realm of nondecision. Alternatively, policy-without-law, with its blend of symbolic reassurances and co-optation, may suffice to keep a potentially threatening issue within the regulatory arena indefinitely. If the challenging groups remain unorganized, the resulting administrative process is likely to be one that the established groups can easily come to dominate. If the challenging groups have attained a degree of formal organization, however, the results of the administrative process become much less certain. Only if the established groups are thoroughly discredited or the challenging groups widely regarded as deserving would redistribution seem likely. Such a progression, though possible, is in no way inevitable.

Changes in demand pattern would seem more likely to generate significant issue movement when such purposively oriented staff organizations can engage in defensive lobbying; the evidence suggests that challenging groups may be most successful in manipulating the defensive advantages posed by the American system of multiple veto points. Groups obtain benefits in the distributive and self-regulatory arenas by keeping conflicts "privatized," in Schattschneider's terms. Although staff organizations may lack the resources and lobbying clout of established membership groups, they need few resources to publicize the existence of distributive subgovernments or instances of regulatory capture. In so doing, they may successfully "socialize" the conflict, arousing the previously inattentive audience. The role of consumer groups in bringing about the demise of the Sugar Act provides a striking example; with the opposition of consumer groups the issue became conflictual and thus shifted from the distributive arena into the realm of nondecision. Lowi argues that this pattern will be general, with issues inevitably becoming increasingly conflictual and thus eventually shifting out of the distributive and regulatory arenas. Although this hypothesis recognizes, at least implicitly, the fundamental importance of demand pattern as the emergence of an aroused opposition to established groups necessitates a shift to one of the conflictual arenas, the emergence of such an opposition is in no way inevitable, and even where it occurs there remains no guarantee of further issue movement.

Issue movement may also occur when the demand pattern shifts as a result of presidential or party efforts to counterbalance interest group pressures. There was, for example, nothing inherently distributive about the tariff in 1930. With the election of a Democratic Congress in 1932 and with the Roosevelt administration's decision to lower tariffs, the Reciprocal Trade Act of 1934 was enacted, delegating the authority to set rates to the executive branch and thus shifting the tariff issue out of the distributive arena once and for all. Between 1930 and 1934 the demand pattern on the issue had become conflictual, not because of any shift in interest group alignments on the issue, but because presidential leadership and party pressures emerged in opposition to interest group demands.

Characteristically, Schattschneider recognized this development. Writing in 1934, he praised the Reciprocal Trade Act for taking the tariff issue out of Congress, citing the president's superior ability to play off competing interests because of his broader constituency.[32] Moreover he recognized the important role of political parties in responding to those groups in the population that fail to organize— indeed that may be only spectators to political conflict.[33] To the extent that political parties form logrolling coalitions with organized groups, as Schattschneider observed they often do,[34] they may fail to offer an effective counterbalance to the bias of the pressure system. Yet the evidence suggests that all too often such a bias is inevitable and that effective opposition must come from the president or the parties if it is to come at all.

VII

Prospects for Reform

Clearly political markets cannot be relied on to remedy automatically the failures of economic markets; yet political markets constitute a last line of defense, for there is no higher authority to intervene and correct their operation. If, as Schattschneider suggested, the proper role of government is to remedy the inevitable imbalances generated by the private sphere, political markets must somehow be made to work.

At least four broad categories of reforms can be identified. Some scholars suggest that all that is needed is to remedy the biases of pluralism. Others have called for the strengthening of those institutions uniquely situated to represent broad national interests: the presidency and especially the parties. A third group suggests a variety of constitutional or institutional reforms designed to constrain or better channel the behavior of politicians. A fourth group suggests that only significant changes in the motivations of politicians and voters will suffice to produce the necessary changes in behavior. Although some of these proposals hold real promise, their prospects are not bright.

REMEDYING THE BIAS TO PLURALISM

The strategy for remedying the bias to pluralism is to restore perfect competition in the demand for public policies. Pluralism presumes that all affected political interests will organize and approach government and that each will be strong enough to produce a just equilibrium to the group struggle. When these assumptions are not met, one obvious remedy is to restore a perfectly functioning and self-correcting pluralism. Galbraith, for example, introduced the

141

notion of countervailing power, whereby the formation of large organizations is seen as generating counterorganization by threatened groups. This process is not automatic, however; where counterorganization fails to occur by itself, the role of government is to step in and subsidize the mobilization of the appropriate groups or, where necessary, exercise countervailing power itself.[1]

To a considerable degree, countervailing power has arisen quite spontaneously through the activity of private entrepreneurs. As McFarland has observed, for example, members of public interest lobbies tend to adhere to a "civic balance" ideology in which remedying the biases to pluralism suffices as a broad, purposive reward. The recent proliferation of such middle-class social movements as public interest lobbies, environmental groups, and gray lobbies suggests that this notion retains considerable appeal.[2]

Yet there are inevitable limits to this process. Some groups find it impossible to overcome the free rider problem. Others prove extremely difficult to mobilize. Participation in political organizations—and political entrepreneurship in particular—is a function of social class. Members of the lower classes, for whom organization might seem to offer the greatest potential benefits, find it hardest to afford the dues and are least likely to possess the feelings of efficacy necessary for involvement. Nor is there any guarantee that such groups, when they do organize, will be in any sense strong enough to produce a just equilibrium to the group struggle. Different interests will inevitably employ different incentive structures, different strategies and tactics, and widely varying resources.

Government efforts to mobilize previously excluded groups are subject to these same limitations; the middle-class bias of participation on Community Action boards provides an instructive example of this.[3] Moreover, as Lowi has convincingly argued, there is ultimately no way to identify all affected interests. Interest group liberalism as a public philosophy never knows whether to stop organizing or whether important groups remain unrepresented.[4] To make matters worse, such a strategy ignores the divergence of interests between group leaders and followers. Group leaders often possess surplus profits and exercise considerable discretion. Insofar as they survive by position taking and plausible credit-claiming, the representation of group interests may take on dramaturgical overtones, with legislators and lobbyists engaging in ritualized conflicts and mutual role taking. To that extent, the rank-and-file members of Pattern A groups may well be every bit as vulnerable to symbolic reassurances as are Edelman's Pattern B groups. Within labor unions, the manipulation of symbols to maintain the quiescence of the rank and file has become institutionalized.[5]

Perhaps most important, the pluralist vision must sooner or later encounter the paradox of logrolling, which would in no way be avoided by remedying the biases to pluralism, for the difficulty does not stem from the failure of some groups to organize but from the inability of rational individuals to weigh the external costs of logrolling. Those insightful enough to anticipate the paradox find themselves powerless to prevent it by their own abstinence and thus engage in vote trading to minimize their own losses. In this regard, Walter Lippman's critique of the New Deal's efforts to organize a "polity of pressure groups" retains its essential validity in the contemporary context:

> There is no reason to think that the self-regarding activities of special groups can be balanced or regulated by organizing more and more of them. . . . By organized restrictions of many sorts the production of wealth has been retarded, the method of monopoly being employed to enrich the favored interests. The imprimatur of respectability having been put upon organized privilege, the whole population has become imbued with the idea that as a matter of right everyone is entitled to invoke the law to increase his income.
>
> This is the vicious paradox of the gradual collectivism which has developed in western society during the past sixty years: it has provoked the *expectation* of universal plenty provided by action of the state while, through almost every action undertaken or tolerated by the state, the production of wealth is *restricted*. By these measures modern states have frustrated the hopes which their policies have aroused. (Emphasis added)[6]

Rose and Peters suggest that this paradox has run its course and that as a consequence most of the industrialized democracies now face imminent political bankruptcy.[7] This cannot be averted by tinkering with the demand side of political markets. The paradox is inescapable inasmuch as the participants are trapped in an n-person prisoner's dilemma; self-discipline will not be forthcoming.

STRENGTHENING AGGREGATIVE INSTITUTIONS

The foregoing analysis focused on the incentives for individual congressmen to logroll when faced with overwhelming group pressures; yet a recurring theme of the transactional theory advanced here is that "pressure" is an inadequate characterization of the relationship between legislators and lobbyists. They engage in mutually beneficial transactions in which groups obtain benefits even as congressmen retain considerable latitude. Ironically, according to Schattschneider, this very latitude is the root of the problem; it is not so much that organized group pressures are overwhelming, but that the parties are so weak:

> Congressmen succumb to pressure by organized minorities, not because the pressure groups are strong, but because congressmen see no reason for fighting at all; the party neither disciplines them nor supports them. . . . Because the congressman is neither punished nor protected by the party, and because in addition he is in doubt about the power of the pressure group to defeat him for re-election, he decides to play safe.[8]

Thus to Schattschneider there was no substitute for vigorous and competitive political parties. His case for party government rested on two underlying assumptions: that the parties would find it *rational* to counterbalance interest group demands and that the parties possessed inherent bargaining advantages enabling them to exercise this countervailing power. Unfortunately each of these assumptions can be called into serious question upon closer examination.

Schattschneider believed that the parties would find it rational to appeal to an otherwise inattentive audience in an effort to mobilize broad national majorities. Indeed the expansion of the practicing electorate constituted, in his view, a profoundly important and largely unrecognized contribution of the parties.[9] In this effort the parties are moreover uniquely situated to broker and integrate the segmented appeals of interest groups and to identify and champion broader public interests:

> No public policy could ever be the mere sum of the demands of the unorganized special interests. . . . The mobilization of majorities in recognition of the great public interests, the integration of special interests with public policy, and the over-all management and planning involved in discriminating among special interests cannot be done by organized special interests on their own initiative. These are functions of an entirely different kind of organization, the political party.[10]

The presidency might seem particularly well suited to this task inasmuch as the president alone is accountable to a national constituency, but Vietnam and Watergate provide striking contemporary reminders that the powers of that office will always be subject to abuse, and they suggest that the routinization of charisma may well be preferable to an imperial presidency. In this respect, Schattschneider believed the parties to be ideally suited, for any tendency toward an imperial presidency would be counterbalanced in a system of strong national parties inasmuch as "political responsibility is more flexible, comprehensive, and powerful than the system of legal responsibility set up in the separation of powers."[11] In his view, until the national parties are strengthened, Congress will remain unable to compete with the president in the discovery and exploitation of new issues, and the presidency will remain "the sole rallying point of the great public interests of the country."[12] Thus it is a "waste of time" to even speak of counterbalancing group pressures except in terms of the parties: "Aside from a strong party system there is no democratic way of protecting the public against the disintegrating tactics of the pressure groups."[13]

Unfortunately the evidence suggests that the parties have failed historically to perform this brokerage function, at least in the United States. Mayhew found, for example, that Republicans in Congress in the 1947–1962 period championed the cause of economy in government against the Democrats' logrolling coalition of farm, city, labor, and western interests.[14] This might suggest that a Republican resurgence to majority status would produce incumbents committed to resisting the wiles of special interests; but as Mayhew observed, when the situation was reversed in the early 1900s, the Republicans fashioned a majority out of a logrolling coalition on the tariff issue while the Democrats championed the cause of a broadly defined public interest. Thus Mayhew reluctantly concluded that such logrolling coalitions may well represent the inevitable path to majority status, while the minority party is left with no recourse but to pay lip service to the public interest even as it tries to break up the dominant coalition and forge a majority of its own.[15] In this respect, even Schattschneider conceded that only minority parties can afford to be principled and programmatic.

> The minor party can evolve a precise, symmetrical, and consistent set of principles and a program that is designed to implement those principles because it does not need to conciliate a multitude of incompatible interests, since it is not seriously trying to win the next election. Minor parties deal in principles divorced from power, but the bid for power is the life of a major party.[16]

Some grounds for optimism remain nevertheless. According to Sundquist, for example, the Democrats in Congress in the 1950s exhibited many of the characteristics of programmatic parties.[17] Greenstone found that labor's increasing dependence on the Democratic party has led to a tempering of that group's demands and a broadening of the range of issues on which it takes positions; yet he attributed this less to the party's inherent strength than to the lack of an alternative acceptable to labor. By and large, labor's stake in Democratic success has been self-evident, and its support has more often than not been voluntarily offered.[18] In short, the case of labor in fact suggests the potential for the party to excercise a much stronger brokerage role for that has largely gone unexercised.

In any event the disappointing performance of American parties is not inherent, according to Schattschneider. The decentralization of power is the most important single characteristic of the American party system. The national parties exercise little or no control over the nomination of congressional candidates. There is little they can do to hold them accountable, and they lack the resources to offer them support. Moreover, American parties, unlike those in a parliamentary system, lack both the power to call elections and, as a consequence, the power to frame the question to be referred to the electorate.[19] Thus increased centralization is a prerequisite for real party government.

In opposition to this argument, however, Downs's economic theory has convincingly demonstrated that vote-maximizing parties will typically converge to the electoral center, obscure their differences, and thus fail to offer voters clear-cut, programmatic choices. Moreover any reform that rests on the assumption that voters will make decisions intelligently on the issues must eventually come to grief over the problem of information cost. Indeed much of the controversy surrounding the call for responsible parties by the American Political Science Association's Committee on Political Parties in 1950 has centered around the feasibility and desirability of such mass-based, ideological parties.[20]

Schattschneider's case for stronger parties did not rest on such a conception of their function, however. He recognized the moderating tendencies of the two-party system and in fact saw this as a virtue. For one thing, both parties must draw support from all across the political spectrum in order to preserve at least a modicum of factor mobility. Such parties are free to shift in response to changes in public opinion, whereas ideological parties will sooner or later find themselves dependent on an isolated minority interest.[21] The lack of clear programmatic alternatives also helps to ensure the essential precondition of party government: that comity and tolerance between the two parties that makes possible the peaceful transfer of power.[22]

To a surprising extent, then, Schattschneider's case for stronger parties can be reconciled with Downs's pessimistic conclusions. It is almost as if Schattschneider, writing in 1941, anticipated Downs's objections and dispensed with them one by one. Schattschneider's argument, though, rests on a fundamentally different conception of the incentives motivating politicians. In Downs's view, politicians behave as cynical vote maximizers; in Schattschneider's, the "task of statesmen" is to "evolve policy amid conflict":[23] to mobilize majorities, take control of government, and assume responsibility for policy.[24]

> If politicians had no principles at all, there would be no real problem involved in the bid for power. The unprincipled politician interested only in staying in office lets himself become a cipher, a mere resultant of the conflicting forces without influence on the course of events. The problem results from the fact that many politicians want to accomplish something, and are not content to let themselves go where they are pushed.[25]

Such a conception of political man is fundamentally at odds with that underlying this volume. It assumes that a broad public interest is in fact identifiable and that politicians will seek, through the parties, to implement it. Such behavior, however desirable, cannot be assumed. Parties by their very nature are compelled to engage in credit-claiming. It is no surprise when they logroll to deliver particularized benefits or engage in symbolic position taking on controversial issues. Insofar as the case for party government rests on a conception of parties as mobilizers of a broad public interest, it comes down to little more than an exhortation to politicians to transcend their narrow self-interest. Ironically, such behavior, were it forthcoming, would eliminate much of the need for party government.

To make matters worse, the case is not much more convincing for Schattschneider's second assumption, that the parties will have, at least potentially, the capacity to exercise countervailing power. Here, in contrast to Downs, Schattschneider focused on the policy-making and brokerage functions of the parties between elections and stressed repeatedly their inherent bargaining power in dealing with organized interests:

> While it is true that the parties compete for the support of the interests, it is also true that the interests compete for the support of the parties. Moreover, there are 1,000 interests and only two parties. For this reason, it is extravagant for a major party to offer too much for the support of any one special interest; as purchasers of political support, the parties have a buyers' market.[26]

Thus any party capable of mobilizing a majority and capturing control of the government will inevitably possess enormous leverage over any individual interest, for it can always go elsewhere for support.

The British political system provides a particularly vexing counterexample, however. Possessed of many of the attributes of genuine party government Schattschneider called for, it remains nevertheless plagued by the same kinds of political market failure discussed earlier. Some analysts regard Britain as even further down the road toward political bankruptcy than the United States.[27] This would suggest that stronger parties are at best a necessary but clearly insufficient prerequisite to properly functioning political service.

The explanation for this surprising finding may lie in the relationship between a nation's political structure and its group activity. According to Wilson, the kinds of associations that exist in a given society will be a function of its political structure. The greater the dispersion of political power, the greater the incentive for the formation of a multitude of organizations. A highly centralized regime may generate a smaller number of large, mass-based, and correspondingly centralized groups.[28] Thus, paradoxically, a successful attempt to strengthen the national parties might have the unanticipated consequence of generating stronger national groups as well, a development that might well more than offset any gains from strengthening the parties.

The British example is again instructive, although far from conclusive. According to Wilson, "Whatever may have produced the essential features of the British government, it is the resultant political structure, and not general attitudes of consensus and deference, that is chiefly responsible for the structure of politically active voluntary associations."[29] In the United States, the separation of powers and federalism have combined to produce a multitude of groups active at all levels. Such national organizations as exist are more often than not relatively loose federations of local units. In Britain, by contrast, the farm, veterans, business, professional, and trade union organizations are, by and large, national in orientation, monolithic, centralized, and noncompetitive.[30] Under such circumstances it should not be surprising that even comparatively disciplined and responsible parties have been unable to exercise countervailing power. This suggests that, if party government could somehow be transplanted into the American context, the dispersion of power imposed by the Constitution might, just possibly, serve to retard the otherwise natural tendency toward the consolidation and centralization of the interest group universe. It would be ironic if federalism and the separation of powers, both of which Schattschneider criticized as obstacles to real party government,[31] ultimately proved essential for its efficient operation.

In any event, one final obstacle to responsible party government seems virtually insurmountable. As Wilson has observed, in a centralized regime the locus of group activity is likely to shift to the bureaucracy:

> Indeed, a national association confronting a centralized national government is likely to play its largest role, not with respect to decisions whether or not to adopt a major policy, but with respect to the administration of those policies that have already been adopted. A bureaucracy provides the many points of access and the details over which to bargain that a legislature in a centralized government cannot.[32]

Thus party control over policy ultimately requires that the bureaucracy be responsive to the national party, and this cannot be achieved in the absence of patronage. As Lowi has insightfully observed, however, civil service reforms and public employee unions have transformed modern bureaucracies into largely autonomous permanent governments.[33] Lowi's provocative contention that reformed cities are well run but badly governed suggests that the corruption commonly associated with urban political machines may well have been a necessary price to pay for political responsiveness. Of course Schattschneider would caution that urban political machines were notoriously noncompetitive; it follows that pathological characteristics of such party systems in no way refute his case for vigorous and competitive parties.[34] The issue Lowi raised, however, is not confined to the urban context; at the national level, these same developments operate to render responsible party government unattainable.

This is not to say that strengthening the parties is altogether without merit. Reforms aimed at strengthening the national parties as electoral and legislative institutions may well be desirable on balance, although the weaknesses underlying the case for party government suggest the need for guarded optimism. At best, stronger parties might serve to reduce the discretion available to bureaucrats by curbing the tendency toward interest group liberalism when congressmen are confronted with conflictual demand patterns, but it is not at all clear that this would actually happen. Failing that, the permanent bureaucracy, and ultimately policy, would seem largely immune to alternations in party control.

INSTITUTIONAL REFORMS

In the context of institutional reform it is worth recalling that there are at least four distinct problems of political markets to be addressed: the tendency toward excessive logrolling, the undersupply of certain kinds of collective benefits, the resulting inequities in income distribution, and the tendency of politicians to avoid hard choices by delegating broad discretion to administrators. Part of the appeal of the case for stronger parties lies of course in the hope that, as aggregative institutions, they might somehow find it rational to correct all these problems. In the absence of party government, constitutional and institutional reforms would seem necessary to better constrain and channel the behavior of politicians. Because scholars have tended to focus on one or another of these problems in isolation as if it were the entire difficulty, reform proposals have tended to come piecemeal and to be oversold. It is no surprise that none of these solutions proves sufficient in and of itself to remedy political market failure. Taken in combination, however, they could make a substantial difference.

Both Rose and Peters and Buchanan and Wagner stress the need to solve the paradox of logrolling. Politicians seeking reelection find it rational to increase spending programs while disguising their true costs. "Because politics today is about what is new, politicians today are rarely content to act as custodians for established programs. Politicians want to do things, and almost always the things they want to do cost money."[35] With the demise of the balanced budget myth, politicians are now free to conceal the real costs of such programs through deficit spending; but sooner or later they must choose between reducing benefits or cutting take-home pay. Either choice may lead to political bankruptcy.

With varying degrees of success, political entrepreneurs have recently advanced a variety of proposals such as Proposition 13 in California, to limit taxes and constitutional amendments to limit governmental outlays as a share of the national income. Buchanan and Wagner favor a constitutional amendment requiring the federal government to maintain a balanced budget, with a carefully circumscribed escape clause for exceptions in congressionally declared national emergencies. In their view, only by agreeing in this manner to bind themselves can politicians successfully escape the n-person prisoner's dilemma that sooner or later culminates with the paradox of logrolling.

> A meaningful constitutional norm is required.... Budgets cannot be left adrift in the sea of democratic politics.... The elected politicians, who must be responsive to their constituents, the governmental bureaucracy as well as the electorate, need something by way of an external and "superior" rule that will allow them to forestall the persistent demands for an increased flow of public-spending benefits along with reduced levels of taxation.[36]

A balanced budget rule is superior to alternative constitutional norms for a variety of reasons. Efforts to limit levels of taxation will have little effect on politicians who remain free to disguise the costs of programs through deficit spending. It is for this reason that Milton Friedman has pointed convincingly to the need to limit federal spending instead.[37] A balanced budget rule is ultimately more flexible, however, because it avoids setting any arbitrary ceiling for the government share of the national product. Citizens may vote for as many public programs as they want, subject only to the constraint that the true costs of those programs be made explicit through the imposition of the necessary taxes. Thus perhaps the greatest virtue of such an amendment would be its potential for limiting the ability of politicians to deflect potentially conflictual issues into the distributive arena by keeping the losers unaware of the real stakes. If Downs is correct in assuming that voters are aware of their tax burdens, any rule making it more difficult to conceal the costs of programs through inflation or higher interest rates would tend to generate conflictual demand patterns, thus shifting such issues out of the distributive arena.

In addition, Rose and Peters, Friedman, and others have suggested that income tax rates be indexed to adjust for inflation. Under such a system, increases in the cost of living would automatically trigger both corresponding increases in the deductions individuals could claim and whatever reductions in tax rates on nominal income were necessary to restore individuals to the same level of tax on their real incomes. This would have the healthy effect of eliminating the need for earnings to increase even faster than the rate of inflation just to stay in place. More significantly, indexing would remove yet another of the primary incentives for politicians to sustain at least moderate rates of inflation: The fact that by pushing individuals into ever higher tax brackets, inflation produces automatic increases in tax revenues as a by-product. This enables politicians to increase spending levels without having to accept the responsibility for formally imposing tax increases. Alternatively, politicians periodically reduce taxes with great fanfare, especially in election years. Although such tax cuts can have the effect of restoring rates to their previous levels in real income terms, they are seldom accompanied by rebates to compensate taxpayers for those excess dollars claimed in taxes during the preceding period solely as a by-product of inflation.[38]

As with the balanced budget amendment, then, indexing tax rates would make it harder for politicians to conceal the true costs of government programs. Increases in revenues would require explicit appeals for higher taxes, thus making it more difficult to keep such issues within the distributive arena. Whereas both of these reforms would help to curb the tendency toward excessive logrolling, tax indexation might prove more effective in practice. A balanced budget rule would have to be painstakingly drafted to prevent its erosion into just another debt ceiling, violated at will by politicians and never really taken seriously. For this reason Buchanan and Wagner argue that such a norm must take the form of a constitutional amendment if it is to have real teeth;[39] whether even such an amendment could in fact be made effectively binding remains unclear. Indexing, by contrast, would seem immune to the wiles of politicians and would almost surely help to curb their logrolling tendencies.

Some critics contend that a balanced budget amendment would limit the capacity of policymakers to manage the economy. A respectable argument can be made that the economy would be better left unmanaged; Friedman, for example, advocates a balanced budget to constrain legislators and a fixed rule governing the growth of the money supply, thus effectively tying the hands of the Federal Reserve Board as well. Too often, he contends, government efforts to fine-tune the economy merely introduce random and disequilibrating disturbances; deficits to "prime the pump," for example, emerge from Congress too late or in the wrong amounts and thus prove counterproductive.[40] Other economists point to monetary policy as a much more flexible instrument of economic management. In any event, the case against Keynesianism is that, whatever its merits on purely economic grounds, in a democratic society politicians simply cannot be relied on to follow its prescriptions. Whatever its theoretical appeal, its political weaknesses are inherent and fatal. At best it is workable only in periods of recession or depression, when politicians will find it electorally appealing to stimulate expansion through deficits. It is unrealistic in the extreme to expect these same politicians to bite the bullet in an overheated economy. Rose and Peters have termed this phenomenon "one-eyed Keynesianism," and economists as divergent on other matters as Friedman and Galbraith have pointed to this serious shortcoming.[41]

The most serious drawback of such reforms is the prior problem of convincing rational politicians to enact them. In a world of self-interested politicians, mere exhortation is not enough, and it is not clear why such politicians should choose to bind themselves in these ways. Experience suggests that the paradox of logrolling probably will not be averted. At best, events will drift until they reach crisis proportions. As with the tariff of 1930 and its contribution to the Depression, political bankruptcy will ensue. Then, perhaps, politicians will pick up the pieces, learn the relevant lessons, and agree to bind themsleves. The Reciprocal Trade Act of 1934, it will be recalled, was just such a calculated response to an earlier paradox, delegating rate-setting authority to the executive branch in the hopes that the Tariff Commission would be better situated to resist group demands. It is also worth recalling that this response came only after Roosevelt's landslide victory and a change in party control of the Congress.

By themselves, these reforms address only one of the failures of political markets. Action to curb excessive logrolling, however desirable, does nothing to remedy the undersupply of public goods or the inequities in income distribution. To these ends, a variety of reforms have been advanced aimed at facilitating majority rule. Some consist of procedural reforms of the legislative process, such as abolishing the filibuster or easing cloture requirements, weakening or eliminating the House Rules Committee, abolishing the seniority system, or reinstating the twenty-one day rule.[42] Some critics would go even further and eliminate the multiple veto points arising from the separation of powers. Dahl stressed the superiority of the "populist" model of democracy to what he termed the "American hybrid," and Lindblom has recently contended that "the problem is not incrementalism, but a structure of veto powers that makes even incremental moves difficult and infrequent."[43]

The relative merits of these reforms, and indeed of the very case for majority rule, have been explored exhaustively elsewhere. For present purposes suffice it to say that while such reforms may well facilitate the passage of legislation, they in no way guarantee that the legislation emerging will remedy either the undersupply of public goods or the inequities in income distribution. They do nothing to remedy the free rider problem or the variation in group styles and resources discussed earlier. More to the point, they fail to address the political incentives facing congressmen to logroll in the consensual arenas and to delegate in the conflictual cases. Elimination of some veto points would reduce but not eliminate the need for legislative entrepreneurs to make compromises on the substance of legislation and would probably shift a number of issues out of the realm of nondecision. The evidence here suggests that often bills languishing in committee or blocked by Rules die with the blessing of congressmen reluctant to vote on them publicly.[44] Making such bills easier to pass does not eliminate the incentive to avoid choice; in the regulatory arena, legislative outcomes are ambiguous by design.

In this regard, it is worth recalling that Medicare and federal aid to education were both passed in 1965, after the Johnson landslide had produced an extraordinary Democratic majority in each house, thus facilitating important changes in procedures and in the composition of key committees. While there can be no doubt that these circumstances were sufficient to shift these issues out of the nondecision arena, they did not produce clear-cut legislative mandates. These bills provide striking examples of the failure of such majoritarian reforms to avert policy-without-law.

This points to the final problem to be addressed: how to constrain the tendencies of politicians to respond to group conflict with legislative delegation. In this regard, Lowi has suggested a number of possible remedies. Foremost, of course, is his call for the Supreme Court to reinvoke the Schecter rule, striking down as unconstitutional such broad grants of legislative authority. In the same vein he has urged presidents to veto such legislation. He has also called on Congress to codify existing laws and urged administrators to return to formal rule making rather than case-by-case adjudication.[45]

The problem with these reforms is much the same as that plaguing indexation and the balanced budget amendment. Although all are promising ideas, it is unrealistic to expect reelection-minded congressmen to tie their own hands. Hence Lowi quite correctly points to the need for external discipline imposed on Congress by the president or the courts. Unfortunately he fails to address the incentives facing these actors to play their assigned roles. He exhorts the Supremo Court to roinvoko tho Schoctor rulo and tho prosidont to exercise the veto power, just as he exhorts the Congress to codify and administrators to return to formal rule making. In short, he admonishes politicians to transcend narrow self-interest.

Ironically, the appeal of the case for party government can be seen to rest less on its own merits than on the inherent inadequacies of the alternatives. Insofar as these reforms require politicians to ignore self-interest, they are unlikely to succeed in the absence of the kind of overarching discipline the parties would seem to provide. Thus the fact that the argument for stronger parties likewise rests on the need for at least some politicians to perform as public interest maximizers at least some of the time takes on even more significance. Unless politicians change their behavior, the prospects for reform do not look promising.

CHANGES IN THE BEHAVIOR OF POLITICIANS

Rose and Peters argue that the success or failure of any reform ultimately depends on the willingness of elected officials to subordinate their immediate self-interest for the sake of the long-term needs of the broader public interest:

No set of procedures or principles by itself can contain the growing costs of public policy. A government can only reduce the risks of political bankruptcy if its leaders are prepared to show the political will to limit growth. If the will is there, the means can be found to safeguard public policy as some Western nations have demonstrated in the 1970s. If there is no political will to act, no amount of institutional tinkering can secure a government from the risk of political bankruptcy.[46]

Yet one of the recurring themes of this volume has been that remedies for political market failure cannot be founded on such an
assumption. Although reelection is not the sole motive of all politicians, it is a prerequisite for all the others; whatever substantive
goals a congressman seeks, he must be reelected to pursue them.[47]
Recall Fiorina's distinction between maximizing and maintaining
congressmen. This distinction recognized that politicians will sometimes ride against the tide of constituency sentiment, but only to a
point; each must set some aspiration level for his electoral margin
below which he will not willingly fall.[48] Thus, though some public
interest–maximizing behavior may indeed occur, in the long run this
is a thin reed indeed on which to place one's hopes.

It seems more realistic to assume that changes in the behavior of
politicians will follow changes in the political attitudes of the electorate. For example, if enough voters demand a balanced budget, this
will have more impact than any arbitrary limits on spending or the
level of the deficit. Likewise, if voters are indifferent to the issue,
even constitutional rules will probably have little more effect than
the existing debt ceilings. Crenson found in this regard that community attitudes affect party behavior. In communities characterized
by a "private-regarding ethos," the parties tended to ignore issues
like pollution that involve broad public interests and narrowly concentrated costs; where a "public-regarding ethos" prevailed, such
issues were much more likely to reach the agenda.[49] Indeed once one
such issue had been dealt with successfully, others tended to follow,
as new actors were drawn into the political process:

> The manpower supply that is created by a collective issue will tend to
> differ in a systematic way from the manpower that is mobilized for a
> specific issue. Citizens who spend their energies in the quest for a col-
> lective good are more likely than other political actors to accept non-
> material, moral gratifications as compensation and, because of their
> public-regarding predispositions, are likely to contribute to the growth
> of other collective issues. A collective issue, then, can be expected to
> cultivate public-regardingness within a town's political stratum, and
> the result is to increase the political stratum's receptivity to other col-
> lective decisions and to create a bias in the composition of the local
> political agenda. In effect, political issues provide one another with
> sustenance.[50]

Thus, an increase in public regardingness could produce a change
in the demands of voters, a shift in the balance of organizational
activity, and ultimately a change in the behavior of politicians.

Whether such a change in orientation would be desirable remains unclear. Wildavsky, for one, has argued for the superiority of what he terms the "partial view of the public interest" over the "total view of the public interest."[51] When citizens subordinate their private desires to some broader conception of the public interest, they forfeit the one piece of valid empirical information they possess: knowledge of their own preferences. By contrast, in a world of selfish actors pursuing their own narrow view of the public interest, a hidden-hand mechanism operates to yield desirable collective choices. Although Wildavsky's optimism on this point would seem misplaced in view of the biases to pluralism discussed at length earlier, his critique of the conception of a total view of the public interest is sobering. Given the significance of imperfect information, it is hard to see how optimal outcomes (whatever that might mean in such a context) can be expected to ensue when political actors disregard the most reliable data they possess.

In any event, both changes in the political attitudes of citizens and in the behavior of their representatives presume a change in the knowledge base of decisions. Perhaps the most important prerequisite for an ideal political market, and almost certainly the least realistic, is the assumption of perfect information. The cost of information makes it irrational for many citizens to vote at all unless they remain largely ignorant of public affairs. It also prevents citizens from properly assessing the benefits they obtain from certain kinds of public policies. It makes symbolic reassurances and interest group liberalism possible, and it serves to provide both legislators and lobbyists with considerable freedom from the demands of their constituents.

Finally, it operates to limit the capacity of even the most dedicated and public-spirited legislators to identify and solve public problems. Though I have focused throughout this volume on the electoral incentives to avoid hard choices among conflicting groups, these are not the only causes of legislative delegation. Policy-without-law may also reflect a perceived need to act on pressing problems in the absence of sufficient knowledge. This is what Jones has termed "speculative augmentation," or legislating beyond capability.[52] Under such circumstances ambiguity is an unavoidable response to complexity and value disagreement. Alternatively, delegation may reflect normal incrementalism, as concessions in legislative mandates or agency resources become the necessary price of securing any legislation at all.

This suggests a potentially significant role for improved policy analysis. If Keynes was indeed correct regarding the power of academic scribblers, the potential contribution of policy analysis could prove to be profound, serving to reduce the costs of information to politicians, voters, and interest group entrepreneurs. Much of that research would have to be contentious, in Rein's terms, challenging prevailing values and conceptions.[53] Any vision of policy analysis that rests on the underlying assumption that policymakers are public interest maximizers just waiting to respond to the best advice of academic theorists ignores one of the fundamental implications of this volume: Policymakers and interest group leaders thrive on imperfect information. It follows that knowledge of the real benefits and costs of public policies threatens the socialization of conflict. Insofar as the symbiotic relationship between legislators and lobbyists frequently hinges on keeping the losers unaware of the real stakes or, failing that, in obfuscating policy outcomes, such knowledge will simply not be welcome.

A prerequisite to usable knowledge, then, is to abandon naïve conceptions of the role of policy analysis. Political science has a unique contribution to make in this respect. The central argument of this volume has been that such a contribution will not be forthcoming until we recognize once again the importance of interest groups and transcend the notion that there is a single, "typical" legislative process to be explained.

Conclusion

My typology was a means to a well-defined end: I wanted to specify the circumstances under which interest groups would play a significant role in the congressional process in the United States. Given this limited purpose, that typology has proven both parsimonious and useful. Though I would hope it has wider applicability, the typology as it stands cannot do justice to the full complexity of the policy process. Both the demand pattern and supply pattern dimensions require a good deal more elaboration. The simple distinction between consensual and conflictual demands does not capture the variety of configurations of distinctively different types of groups, not to mention the countervailing pressures of party or presidential leadership. Similarly, legislative delegations take on a wide variety of distinct forms depending on the configuration of demand.

More significantly, however, the policy process is ultimately too complex to be adequately captured by any simple, two-dimensional typology. In reality, as Jones has convincingly argued, the policy process must be understood as a series of functional activities, beginning with the process of agenda formation and continuing on through policy adoption, implementation, and feedback.[1] Seen in this light, the various attempts at policy typologies (including my own) can all be seen to focus exclusively on some of these stages while ignoring others entirely.

For example my demand pattern dimension is confined almost exclusively to the configuration of interest group demands while largely ignoring the role of political parties in interest aggregation. The weakness of the American parties led me to ignore this dimension in deriving my own typology. In a comparative context, however, such an omission could be highly misleading. Party systems vary enormously across urban settings, by state, and cross-nationally. Much more research is clearly needed on how parties perform, or fail to perform, this vital aggregating function. Greenstone's study of the relationship between the AFL-CIO and the Democratic party offers a promising model in this respect. He found for example that the conventional assumption that interest groups confine themselves to interest articulation whereas the parties engage in aggregation was simply not borne out; the interpenetration of labor and the party frequently led to a reversal of these roles. He found, moreover, that this relationship varied enormously across the cities he examined, as a function of the relative resources of labor and the local party organization, their respective incentive systems, and the local political structure.[2]

My supply pattern dimension focuses on the incentives facing individual legislators confronted with varying configurations of demand, thus largely ignoring the constitutional and institutional characteristics of a given political system. Salisbury pointed to the relevance of these characteristics in his decisional system integration-fragmentation dimension. Wilson likewise pointed to the significance of what he termed the society's political structure. Because I chose to focus on the American legislative context, where the dispersion of power may be taken as a given, this dimension could be ignored as largely irrelevant. As with the interest aggregation dimension, however, such an omission could be misleading in a comparative context. Urban political systems, for example, vary widely in this respect, ranging from machine cities with strong mayors and highly centralized control over patronage, to cities with weak mayors, decentralized institutional structures, nonpartisan elections, merit systems, and so forth. Here again, Greenstone's comparison of Chicago, Detroit, and Los Angeles is illustrative of the kinds of analyses that might be done.

Although both Salisbury and Wilson point to the importance of this variable, they suggest that its effects are ultimately mixed and unclear. Salisbury observed that fragmentation of the decisional system can be desirable insofar as it encourages innovation and experimentation, provides multiple access points, encourages a consensus on rules and thus enhances system stability, and (following Lindblom) leads to efficient resource allocation in solving problems too complex for synoptic analysis. At the same time, however, such fragmentation can make problem identification more difficult and make nonincremental change almost impossible, thus leading at times to irrational or ineffectual responses and threatening system stability in times of crisis.[3] In a different vein, Wilson notes that centralization of the political structure may well increase the capacity of decision makers to manage conflict and broker interest group demands. At the same time, however, a centralized regime may also generate correspondingly centralized groups, thus offsetting to some degree the capacity of such a decision system to exercise such countervailing power.[4] These tentative propositions testify both to the relevance of this dimension in a comparative context and to how much remains to be learned about it.

Thus various efforts at policy typologies can ultimately be seen to be quite complementary in that they simply highlight different aspects of the same overall process. Because different dimensions are relevant for each stage of the process, depending on the purposes of a given researcher, any one typology might prove useful. No two-dimensional typology can hope to do justice to the complexity of the whole; for that purpose a multivariate analysis is clearly in order. In such an analysis a variety of typologies may have something to offer along the way. More likely, the attempt to generate such typologies will ultimately prove too confining and have to be discarded. This is why I have stressed the value of my typology not as a device for categorization but as a vehicle for identifying the underlying variables that contribute to an understanding of the role of interest groups in the American context.

In the long run, the larger challenge facing political science is to explain the *flow* of policy and how it varies, across issues as well as across different political systems—a formidable task and one that we have barely begun. In this effort a variety of typologies may be of heuristic value, pointing to variables that may be relevant at each stage. Eventually, however, we need to transcend these typologies, treating their underlying dimensions as continuous rather than as nominal or ordinal variables, and moving to operationalize and test the interrelationships among these variables rigorously and systematically. Again, it is multivariate analyses that are called for. One of the greatest difficulties posed by Lowi's original effort stemmed, after all, from his attempt to capture too many different things (expectations, group configurations, institutional foci, outcomes, etc.) employing only three nominal categories.

Unfortunately the empirical studies reviewed suggest that crucial variables will be all too often virtually impossible to operationalize.

Such concepts as decisional system integration or the aggregative capacities of the parties would seem no less difficult to measure; yet if there is one lesson that must be drawn from these studies, it is that such variables cannot be ignored. The temptation to draw unwarranted inferences from those that can be successfully operationalized would seem too great.

This suggests, at least for the foreseeable future, a continuing role for case studies. It goes without saying that one cannot draw reliable inferences from an examination of any single case; but case studies do remain an invaluable data base when examined comparatively and in the context of good theory—a commodity that is unfortunately always in short supply. In the generation of such theories, policy typologies may also have a place, at least for a time.

A necessary first step, at least in the U.S. context, is to change the way we think about interest groups and Congress. Legislators and lobbyists are interdependent; their relationsip is genuinely transactional, inasmuch as both parties benefit. Congressmen and interest group leaders each retain a surprising degree of latitude vis-à-vis their respective constituencies by taking advantage of the complexity of self-interest that provides the potential for obfuscation. The policy stakes are seldom zero-sum for congressmen, and they need not be for group leaders. In the distributive arena, both legislators and lobbyists profit from the exchange of electoral support for particularized benefits. In the regulatory arena, legislators avoid the electoral repercussions of explicit choices among contending groups through legislative delegation even as they create avenues for electorally rewarding casework in the long run. Delegative outcomes similarly benefit interest group leaders, allowing them to claim legislative victories and providing them with institutionalized access to the ongoing administrative process. Such outcomes provide both legislators and lobbyists with the best of all possible worlds: steady progress toward goals that are never fully achieved.

Notes

INTRODUCTION

1. Earl Latham, *The Group Basis of Politics*, pp. 35–36.
2. Raymond A. Bauer, Ithiel de Sola Pool, and Lewis Anthony Dexter, *American Business and Public Policy*.
3. Ibid., pp. 456–457.
4. Quoted in Tom Mathews, et al., "Single Issue Politics," p. 48.
5. Ibid., p. 57.
6. Theodore J. Lowi, "American Business, Public Policy, Case Studies, and Political Theory."
7. Mancur Olson, Jr., *The Logic of Collective Action*.
8. Robert H. Salisbury, "An Exchange Theory of Interest Groups"; and James Q. Wilson, *Political Organizations*.
9. Anthony Downs, *An Economic Theory of Democracy*; David R. Mayhew, *Congress*; and Morris P. Fiorina, *Representatives, Roll Calls, and Constituencies*.
10. Bauer, Pool, and Dexter, *American Business and Public Policy*, p. 478; see also Murray Edelman, *The Symbolic Uses of Politics*; and Theodore J. Lowi, *The End of Liberalism: Ideology*.
11. E. E. Schattschneider, *The Semi-sovereign People*.

CHAPTER ONE

1. Theodore J. Lowi, "American Business, Public Policy, Case Studies, and Political Theory," p. 679.
2. The phrase is Latham's; see his *The Group Basis of Politics*.
3. David B. Truman, *The Governmental Process*, p. 48.
4. Latham, *Group Basis of Politics*, p. 36.
5. Lowi, "American Business," p. 678.
6. Ibid., p. 681.
7. Stephen Kemp Bailey, *Congress Makes a Law*.
8. E. E. Schattschneider, *Politics, Pressures and the Tariff*.

9. Raymond A. Bauer, Ithiel de Sola Pool, and Lewis Anthony Dexter, *American Business and Public Policy.*

10. Schattschneider, *Politics, Pressures and the Tariff,* pp. 19–20.

11. Ibid., p. 22.

12. Ibid., pp. 135–136.

13. Ibid., p. 109.

14. Ibid., pp. 288–289.

15. Bauer, Pool, and Dexter, *American Business and Public Policy,* p. 324.

16. Ibid., pp. 258–261, 265–276, 317–318.

17. Ibid., chap. 9, "The Roots of Conviction—Self-interest and Ideology," pp. 127–153.

18. Bauer, Pool, and Dexter, *American Business and Public Policy,* pp. 372–374.

19. Ibid., p. 324.

20. Ibid., p. 345.

21. Ibid., chap. 24, "Pressure Group or Service Bureau?" pp. 350–357.

22. Bauer, Pool, and Dexter, *American Business and Public Policy,* p. 478.

23. Ibid., pp. 456–457.

24. Dexter, in particular, has written extensively concerning the tendency for theories to become fashionable within academic disciplines and in the process to gain widespread currency as something approaching caricatures of the more sophisticated and cautious formulations of their originators. In this regard Dexter has stressed the need for what he terms "countervailing intellectual power." See his "On the Use and Abuse of Social Science by Practitioners"; and *The Sociology and Politics of Congress,* pp. 179–210; see also his *How Organizations Are Represented in Washington.*

25. Lester Milbrath, *The Washington Lobbyists.*

26. Donald R. Matthews, *U.S. Senators and Their World,* chap. 8, "Senators and Lobbyists," pp. 176–196.

27. Donald R. Matthews and James A. Stimson, *Yeas and Nays.*

28. Leroy N. Rieselbach, *Congressional Politics,* p. 204. For a similar review of the literature of that period, see Malcolm E. Jewell and Samuel C. Patterson, *The Legislative Process in the United States,* chap. 12, "The Lobbyists," especially pp. 351–352.

29. Randall B. Ripley, *Congress,* chap. 8, "Congress, Interest Groups, and Constituents," pp. 201–223. See especially pp. 210–212 for the section on conditions for interest group influence. The revised edition of Ripley's text (*Congress,* 1979) provides evidence that this weakness in the literature remains a problem; see especially pp. 274–275, where Ripley graciously acknowledges the validity of this criticism, made previously in my "The Semi-sovereign Pressure Groups," p. 136.

30. Stanley S. Surrey, "How Special Tax Provisions Get Enacted"; and Bruce Ian Oppenheimer, "The Effects of Policy Variation on Interest Group Behavior in the Congressional Process."

31. For an early work on the subject, see Samuel P. Huntington, "Clientelism." More recently, see J. Leiper Freeman, *The Political Process;* and Douglas Cater, *Power in Washington.* See also Francis E. Rourke, *Bureaucracy, Politics, and Public Policy,* especially chap. 3, "The Mobilization of Political Support," pp. 42–80.

32. Cater, *Power in Washington,* pp. 17–20. I have chosen, somewhat arbitrarily in order to make the discussion manageable, to focus on the extensions of the Sugar Act from 1961 to its demise in 1974. The account that follows draws heavily on the

excellent analyses of these bills appearing in various editions of the *Congressional Quarterly Almanac* (Washington, D.C.: Congressional Quarterly, Inc., annual). For detailed coverage, see "Cuba, Dominican Republic Penalized by Sugar Act," *1961 CQ Almanac*, pp. 125-132: "Congress Again Revises Sugar Quotas," *1962 CQ Almanac*, pp. 127-143; "Congress Fails to Extend Foreign Sugar Quotas," *1964 CQ Almanac*, pp. 119-123; "Sugar Act Extended to December 31, 1971," *1965 CQ Almanac*, pp. 140-148; and "Sugar Quotas: 1948 Act Extended Through 1974," *1971 CQ Almanac*, pp. 481-493.

33. In Schattschneider's era, the tariff bill incorporated all items into a single omnibus bill. Thus, although there was little opposition to the tariff, hordes of lobbyists would attend, seeking protection. Import quota bills in the contemporary period apply to a narrower range of products, with separate legislation for meat, cotton textiles, etc. Hearings typically attract only a handful of lobbyists, all in support of the legislation and seeking a piece of the action. By contrast, the number of groups active on the contemporary tariff generally runs in the hundreds and, as Bauer, Pool, and Dexter observed, these groups tend to cancel each other out.

34. Gilbert Y. Steiner and Samuel K. Gove, *Legislative Politics in Illinois.*

35. "Congress Fails to Extend Foreign Sugar Quotas," *1964 CQ Almanac*, p. 119.

36. On the events leading to the eventual demise of the Sugar Act in 1974, see Randall B. Ripley and Grace A. Franklin, *Congress, the Bureaucracy, and Public Policy*, pp. 117 119; see also the coverage in *Congressional Quarterly Weekly Reports* (Washington, D.C.: Congressional Quarterly, Inc.): "The Battle to Overhaul the Sugar Act May Be Over," 16 February 1974, pp. 365-368; "Sugar Act," 9 March 1974, pp. 629-630; "Sugar Act: Lobby Scramble among Foreign Interests," 6 April 1974, pp. 876-877; "Sugar Act Extension," 18 May 1974, p. 1312; "Sugar Act Extension: Subsidies Pared by House Panel," 1 June 1974, pp. 1436-1438; and "Sugar Act Defeat," 8 June 1974, pp. 1529-1530.

37. Theodore J. Lowi, *The End of Liberalism: Ideology*; and idem, *The Politics of Disorder.*

38. Grant McConnell, *The Decline of Agrarian Democracy.*

39. Grant McConnell, *Private Power and American Democracy.*

40. Mark V. Nadel, *Corporations and Political Accountability.*

41. Charles E. Lindblom, *Politics and Markets.*

42. Charles E. Lindblom, *The Policy-making Process*, pp. 65-66, 73-74.

43. Lester M. Salamon and John J. Siegfried, "Economic Power and Political Influence."

44. George J. Stigler, "The Theory of Economic Regulation."

45. Theodore J. Lowi, "How the Farmers Get What They Want."

46. J. David Greenstone, *Labor in American Politics*; Nicholas A. Masters, "The Organized Labor Bureaucracy as a Base of Support for the Democratic Party"; and Harry M. Scoble, "Organized Labor in Electoral Politics."

47. Henry J. Pratt, *The Gray Lobby.*

48. See Michael Lipsky, *Protest in City Politics*; William A. Gamson, *The Strategy of Social Protest*; Jack L. Walker, "Protest and Negotiation"; James Q. Wilson, "The Strategy of Protest"; and Nick Kotz and Mary Lynn Kotz, *A Passion for Equality.*

49. See Mark V. Nadel, *The Politics of Consumer Protection*; Andrew S. McFarland, *Public Interest Lobbies*; and Jeffrey M. Berry, *Lobbying for the People.*

50. Mancur Olson, Jr., *The Logic of Collective Action.*

51. Robert H. Salisbury, "An Exchange Theory of Interest Groups."

52. James Q. Wilson, *Political Organizations.*
53. Anthony Downs, *An Economic Theory of Democracy,* chap. 15, "A Comment on Economic Theories of Government Behavior," pp. 279–294. On this point, see also James M. Buchanan and Richard E. Wagner, *Democracy in Deficit,* pp. 77–81.
54. Stigler, "Theory of Economic Regulation," pp. 3–5; see also Richard A. Posner, "Theories of Economic Regulation," p. 344.

CHAPTER TWO

1. Theodore J. Lowi, "American Business Public Policy, Case Studies, and Political Theory."
2. Ibid., p. 690–691.
3. Ibid., p. 692–715.
4. Ibid., p. 689.
5. Ibid., pp. 699–703.
6. For a thorough review of these efforts, see Lewis A. Froman, Jr., "The Categorization of Policy Contents"; and Michael T. Hayes, "An Economic Theory of Interest Groups and Public Policy," especially chap. 3, "Does Policy Area Make a Difference?" p. 38–73. For Lowi's own subsequent efforts to expand his original typology, see his "Decision-making vs. Policy-making"; and idem, "Four Systems of Policy, Politics, and Choice." Lowi does introduce a fourth policy area into this revised typology, but it is ultimately no more clearly defined than the others, and he is explicitly content in defining those to rely on footnote references to his original work. For a particularly insightful recent application of Lowi's typology, see Randall B. Ripley and Grace A. Franklin, *Congress, the Bureaucracy, and Public Policy.* Ripley and Franklin modify Lowi's original categories somewhat, but they do not really go beyond the cataloging of attributes that characterized Lowi's effort. For an application of Lowi's typology to the comparative context, see T. Alexander Smith, "Toward a Comparative Theory of the Policy Process."
7. Robert H. Salisbury, "The Analysis of Public Policy"; and Robert H. Salisbury and John P. Heinz, "A Theory of Policy Analysis and Some Preliminary Applications."
8. Salisbury, "Analysis of Public Policy," pp. 164–170.
9. Ibid., pp. 158–159.
10. Salisbury and Heinz, "Theory of Policy Analysis," p. 41; and Salisbury, "Analysis of Public Policy," pp. 165–166.
11. Salisbury and Heinz, "Theory of Policy Analysis," p. 48.
12. Salisbury, "Analysis of Public Policy," p. 167.
13. Salisbury and Heinz, "Theory of Policy Analysis," pp. 41–42.
14. Salisbury, "Analysis of Public Policy," pp. 167–168.
15. Salisbury and Heinz, "Theory of Policy Analysis," pp. 42–43.
16. Ibid., p. 42.
17. Ibid., pp. 48–49.
18. Ibid., p. 43.
19. Ibid., pp. 43–47.
20. Lowi, "American Business," p. 688.
21. Salisbury, "Analysis of Public Policy," pp. 157–165.
22. See David Easton, *The Political System;* and idem, *A Systems Analysis of Political Life.*

23. Raymond A. Bauer, Ithiel de Sola Pool, and Lewis Anthony Dexter, *American Business and Public Policy*, p. 324.
24. David B. Truman, *The Governmental Process*, pp. 511–513.
25. Mancur Olson, Jr., *The Logic of Collective Action.*
26. Robert H. Salisbury, "An Exchange Theory of Interest Groups."
27. Bauer, Pool, and Dexter, *American Business and Public Policy*, pp. 211, 221.
28. John W. Kingdon, *Congressmen's Voting Decisions*, p. 142.
29. Robert L. Ross, "Dimensions and Patterns of Relations among Interest Groups at the Congressional Level of Government," pp. 281–286; see also idem, "Relations among National Interest Groups."
30. Salisbury explicitly rejected such a formulation in his original typology ("Analysis of Public Policy," pp. 158–159) on the grounds that even most redistributive policies are actually formulated in non-zero-sum games. Although I believe Salisbury is absolutely correct on this point, the zero-sum versus non-zero-sum distinction nonetheless offers advantages over Salisbury's own formulation insofar as it addresses itself explicitly to the fundamental importance of opposition.
31. Bauer, Pool, and Dexter, *American Business and Public Policy*, p. 455.
32. Ibid., pp. 426–427.
33. Theodore J. Lowi, *The End of Liberalism: Ideology*, especially chap. 5, "Liberal Jurisprudence," pp. 125–156.
34. Salisbury and Heinz, "Theory of Policy Analysis," pp. 43, 47.
35. Theodore J. Lowi, *The Politics of Disorder*, p. 59.
36. Murray Edelman, *The Symbolic Uses of Politics*, p. 141.
37. Bauer, Pool, and Dexter, *American Business and Public Policy*, chap. 9, "The Roots of Conviction—Self-interest and Ideology," pp. 127–153.
38. David R. Mayhew, *Congress*, pp. 53–59.
39. Stanley S. Surrey, "How Special Tax Provisions Get Enacted"; Arthur A. Maass, "Congress and Water Resources"; and John Ferejohn, *Pork Barrel Politics.*
40. Mayhew, *Congress*, pp. 111–116.
41. Edelman, *Symbolic Uses of Politics*, chap. 2, "Symbols and Political Quiescence," pp. 22–43.
42. Roger Noll, *Reforming Regulation*, pp. 47–52.
43. On this point, see especially Daniel P. Moynihan, *Maximum Feasible Misunderstanding*; see also John C. Donovan, *The Politics of Poverty.*
44. Frances Fox Piven and Richard A. Cloward, *Regulating the Poor*; see also their "The Professional Bureaucracies," in Cloward and Piven, *The Politics of Turmoil*, pp. 7–27.
45. George J. Stigler, "The Theory of Economic Regulation"; see also Richard A. Posner, "Theories of Economic Regulation."
46. Stigler, "Theory of Economic Regulation," pp. 13–17.
47. Merle Fainsod, Lincoln Gordon, and Joseph C. Palamountain, Jr., *Government and the American Economy*, pp. 427–528; see also Ellis W. Hawley, *The New Deal and the Problem of Monopoly*; and Grant McConnell, *Private Power and American Democracy*, chap. 8, "Self-Regulation," pp. 246–297.
48. See Martin Anderson, *The Federal Bulldozer*; Leonard Freedman, *Public Housing*; and Harold L. Wolman, *Politics of Federal Housing.*
49. Theodore R. Marmor, *The Politics of Medicare.*
50. Daniel P. Moynihan, *The Politics of a Guaranteed Income.*
51. E. E. Schattschneider, *The Semi-sovereign People*, chap. I, "The Contagiousness of Conflict," pp. 1–19. It is worth noting that Truman also recognized the impor-

tance of this struggle over the scope of conflict; see Truman, *Governmental Process*, pp. 358–362, for his insightful discussion of the ways in which groups can manipulate the size of the attentive public on any given issue to suit their own advantage.

52. Sidney Verba and Norman H. Nie, *Participation in America*.
53. Peter Bachrach and Morton S. Baratz, *Power and Poverty*.
54. Matthew A. Crenson, *The Un-politics of Air Pollution*; and Bruce Ian Oppenheimer, *Oil and the Congressional Process*.
55. Bachrach and Baratz, *Power and Poverty*, pp. 44–51; also fig. 2, p. 54; and especially pp. 59–60.
56. Truman, *Governmental Process*, pp. 353–362; see also Lewis Anthony Dexter, *How Organizations Are Represented in Washington*, pp. 62–63.
57. Truman, *Governmental Process*, pp. 322–332, 507–508; see also Robert Bendiner, *Obstacle Course on Capitol Hill* (New York: McGraw-Hill, 1964); and James MacGregor Burns, *The Deadlock of Democracy*. For an excellent analysis of the implications of the legislative process for majority rule, see Lewis A. Froman, *The Congressional Process*.
58. Randall B. Ripley, *Majority Party Leadership in Congress*, pp. 11–14.
59. Crenson, *Un-politics of Air Pollution*, pp. 102–146.
60. Oppenheimer, *Oil and the Congressional Process*.
61. Mark V. Nadel, *The Politics of Consumer Protection*.
62. McConnell, *Private Power and American Democracy*; idem, *The Decline of Agrarian Democracy*; Theodore J. Lowi, "How the Farmers Get What They Want"; and Mark V. Nadel, *Corporations and Political Accountability*.
63. Nadel, *Corporations and Political Accountability*, pp. 107–196.
64. Posner, "Theories of Economic Regulation," pp. 344–345.

CHAPTER THREE

1. George J. Stigler, "The Theory of Economic Regulation."
2. Charles P. McPherson, "Tariff Structures and Political Exchange"; and Jonathan J. Pincus, "Pressure Groups and the Pattern of Tariffs."
3. Lester M. Salamon and John J. Siegfried, "Economic Power and Political Influence."
4. Mancur Olson, Jr., *The Logic of Collective Action*.
5. Mark V. Nadel, *Corporations and Political Accountability*; and Charles E. Lindblom, *Politics and Markets*.
6. Robert H. Salisbury, "An Exchange Theory of Interest Groups"; and James Q. Wilson, *Political Organizations*.
7. For a critique of this economic conception of rationality, see Wilson, *Political Organizations*, chap. 2, "Rationality and Self-interest," pp. 19–29.
8. Olson, *Logic of Collective Action*, pp. 5–65.
9. Ibid., pp. 132–135.
10. Ibid., pp. 66–97, 135–137.
11. George J. Stigler, "Free Riders and Collective Action," p. 362.
12. Wilson, *Political Organizations*, chap. 8, "Business Associations," pp. 143–170.
13. For good reviews of the evidence, see Richard A. Posner, "Theories of Economic Regulation"; William A. Jordan, "Producer Protection, Prior Market Structure,

and the Effects of Government Regulation"; and Thomas K. McCraw, "Regulation in America."

14. On the life-cycle phenomenon, see Marver P. Bernstein, *Regulating Business by Independent Commission*. For an application to the ICC, see Samuel P. Huntington, "The Marasmus of the ICC"; see also Avery Leiserson, *Administrative Regulation*.

15. Posner, "Theories of Economic Regulation," p. 342.

16. Stigler, "Theory of Economic Regulation," pp. 3–5.

17. Ibid., pp. 13–17.

18. McPherson, "Tariff Structures and Political Exchange," pp. 22–24. For data on concentration ratios, see U.S. Bureau of the Census, *Concentration in U.S. Manufacturing, 1954 and 1963*.

19. McPherson, "Tariff Structures and Political Exchange," pp. 15–28, 50–53.

20. Pincus, "Pressure Groups," p. 773.

21. Ibid., p. 771, table 1.

22. Salamon and Siegfried, "Economic Power and Political Influence," pp. 1031–1034.

23. Ibid., p. 1034, table 1.

24. Ibid., p. 1038.

25. Ibid., p. 1037, table 2.

26. Ibid., pp. 1039–1042.

27. Raymond A. Bauer, Ithiel de Sola Pool, and Lewis Anthony Dexter, *American Business and Public Policy*, p. 324.

28. On this point see Beatrice N. Vaccara, *Employment and Output in Protected Manufacturing Industries*.

29. McPherson, "Tariff Structures and Political Exchange," pp. 40–41.

30. Pincus, "Pressure Groups," pp. 775–776.

31. E. E. Schattschneider, *The Semi-sovereign People*, chap. 1, "The Contagiousness of Conflict," pp. 1–19.

32. Stanley E. Surrey, "How Special Tax Provisions Get Enacted."

33. Salamon and Siegfried, "Economic Power and Political Influence," p. 1038.

34. Stigler, "Theory of Economic Regulation," pp. 13–17.

35. Ibid., pp. 3–5.

36. John W. Kingdon, *Congressmen's Voting Decisions*, pp. 145–146.

37. Posner, "Theories of Economic Regulation," pp. 344–347.

38. Bauer, Pool, and Dexter, *American Business and Public Policy*, pp. 251–276.

39. Ibid., p. 258.

40. See Vaccara, *Employment and Output*; and John H. Cheh, "United States Concessions in the Kennedy Round and Short-run Labor Adjustment Costs."

41. Pincus, "Pressure Groups," pp. 770–772.

42. Stigler, "Theory of Economic Regulation," pp. 13–15.

43. Ibid., p. 14.

44. Salamon and Siegfried, "Economic Power and Political Influence," pp. 1037–1039.

45. Ibid., p. 1039.

46. Bruce Ian Oppenheimer, "The Effects of Policy Variation on Interest Group Behavior in the Congressional Process," pp. 216–222.

47. Earl Latham, *The Group Basis of Politics*, pp. 35–36. Latham goes on to caution however that "in these adjustments of group interest, the legislature does not play

the inert part of cash register, ringing up the additions and withdrawals of strength, a mindless balance pointing and marking the weight and distribution of power among the contending groups" (ibid., p. 37). Though Latham does not dwell long on this point and soon reverts back to what can justifiably be interpreted as a mechanistic conception of the legislative process, this does suggest that a good number of writers (myself included) may have been guilty at times of unfairly treating Latham's work as something of a straw man.

48. Pincus, "Pressure Groups," p. 760.
49. Ibid., p. 761.
50. Bauer, Pool, and Dexter, *American Business and Public Policy*, pp. 456–457.
51. Robert A. Dahl, "A Critique of the Ruling Elite Model."
52. Robert H. Haveman, *The Economics of the Public Sector*, pp. 145–151.
53. Robert A. Dahl and Charles E. Lindblom, *Politics, Economics, and Welfare*.
54. Charles E. Lindblom, "The Science of Muddling Through"; and David Braybrooke and Charles E. Lindblom, *A Strategy of Decision*.
55. Charles E. Lindblom, *The Intelligence of Democracy*.
56. Here, see especially Lindblom, "Science of Muddling Through"; and Braybrooke and Lindblom, *Strategy of Decision*.
57. Lindblom, "Science of Muddling Through," p. 85.
58. Charles E. Lindblom, *The Policy-making Process*, especially pp. 65–66, 73–74.
59. Lindblom, *Politics and Markets*.
60. James Q. Wilson, "Democracy and the Corporation."
61. Lindblom, *Politics and Markets*, pp. 179–180; see also C. Wright Mills, *The Power Elite*.
62. Salisbury, "Exchange Theory of Interest Groups."
63. Anthony Downs, *An Economic Theory of Democracy*, chap. 8, "The Statics and Dynamics of Party Ideologies," pp. 114–141.
64. On Mills, see Theodore R. Marmor, *The Politics of Medicare*. On Long's role in blocking the FAP, see Daniel P. Moynihan, *The Politics of a Guaranteed Income*.
65. Richard A. Cloward and Frances Fox Piven, "The Professional Bureaucracies," in Cloward and Piven, *The Politics of Turmoil*, pp. 7–27.
66. L. Harmon Zeigler and G. Wayne Peak, *Interest Groups in American Society*, pp. 178–180.
67. Herbert Kaufman, *Are Government Organizations Immortal?*
68. Aaron B. Wildavsky, *The Politics of the Budgetary Process*.
69. Lindblom, "Science of Muddling Through," p. 84; and Braybrooke and Lindblom, *Strategy of Decision*, pp. 83–93.
70. Kingdon, *Congressmen's Voting Decisions*, pp. 254–257.
71. Ibid., pp. 150–153, 161.
72. For a discussion, see Haveman, *Economics of the Public Sector*, pp. 32–40.
73. William H. Riker and Steven J. Brams, "The Paradox of Vote Trading"; see also Steven J. Brams, *Paradoxes in Politics*, pp. 102–109.
74. In game theory, the prisoner's dilemma centers around two suspects, interrogated separately and thus unable to communicate with each other. If each remains silent, both will get off with light sentences, as the state has insufficient evidence for a felony conviction. If either talks while the other remains silent, however, the prisoner turning state's evidence goes free while the other receives a long sentence. Both prisoners face the same situation: the only way to avoid the long sentence (and at the same time, the only chance of getting off altogether) lies in a full

confession. As a result both players will find it "rational" to talk, and both will go to prison for intermediate sentences. An n-person prisoner's dilemma is simply one involving more than two players. See Brams, *Paradoxes in Politics*, pp. 81–91.

75. James M. Buchanan and Gordon Tullock, *The Calculus of Consent*.
76. David R. Mayhew, *Congress*, pp. 53–59.
77. Herbert A. Simon, *Models of Man*.
78. This is a recurrent theme in Lindblom's writings; it is advanced most cogently in "Science of Muddling Through," and in Braybrooke and Lindblom, *Strategy of Decision*. On the implications of imperfect information for incumbents' electoral fortunes, see Downs, *Economic Theory of Democracy*, pp. 61–62.
79. Kingdon, *Congressmen's Voting Decisions*, pp. 142–143.
80. Leonard A. Marascuilo and Harriet Amster, "Survey of 1961–62 Congressional Polls," *Public Opinion Quarterly* 2 (Fall 1964):497–506.
81. Kingdon, *Congressmen's Voting Decisions*, pp. 30–31.
82. Ibid., pp. 143–145.
83. Ibid., pp. 42–44.
84. Ibid., pp. 55–57. For excellent discussions of the intensity problem, see Robert A. Dahl, *A Preface to Democratic Theory*, chap. 4, "Equality, Diversity, and Intensity," pp. 90–123; and Willmoore Kendall and George W. Carey, "The 'Intensity' Problem and Democratic Theory."
85. Kingdon, *Congressmen's Voting Decisions*, pp. 36–38.
86. Schattschneider, *Semi-sovereign People*, pp. 49–53.
87. James Q. Wilson, "The Strategy of Protest," p. 292.
88. Salisbury, "Exchange Theory of Interest Groups," pp. 3–19.
89. Wilson, *Political Organizations*, chap. 3, "Organizational Maintenance and Incentives," pp. 30–55. For an earlier version of Wilson's argument, see Peter B. Clark and James Q. Wilson, "Incentive Systems."
90. Wilson, *Political Organizations*, chap. 4, "Social Structure and Organizations," pp. 56–77.
91. Wilson, *Political Organizations*, pp. 196–198.
92. J. David Greenstone, *Labor in American Politics*.
93. Salisbury, "Exchange Theory of Interest Groups," pp. 26–29; see also V. O. Key, Jr., *Public Opinion and American Democracy*, pp. 481–499.
94. Wilson, *Political Organizations*, pp. 208–209, 226–227.
95. Ibid., chap. 5, "Political Structure and Organizations," pp. 78–91.
96. Wilson, *Political Organizations*, pp. 327–337.

CHAPTER FOUR

1. James Q. Wilson, *Political Organizations*, pp. 331–332.
2. Ibid., p. 332.
3. Ibid., pp. 330–331.
4. Ibid., pp. 331–337. The following paragraphs draw heavily on Wilson's discussion.
5. James M. Buchanan and Gordon Tullock, *The Calculus of Consent*, chap. 11, "Simple Majority Voting and the Theory of Games," pp. 147–169.
6. Anthony Downs, *An Economic Theory of Democracy*, p. 198.
7. Ibid., pp. 199–201.
8. Paul Sabatier, "Social Movements and Regulatory Agencies."

9. David B. Truman, *The Governmental Process*, pp. 112–115.
10. John W. Kingdon, *Congressmen's Voting Decisions*, pp. 142–143.
11. Ibid., pp. 42–44.
12. Murray Edelman, *The Symbolic Uses of Politics*, pp. 35–36.
13. Ibid., pp. 22–23.
14. Downs, *Economic Theory of Democracy*, especially pt. 3, "Specific Effects of Information Costs," pp. 207–276; see also Gordon Tullock, *Toward a Mathematics of Politics*, chap. 7, "Political Ignorance," pp. 100–114.
15. David E. RePass, "Issue Salience and Party Choice."
16. Edelman, *Symbolic Uses of Politics*, pp. 35–36.
17. Raymond A. Bauer, "The Audience."
18. On organizations as open systems, see for example Richard M. Cyert and James G. March, *A Behavioral Theory of the Firm*; James G. March and Herbert A. Simon, *Organizations*; James D. Thompson, *Organizations in Action*; and Donald P. Warwick, Marvin Meade, and Theodore Reed, *A Theory of Public Bureaucracy*.
19. This paragraph owes much to Warwick et al., *Theory of Public Bureaucracy*, chap. 4, "The External Environment," pp. 59–83.
20. Herbert Simon, *Models of Man*, p. 200.
21. Ibid., p. 204 ff.; see also March and Simon, *Organizations*, p. 140 ff.
22. Lewis Anthony Dexter, *How Organizations Are Represented in Washington*, pp. 60–63; see also Raymond A. Bauer, Ithiel de Sola Pool, and Lewis Anthony Dexter, *American Business and Public Policy*, pp. 348–349.
23. Jeffrey M. Berry, *Lobbying for the People*, pp. 202–206.
24. Harry M. Scoble, *Ideology and Electoral Action*, p. 16.
25. Truman, *Governmental Process*, pp. 115–129.
26. Scoble, *Ideology and Electoral Action*, pp. 16–18.
27. Ibid., pp. 18–19.
28. Berry, *Lobbying for the People*, pp. 202–206.
29. David J. O'Brien, *Neighborhood Organization and Interest-group Processes*, pp. 43–51.
30. Andrew S. McFarland, *Public Interest Lobbies*, p. 54.
31. Berry, *Lobbying for the People*, pp. 28–29.
32. Ibid., pp. 179–186.
33. Ibid., p. 188.
34. Ibid., p. 196.
35. Ibid., pp. 197–199.
36. O'Brien, *Neighborhood Organization*, p. 112.
37. Nick Kotz and Mary Lynn Kotz, *A Passion for Equality*, pp. 238–248.
38. Berry, *Lobbying for the People*, pp. 41–43.
39. Wilson, *Political Organizations*, pp. 196–198.
40. Berry, *Lobbying for the People*, pp. 41–43.
41. Scoble, *Ideology and Electoral Action*, p. 18.
42. Kingdon, *Congressmen's Voting Decisions*, pp. 145–146.
43. Berry, *Lobbying for the People*, pp. 46–48.
44. Ibid., p. 238.
45. Kotz and Kotz, *Passion for Equality*, pp. 291–292; see also Berry, *Lobbying for the People*, pp. 48–55.
46. William A. Gamson, *Power and Discontent*; and idem, *The Strategy of Social Protest*.
47. O'Brien, *Neighborhood Organization*, pp. 54–57.

48. James Q. Wilson, "The Strategy of Protest," p. 292.
49. Jack L. Walker, "Protest and Negotiation"; see also Wilson, "Strategy of Protest"; and Michael Lipsky, *Protest in City Politics*.
50. This discussion is heavily indebted to Richard E. Neustadt's analysis of the bargaining resources available to presidents in *Presidential Power*.
51. O'Brien, *Neighborhood Organization*, pp. 104–106.
52. J. David Greenstone, *Labor in American Politics*, pp. 21–22.
53. Grant McConnell, *The Decline of Agrarian Democracy*, chap. 4, "The Heirs of Populism," pp. 36–43.
54. Wilson, *Political Organizations*, pp. 46–47.
55. Ibid., pp. 47–49.
56. Ibid., p. 173.
57. Ibid., p. 264.
58. McFarland, *Public Interest Lobbies*, pp. 4–12.
59. Berry, *Lobbying for the People*, p. 205.
60. David B. Mayhew, *Congress*, pp. 52–53.
61. Ibid., pp. 61–62, 118, 119.
62. Mark V. Nadel, *The Politics of Consumer Protection*, pp. 113–114.
63. Berry, *Lobbying for the People*, pp. 218–220.
64. Ibid., pp. 225–230, 243–252.
65. Ibid., pp. 280–284.
66. Ibid., pp. 254–261.
67. Robert H. Salisbury, "An Exchange Theory of Interest Groups," pp. 17–20.
68. Wilson, *Political Organizations*, p. 197.
69. Ibid., pp. 204–205.
70. Greenstone, *Labor in American Politics*, pp. 23–24.
71. Ibid., p. 26.
72. Ibid., p. 26.
73. Wilson, *Political Organizations*, pp. 174–176.
74. Walker, "Protest and Negotiation."
75. Derek C. Bok and John T. Dunlop, *Labor and the American Community*, pp. 388–389.
76. Mayer N. Zald and Roberta Ash, "Social Movement Organizations," p. 333.
77. Kotz and Kotz, *Passion for Equality*, pp. 181–306; see also Frances Fox Piven and Richard A. Cloward, *Poor People's Movements*, chap. 5, "The Welfare Rights Movement," pp. 264–361.
78. Theodore J. Lowi, *The Politics of Disorder*, especially pp. 3–61.
79. Hans Toch, *The Social Psychology of Social Movements*, p. 228.
80. Robert Michels, *Political Parties*, p. 342 ff.
81. Ibid., pp. 340–341.
82. Zald and Ash, "Social Movement Organizations," pp. 338–339.
83. Greenstone, *Labor in American Politics*, pp. 58–66.
84. Wilson, *Political Organizations*, pp. 226–227.
85. Greenstone, *Labor in American Politics*, especially chap. 8, "The Labor-party Alliance," pp. 246–287; chap. 9, "Party Pressures on Labor," pp. 288–318; and chap. 10, "Labor and Congress," pp. 319–359.
86. Greenstone, *Labor in American Politics*, especially chap. 11, "Conclusion," pp. 360–408.
87. Bauer, Pool, and Dexter, *American Business and Public Policy*, chap. 22, "Quasi-Unanimity—Premise of Action," pp. 332–340.
88. Wilson, *Political Organizations*, pp. 310–312.

89. Dexter, *How Organizations Are Represented in Washington*, chap. 5, "Helping and Seeking Help on Capitol Hill," pp. 80–101.
90. On the importance of obtaining a distinctive organizational competence, see Wilson, *Political Organizations*, pp. 32, 204–205, 263–267. The informal division of labor between the NAACP and the Urban League provides an excellent example of this; see Wilson, "Strategy of Protest," p. 299.
91. Albert A. Blum, "Collective Bargaining," pp. 63–69.
92. Bok and Dunlop, *Labor and the American Community*, pp. 84–90; see also Wilson, *Political Organizations*, pp. 251–253.
93. Greenstone, *Labor in American Politics*, pp. 334–336; see also Wilson, *Political Organizations*, pp. 313–315.
94. Charles O. Jones, *Clean Air*, chap. 7, "Speculative Augmentation in Washington, 1970," pp. 175–210.
95. Henry J. Pratt, *The Gray Lobby*, chap. 5, "Senior Citizens for Kennedy," pp. 56–85, 88–89. On the role of government in organizing farm, labor, and business groups, see Grant McConnell, *Private Power and American Democracy*; and idem, *Decline of Agrarian Democracy*.
96. Wilson, *Political Organizations*, pp. 309–310.
97. Matthew A. Crenson, *The Un-politics of Air Pollution*, pp. 133–176.

CHAPTER FIVE

1. Anthony Downs, *An Economic Theory of Democracy*, chap. 15, "A Comment on Economic Theories of Government Behavior," pp. 279–294.
2. David R. Mayhew, *Congress*; and Morris P. Fiorina, *Representatives, Roll Calls, and Constituencies*.
3. Mayhew, *Congress*, especially pp. 112–114.
4. Fiorina, *Representatives, Roll Calls, and Constituencies*, pp. 22–23.
5. Ibid., p. 39.
6. John E. Mueller, "Presidential Popularity from Truman to Johnson."
7. Fiorina, *Representatives, Roll Calls, and Constituencies*, pp. 44–49.
8. Ibid., pp. 49–67.
9. Ibid., p. 75.
10. Morris P. Fiorina, *Congress*.
11. Theodore J. Lowi, *The End of Liberalism: Ideology*, p. 76.
12. More precisely, Fiorina posits that congressmen will assume that any issue may be turned into a campaign issue by potential opponents. This is both a much weaker and a more realistic conception that I have implied. Even so, imperfect information and differential vulnerabilities to symbolic reassurances among different voting groups would suffice to limit the extent to which opponents could capitalize on any given issue. See Fiorina, *Representatives, Roll Calls, and Constituencies*, p. 33. On information costs, see Downs, *Economic Theory of Democracy*, pp. 207–276; and Gordon Tullock, *Toward a Mathematics of Politics*, pp. 100–114. On symbolic reassurances, see Murray Edelman, *The Symbolic Uses of Politics*.
13. Fiorina, *Representatives, Roll Calls, and Constituencies*, pp. 49–67.
14. Merle Fainsod, Lincoln Gordon, and Joseph C. Palamountain, Jr., *Government and the American Economy*, pp. 427–528; see also Ellis W. Hawley, *The New Deal and the Problem of Monopoly*; and Grant McConnell, *Private Power and American Democracy*, chap. 8, "Self-regulation," pp. 246–297.

15. George J. Stigler, "The Theory of Economic Regulation," pp. 3–5.
16. Edelman, *Symbolic Uses of Politics*, p. 65.
17. Theodore J. Lowi, "How the Farmers Get What They Want."
18. Grant McConnell, *The Decline of Agrarian Democracy*.
19. Randall B. Ripley and Grace A. Franklin, *Congress, the Bureaucracy, and Public Policy*, pp. 117–119.
20. Charles O. Jones, "Speculative Augmentation in Federal Air Pollution Policy-making."
21. Mark V. Nadel, *Corporations and Political Accountability*.
22. Lowi, *End of Liberalism: Ideology*.
23. Matthew A. Crenson, *The Un-politics of Air Pollution*, pp. 141–147.
24. Jack L. Walker, "Setting the Agenda in the U.S. Senate."
25. Crenson, *Un-politics of Air Pollution*; Charles O. Jones, *Clean Air*, chap. 3, "Air Pollution Policy Development, 1941–1967," pp. 40–86; see also James L. Sundquist, *Politics and Policy*, chap. 8, "For All a Better Outdoor Environment," pp. 322–381; and Jones, "Speculative Augmentation."
26. Jones, *Clean Air*, pp. 56–57; and Sundquist, *Politics and Policy*, p. 349.
27. J. Clarence Davies III and Barbara S. Davies, *The Politics of Pollution*, p. 90; see also Jones, *Clean Air*, chap. 5, "The Rise in Public Concern for the Environment, 1969–1970," pp. 137–155.
28. Jones, *Clean Air*, p. 202 ff.
29. According to Posner, "the typical regulatory agency operates with reasonable efficiency to attain deliberately inefficient or inequitable goals set by the legislature that created it." Richard A. Posner, "Theories of Economic Regulation," p. 337.
30. Philip Shabecoff, "Ecologists Disagree on Clean-water Bill."
31. Posner, "Theories of Economic Regulation," pp. 342, 351–353.
32. John Kenneth Galbraith, *The Affluent Society*.
33. Tullock, *Toward a Mathematics of Politics*, chap. 1, "Models of Man," pp. 1–17.
34. Mark V. Nadel, *The Politics of Consumer Protection*, pp. 158–160.
35. Ibid., pp. 176–191.
36. Ibid., p. 34.
37. Ibid., p. 41.
38. Ibid., pp. 108–112.
39. Ibid., pp. 113–114.
40. Ibid., pp. 180–184.
41. Ibid., pp. 224–229.
42. Roger Noll, *Reforming Regulation*, p. 48.
43. Lowi, *The End of Liberalism: Ideology*, p. 153.
44. Noll, *Reforming Regulation*, pp. 48–51.
45. Posner, "Theories of Economic Regulation," pp. 351–352.
46. Sundquist, *Politics and Policy*, pp. 156–173, 180–195; see also Eugene Eidenberg and Roy D. Morey, *An Act of Congress*, chap. 2, "A Legacy of Conflict," pp. 10–25.
47. Eidenberg and Morey, *Act of Congress*, pp. 59–69.
48. Ibid., pp. 62–64.
49. Ibid., p. 77.
50. Ibid., pp. 87–91.
51. Ibid., pp. 204–205. On this point, see also Stephen K. Bailey and Edith K. Mosher, *ESEA*.

52. Theodore R. Marmor, *The Politics of Medicare*, pp. 23–28.
53. Henry J. Pratt, *The Gray Lobby*, p. 117.
54. J. David Greenstone, *Labor in American Politics*, pp. 337–339.
55. Marmor, *Politics of Medicare*, pp. 20–23, 119–121.
56. Ibid., p. 16.
57. Ibid., pp. 85–86, 122–123.
58. Ibid., p. 122.
59. Ibid., pp. 87–88.
60. Pratt, *Gray Lobby*, p. 117.
61. Ibid., pp. 116–117.
62. William A. Gamson, *Power and Discontent*, p. 47.
63. Pratt, *Gray Lobby*, chap. 15, "The Old-age Policy System," pp. 208–218.
64. Pratt, *Gray Lobby*, pp. 212–213.
65. Ibid., pp. 11–25.
66. Ibid., pp. 39–94.
67. Ibid., pp. 96–100.
68. Ibid., pp. 94–96.
69. Ibid., pp. 129–144.
70. Ibid., pp. 147–153.
71. Sundquist, *Politics and Policy*, pp. 221–253; see also Daniel M. Berman, *A Bill Becomes a Law*.
72. Berman, *Bill Becomes a Law*, p. 114; on privatization and socialization of conflict, see E. E. Schattschneider, *The Semi-sovereign People*, pp. 1–19.
73. Sundquist, *Politics and Policy*, pp. 268–269.
74. Greenstone, *Labor in American Politics*, pp. 341–342.
75. Quoted in Nathan Glazer, *Affirmative Discrimination*, p. 44.
76. Quoted in ibid., p. 45.
77. Quoted in ibid., p. 53.
78. Supreme Court of the United States, *United Steelworkers of America, AFL-CIO-CLC v. Weber et al.*, Slip Opinion, 27 June 1979.
79. See for example Charles E. Lindblom, *The Intelligence of Democracy*; idem, *The Policy-making Process*; and Aaron Wildavsky, *The Politics of the Budgetary Process*.
80. Glazer, *Affirmative Discrimination*, pp. 44, 51–53.
81. Ibid., pp. 46–47.
82. Ibid., pp. 47–48.
83. Ibid., pp. 48–49.
84. Ibid., p. 62.
85. Sundquist, *Politics and Policy*, pp. 271–275.
86. "Effective Lobbying Put Open Housing Bill Across."
87. Sundquist, *Politics and Policy*, pp. 275–286.
88. Ibid., p. 279.
89. Ibid.
90. "Effective Lobbying," p. 166.
91. Ibid.
92. Rochelle L. Stanfield, "Housing Integration Remains a Distant Dream."
93. Harold L. Wolman and Norman C. Thomas, "Black Interests, Black Groups, and Black Influence in the Federal Policy Process."
94. Murray Edelman, *Politics as Symbolic Action*, pp. 155–171.

95. Sundquist, *Politics and Policy*, pp. 112–113.
96. Thomas E. Cronin, "The War on Crime and Unsafe Streets, 1960–76," pp. 208–233.
97. Ibid., p. 221.
98. Ibid., p. 222.
99. Ibid., pp. 233–239.
100. Ibid., p. 255.
101. For a detailed case study of the legislative origins of the War on Poverty that documents this absence of organized group involvement, see John C. Donovan, *The Politics of Poverty*.
102. Daniel P. Moynihan, *Maximum Feasible Misunderstanding*.
103. Donovan, *Politics of Poverty*, especially chap. 4, "Community Action in Action," pp. 49–61.
104. Ibid., chap. 6, "Head Start—and Reverse," pp. 81–92.
105. Ibid., chap. 7, "Negro Poverty and Negro Politics," pp. 93–110; and Moynihan, *Maximum Feasible Misunderstanding*, chap. 5, "The War on Poverty," pp. 75–101.
106. Frances Fox Piven and Richard A. Cloward, *Regulating the Poor*, chap. 9, "The Great Society and Relief," pp. 248–284.
107. Sundquist, *Politics and Policy*, pp. 498–499.
108. Daniel P. Moynihan, *The Politics of a Guaranteed Income*, p. 156.
109. Ibid., p. 157.
110. Ibid., pp. 302–327.
111. Ibid., pp. 327–345. It is worth noting that NWRO constitutes a by-product group in terms of Olson's theory. Moynihan observes (ibid., p. 331) that roughly half the money raised to support the organization came from the federal government and that VISTA volunteers were the prime organizers of the group. Piven and Cloward characteristically see the government's rationale for subsidizing welfare rights organizations as an effort to co-opt the poor (*Regulating the Poor*, pp. 320–330).
112. Gamson, *Power and Discontent*, p. 47.
113. Moynihan, *Politics of a Guaranteed Income*, p. 158.

CHAPTER SIX

1. Mancur Olson, Jr., *The Logic of Collective Action*.
2. John Kenneth Galbraith, *The Affluent Society*.
3. Anthony Downs, "Why the Government Budget Is Too Small in a Democracy."
4. Ibid., p. 547.
5. Ibid., pp. 544–555.
6. Ibid., p. 546.
7. Ibid., p. 551.
8. See James M. Buchanan and Gordon Tullock, *The Calculus of Consent*; William H. Riker and Steven J. Brams, "The Paradox of Vote Trading"; and David R. Mayhew, *Congress*.
9. Downs, "Budget," pp. 557–559.
10. James M. Buchanan and Richard E. Wagner, *Democracy in Deficit*.
11. John E. Mueller, "Presidential Popularity from Truman to Johnson."

12. Aaron Wildavsky, *The Politics of the Budgetary Process*.
13. Richard Rose and Guy Peters, *Can Government Go Bankrupt?* p. 9.
14. Richard A. Musgrave and Peggy B. Musgrave, *Public Finance in Theory and Practice*, pp. 98–103.
15. Charles O. Jones, *An Introduction to the Study of Public Policy*, p. 8.
16. Although this proposition seems in accord with the bulk of the empirical evidence on the subject, at least some recent evidence suggests that cash and in-kind transfers have increased dramatically as a result of the War on Poverty, thus producing a substantial redistribution of income downward. On this point, see Henry J. Aaron, *Politics and the Professors*, pp. 4–10; and Martin Anderson, *Welfare*, chap. 1, "Winning the War on Poverty," pp. 15–42. To whatever extent this revisionist view is correct, this development is largely attributable to presidential and party pressures leading to the Great Society programs; the effects of such pressures on demand pattern are discussed at some length later in this chapter.
17. Frances Fox Piven and Richard A. Cloward, *Poor People's Movements*, pp. xi–xii.
18. Jack L. Walker, "Setting the Agenda in the U.S. Senate."
19. Roger W. Cobb and Charles D. Elder, *Participation in American Politics*, p. 112; see also V. O. Key, Jr., *Politics, Parties, and Pressure Groups*, p. 42.
20. Frances Fox Piven and Richard A. Cloward, *Regulating the Poor*; see also Richard A. Cloward and Frances Fox Piven, "The Professional Bureaucracies: Benefit Systems as Influence Systems," in Cloward and Piven, *The Politics of Turmoil*, pp. 7–27.
21. Paul Sabatier, "Social Movements and Regulatory Agencies."
22. William A. Gamson, *Power and Discontent*, pp. 116–120, 135–142.
23. Ibid., pp. 136–137.
24. David J. O'Brien, *Neighborhood Organization and Interest-group Processes*, chap. 2, "Resource Needs and Environmental Problems," pp. 43–63.
25. Ibid., p. 60.
26. J. David Greenstone, *Labor in American Politics*, chap 11, "Conclusion," pp. 360–408.
27. James Q. Wilson, *Political Organizations*, pp. 208–209, 226–227.
28. Theodore J. Lowi, "American Business, Public Policy, Case Studies, and Political Theory," p. 689.
29. Bruce Ian Oppenheimer, "The Effects of Policy Variation on Interest Group Behavior in the Congressional Process," p. 286, chart 1.
30. Murray Edelman, *The Symbolic Uses of Politics*, pp. 152–171.
31. Randall B. Ripley and Grace A. Franklin, *Congress, the Bureaucracy, and Public Policy*, p. 170.
32. E. E. Schattschneider, *Politics, Pressures and the Tariff*, pp. 288–289.
33. E. E. Schattschneider, *The Semi-sovereign People*, especially pp. 47–61.
34. Ibid., pp. 56–57.

CHAPTER SEVEN

1. John Kenneth Galbraith, *American Capitalism*.
2. Andrew S. McFarland, *Public Interest Lobbies*, pp. 6–20; see also idem, "Recent Social Movements and Theories of Power in America."
3. James Q. Wilson, *Political Organizations*, p. 68.

5. Harold Wilensky, *Intellectuals in Labor Unions.*
6. Walter Lippmann, *An Inquiry into the Principles of the Good Society,* p. 119.
7. Richard Rose and Guy Peters, *Can Government Go Bankrupt?*
8. E. E. Schattschneider, *Party Government,* p. 196.
9. Ibid., pp. 48–49.
10. Ibid., p. 31.
11. Ibid., p. 210.
12. Ibid.
13. Ibid., pp. 197–198.
14. David R. Mayhew, *Party Loyalty among Congressmen.*
15. Ibid., pp. 146–168.
16. Schattschneider, *Party Government,* p. 63.
17. James L. Sundquist, *Politics and Policy.*
18. J. David Greenstone, *Labor in American Politics,* especially pp. 246–359.
19. Schattschneider, *Party Government,* pp. 126–129.
20. Committee on Political Parties of the American Political Science Association, *Toward a More Responsible Two-party System.* For a critique of this view, see Austin Ranney, "Toward a More Responsible Two-party System." For a variety of views, see Jeff Fishel, ed., *Parties and Elections in an Anti-party Age.*
21. Schattschneider, *Party Government,* p. 88.
22. Ibid., p. 37.
23. Ibid., p. 197.
24. Ibid., p. 63.
25. Ibid.
26. Ibid., p. 86.
27. Rose and Peters, *Can Government Go Bankrupt?* pp. 161–173; see also Milton Friedman and Rose Friedman, *Free to Choose,* pp. 100–101. According to Rose and Peters (*Can Government Go Bankrupt?* p. 171), the British government has in fact been quite successful in holding down public spending, contrary to public belief; its real problem has been its inability to generate economic growth sufficient to maintain public programs without cutting take-home pay.
28. Wilson, *Political Organizations,* chap. 5, "Political Structure and Organizations," pp. 70–91.
29. Ibid., p. 81.
30. Ibid., pp. 81–83; Samuel H. Beer, "Group Representation in Britain and the United States."
31. Schattschneider, *Party Government,* pp. 1–11.
32. Wilson, *Political Organizations,* p. 80.
33. Theodore J. Lowi, "Machine Politics—Old and New."
34. Schattschneider, *Party Government,* chap. 7, "The Local Bosses," pp. 170–186.
35. Rose and Peters, *Can Government Go Bankrupt?* p. 225.
36. James M. Buchanan and Richard E. Wagner, *Democracy in Deficit,* p. 175.
37. Friedman and Friedman, *Free to Choose,* pp. 301–304.
38. Rose and Peters, *Can Government Go Bankrupt?* pp. 228–230; see also Friedman and Friedman, *Free to Choose,* pp. 308–309.
39. Buchanan and Wagner, *Democracy in Deficit,* p. 175.
40. Milton Friedman, *Capitalism and Freedom,* chap. 3, "The Control of Money," pp. 37–55; and chap. 5, "Fiscal Policy," pp. 75–84.

41. Rose and Peters, *Can Government Go Bankrupt?* pp. 135–141; see also Friedman, *Capitalism and Freedom*, pp. 75–79; and Galbraith, *American Capitalism*, pp. 187–201.
42. For a thorough review of these proposals, see Lewis A. Froman, Jr., *The Congressional Process*. A more-or-less typical example of the argument for such reform is provided by Joseph S. Clark and other senators, *The Senate Establishment* (New York: Hill & Wang, 1963).
43. Robert A. Dahl, *A Preface to Democratic Theory*; and Charles E. Lindblom, "Still Muddling, Not Yet Through."
44. Froman, *Congressional Process*, especially chap. 11, "Congressional Reform," pp. 183–217. On the Rules Committee, see James A. Robinson, *The House Rules Committee*.
45. Lowi, *End of Liberalism: Ideology*, pp. 297–303; see also Lowi, *The End of Liberalism: Second Republic*, 2nd ed., rev., pp. 298–310.
46. Rose and Peters, *Can Government Go Bankrupt?* p. 232.
47. Richard F. Fenno, Jr., *Congressmen in Committees*, chap. 1, "Member Goals," pp. 1–14.
48. Morris P. Fiorina, *Representatives, Roll Calls, and Constituencies*, pp. 35–38.
49. Matthew A. Crenson, *The Un-politics of Air Pollution*, pp. 159–176.
50. Ibid., p. 176.
51. Aaron B. Wildavsky, *The Politics of the Budgetary Process*, pp. 165–167.
52. Charles O. Jones, *Clean Air*, p. 176.
53. Martin Rein, *Social Science and Public Policy*, pp. 125–126.

CONCLUSION

1. Charles O. Jones, *An Introduction to the Study of Public Policy*; see also James E. Anderson, *Public Policy-making*, 2nd ed., rev. (New York: Holt, Rinehart & Winston, 1979).
2. J. David Greenstone, *Labor in American Politics*; for a study of the relationship of the party system to interest group strength in the states, see L. Harmon Zeigler and Hendrik van Dalen, "Interest Groups in the States."
3. Robert H. Salisbury, "The Analysis of Public Policy," pp. 162–163; for an examination of the relationship between interest group strength and the political structure in the states, see Lewis A. Froman, Jr., "Some Effects of Interest Group Strength in State Politics."
4. James Q. Wilson, *Political Organizations*, chap. 5, "Political Structure and Organizations," pp. 70–91.

Bibliography

Aaron, Henry J. *Politics and the Professors: The Great Society in Perspective*. Washington, D.C.: Brookings Institution, 1978.

Allison, Graham T. *Essence of Decision: Explaining the Cuban Missile Crisis*. Boston: Little, Brown, 1971.

Anderson, Martin. *The Federal Bulldozer*. Cambridge, Mass.: M.I.T. Press, 1964.

———. *Welfare: The Political Economy of Welfare Reform in the United States*. Stanford, Calif.: Hoover Institution, 1979.

Bachrach, Peter, and Baratz, Morton S. *Power and Poverty: Theory and Practice*. New York: Oxford University Press, 1970.

Bailey, Stephen Kemp. *Congress Makes a Law: The Story Behind the Employment Act of 1946*. New York: Columbia University Press, 1950.

Bailey, Stephen K., and Mosher, Edith K. *ESEA: The Office of Education Administers a Law*. Syracuse, N.Y.: Syracuse University Press, 1968.

Bauer, Raymond A. "The Audience." In *Handbook of Communication*, edited by Ithiel de Sola Pool, Frederick W. Frey, Wilbur Schramm, Nathan Maccoby, and Edwin B. Parker, pp. 141–152. Chicago: Rand McNally College Publishing, 1973.

Bauer, Raymond A.; Pool, Ithiel de Sola; and Dexter, Lewis Anthony. *American Business and Public Policy: The Politics of Foreign Trade*. New York: Atherton, 1963.

———. *American Business and Public Policy: The Politics of Foreign Trade*. 2d ed. Chicago: Aldine-Atherton, 1972.

Beer, Samuel H. "Group Representation in Britain and the United States." *The Annals of the American Academy of Political and Social Science* 319 (September 1958):130–140.

Bentley, Arthur F. *The Process of Government: A Study of Social Pressures*. Chicago: University of Chicago Press, 1908.

Berman, Daniel M. *A Bill Becomes a Law: Congress Enacts Civil Rights Legislation*. 2d ed., rev. New York: Macmillan, 1966.

Bernstein, Marver P. Regulating Business by Independent Commission. Princeton, N.J.: Princeton University Press, 1955.

Berry, Jeffrey M. Lobbying for the People: The Political Behavior of Public Interest Groups. Princeton, N.J.: Princeton University Press, 1977.

Blum, Albert A. "Collective Bargaining: Ritual or Reality?" Harvard Business Review 39 (November–December 1961):63–69.

Bok, Derek C., and Dunlop, John T. Labor and the American Community. New York: Simon & Schuster, Touchstone Books, 1970.

Brams, Stephen J. Paradoxes in Politics: An Introduction to the Nonobvious in Political Science. New York: Free Press, 1976.

Braybrooke, David, and Lindblom, Charles E. A Strategy of Decision: Policy Evaluation as a Social Process. New York: Free Press of Glencoe, 1963.

Buchanan, James M., and Tullock, Gordon. The Calculus of Consent: Logical Foundations of Constitutional Democracy. Ann Arbor: University of Michigan Press, 1962.

Buchanan, James M., and Wagner, Richard E. Democracy in Deficit: The Political Legacy of Lord Keynes. New York: Academic, 1977.

Burns, James MacGregor. The Deadlock of Democracy: Four Party Politics in America. Englewood Cliffs, N.J.: Prentice-Hall, 1963.

Cater, Douglas. Power in Washington: A Critical Look at Today's Struggle to Govern in the Nation's Capital. New York: Random House, 1964.

Cheh, John H. "United States Concessions in the Kennedy Round and Short-run Labor Adjustment Costs." Journal of International Economics 4 (1974):323–340.

Clark, Peter B., and Wilson, James Q. "Incentive Systems: A Theory of Organizations." Administrative Science Quarterly 6 (1961):219–266.

Cloward, Richard A., and Piven, Frances Fox. The Politics of Turmoil: Poverty, Race, and the Urban Crisis. New York: Random House, 1974.

Cobb, Roger W., and Elder, Charles D. Participation in American Politics: The Dynamics of Agenda Building. Boston: Allyn & Bacon, 1972.

Committee on Political Parties of the American Political Science Association. Toward a More Responsible Two-party System. New York: Rinehart, 1950.

Crenson, Matthew A. The Un-politics of Air Pollution: A Study of Nondecisionmaking in the Cities. Baltimore: Johns Hopkins University Press, 1971.

Cronin, Thomas E. "The War on Crime and Unsafe Streets, 1960–76: Policymaking for a Just and Safe Society." In America in the Seventies: Problems, Policies, and Politics, edited by Allan P. Sindler, pp. 208–259. Boston: Little, Brown, 1977.

Cyert, Richard M., and March, James G. A Behavioral Theory of the Firm. Englewood Cliffs, N.J.: Prentice-Hall, 1963.

Dahl, Robert A. A Preface to Democratic Theory. Chicago: University of Chicago Press, 1956.

————. "A Critique of the Ruling Elite Model." *American Political Science Review* 52 (1958):463–469.

Dahl, Robert A., and Lindblom, Charles E. *Politics, Economics, and Welfare: Politico-Economic Systems Resolved into Basic Social Processes.* New York: Harper, 1953.

Davies, J. Clarence III, and Davies, Barbara S. *The Politics of Pollution.* 2d ed. Indianapolis: Bobbs-Merrill, Pegasus Books, 1975.

Dexter, Lewis A. "On the Use and Abuse of Social Science by Practitioners." *The American Behavioral Scientist* 19 (1965):25–29.

————. *How Organizations Are Represented in Washington.* Indianapolis: Bobbs-Merrill, 1969.

————. *The Sociology and Politics of Congress.* Chicago: Rand McNally, 1970.

————. "The Representative and His District." In *Legislative Politics U.S.A.,* 3d ed., edited by Theodore J. Lowi and Randall B. Ripley, pp. 175–184. Boston: Little, Brown, 1973.

Donovan, John C. *The Politics of Poverty.* 2d ed., rev. Indianapolis: Bobbs-Merrill, Pegasus Books, 1973.

Downs, Anthony. *An Economic Theory of Democracy.* New York: Harper & Row, 1957.

————. "Why the Government Budget Is Too Small in a Democracy." *World Politics* 12 (1960):541–563.

Easton, David. *The Political System: An Inquiry into the State of Political Science.* New York: Knopf, 1953.

————. *A Systems Analysis of Political Life.* New York: Wiley, 1965.

Edelman, Murray. *The Symbolic Uses of Politics.* Urbana: University of Illinois Press, 1964.

————. *Politics As Symbolic Action: Mass Arousal and Quiescence.* Chicago: Markham, 1971.

"Effective Lobbying Put Open Housing Bill Across." In *Congressional Quarterly Almanac,* pp. 166–168. Washington, D.C.: Congressional Quarterly, 1968.

Eidenberg, Eugene, and Morey, Roy D. *An Act of Congress: The Legislative Process and the Making of Education Policy.* New York: Norton, 1969.

Fainsod, Merle; Gordon, Lincoln; and Palamountain, Joseph C., Jr. *Government and the American Economy.* 3d ed., rev. New York: Norton, 1959.

Fenno, Richard F., Jr. *Congressmen in Committees.* Boston: Little, Brown, 1973.

Ferejohn, John. *Pork Barrel Politics: Rivers and Harbors Legislation, 1947–1968.* Stanford, Calif.: Stanford University Press, 1974.

Fiorina, Morris P. *Representatives, Roll Calls, and Constituencies.* Lexington, Mass.: Heath, Lexington Books, 1975.

————. *Congress: Keystone of the Washington Establishment.* New Haven, Conn.: Yale University Press, 1977.

Fishel, Jeff, ed. *Parties and Elections in an Anti-party Age: American Politics and the Crisis of Confidence.* Bloomington: Indiana University Press, 1978.

Freedman, Leonard. *Public Housing: The Politics of Poverty.* New York: Holt, Rinehart, and Winston, 1969.

Freeman, J. Leiper. *The Political Process: Executive-Legislative Committee Relations.* 2d ed. New York: Random House, 1965.

Friedman, Milton. *Capitalism and Freedom.* With the assistance of Rose D. Friedman. Chicago: University of Chicago Press, 1962.

Friedman, Milton, and Friedman, Rose. *Free to Choose: A Personal Statement.* New York: Harcourt Brace Jovanovich, 1980.

Froman, Lewis A., Jr. "Some Effects of Interest Group Strength in State Politics." *American Political Science Review* 60 (1966):952–962.

———. *The Congressional Process: Strategies, Rules, and Procedures.* Boston: Little, Brown, 1967.

———. "The Categorization of Policy Contents." In *Political Science and Public Policy,* edited by Austin Ranney, pp. 41–52. Chicago: Markham, 1968.

Galbraith, John Kenneth. *American Capitalism: The Concept of Countervailing Power.* Boston: Houghton Mifflin, 1952.

———. *The Affluent Society.* Boston: Houghton Mifflin, 1958.

Gamson, William A. *Power and Discontent.* Homewood, Ill.: Dorsey, 1968.

———. *The Strategy of Social Protest.* Homewood, Ill.: Dorsey, 1975.

Glazer, Nathan. *Affirmative Discrimination: Ethnic Inequality and Public Policy.* New York: Basic Books, 1975.

Greenstone, J. David. *Labor in American Politics.* 2d ed. Chicago: University of Chicago Press, 1977.

Haveman, Robert H. *The Economics of the Public Sector.* 2d ed., rev. New York: Wiley, 1976.

Hawley, Ellis W. *The New Deal and the Problem of Monopoly: A Study in Economic Ambivalence.* Princeton, N.J.: Princeton University Press, 1966.

Hayes, Michael T. "An Economic Theory of Interest Groups and Public Policy." Ph.D. dissertation, Indiana University, 1977.

———. "The Semi-sovereign Pressure Groups: A Critique of Current Theory and an Alternative Typology." *Journal of Politics* 40 (1978):134–161.

———. "Interest Groups and Congress: Toward a Transactional Theory." In *The Congressional System: Notes and Readings,* 2d ed., rev., edited by Leroy N. Rieselbach, pp. 252–273. North Scituate, Mass.: Duxbury, 1979.

Huntington, Samuel P. "Clientelism: A Study in Administrative Politics." Ph.D. dissertation, Harvard University, 1950.

———. "The Marasmus of the ICC: The Commission, the Railroads, and the Public Interest." *Yale Law Journal* 61 (1952):467–509.

Jewell, Malcolm E., and Patterson, Samuel G. *The Legislative Process in the United States.* 2d ed., rev. New York: Random House, 1972.

Jones, Charles O. "Speculative Augmentation in Federal Air Pollution Policy-making." *Journal of Politics* 36 (1974):438–464.

———. *Clean Air: The Policies and Politics of Pollution Control.* Pittsburgh: University of Pittsburgh Press, 1975.

———. *An Introduction to the Study of Public Policy.* 2d ed., rev. North Scituate, Mass.: Duxbury, 1977.

Jordan, William A. "Producer Protection, Prior Market Structure, and the Effects of Government Regulation." *Journal of Law and Economics* 15 (1972):151–176.

Kaufman, Herbert. *Are Government Organizations Immortal?* Washington, D.C.: Brookings Institution, 1976.

Kendall, Willmoore, and Carey, George W. "The 'Intensity' Problem and Democratic Theory." *American Political Science Review* 62 (March 1968):5–24.

Key, V. O., Jr. *Politics, Parties, and Pressure Groups.* 5th ed., rev. New York: Crowell, 1964.

———. *Public Opinion and American Democracy.* New York: Knopf, 1965.

———. *The Responsible Electorate: Rationality in Presidential Voting, 1936–1960.* Cambridge, Mass.: Harvard University Press, 1966.

Kingdon, John W. *Candidates for Office: Beliefs and Strategies.* New York: Random House, 1966.

———. *Congressmen's Voting Decisions.* New York: Harper & Row, 1973.

Kotz, Nick, and Kotz, Mary Lynn. *A Passion for Equality: George Wiley and the Movement.* New York: Norton, 1977.

Latham, Earl. *The Group Basis of Politics: A Study of Basing-point Legislation.* Ithaca, N.Y.: Cornell University Press, 1952.

Leiserson, Avery. *Administrative Regulation: A Study in Representation of Interests.* Chicago: University of Chicago Press, 1942.

Lindblom, Charles E. "The Science of Muddling Through." *Public Administration Review* 19 (1959):79–88.

———. *The Intelligence of Democracy: Decision Making through Mutual Adjustment.* New York: Free Press, 1965.

———. *The Policy-making Process.* Englewood Cliffs, N.J.: Prentice-Hall, 1968.

———. *Politics and Markets: The World's Political-Economic Systems.* New York: Basic Books, 1977.

———. "Still Muddling, Not Yet Through." *Public Administration Review* 39 (1979):517–526.

Lippmann, Walter. *An Inquiry into the Principles of the Good Society.* Boston: Little, Brown, 1937.

Lipsky, Michael. *Protest in City Politics: Rent Strikes, Housing, and the Power of the Poor.* Chicago: Rand McNally, 1970.

Lowi, Theodore J. "How the Farmers Get What They Want." *Reporter,* 14 September 1954, pp. 34–37.

———. "American Business, Public Policy, Case Studies, and Political Theory." *World Politics* 16 (1964):677–715.

———. "Machine Politics—Old and New." *The Public Interest* 9 (1967):83–92.

——. *The End of Liberalism: Ideology, Policy, and the Crisis of Public Authority.* New York: Norton, 1969.

——. "Decision-making vs. Policy-making: Toward an Antidote for Technocracy." *Public Administration Review* 30 (1970):314–325.

——. *The Politics of Disorder.* New York: Basic Books, 1971.

——. "Four Systems of Policy, Politics, and Choice." *Public Administration Review* 32 (1972):298–310.

——. *The End of Liberalism: The Second Republic of the United States.* 2d ed., rev. New York: Norton, 1979.

Maass, Arthur A. "Congress and Water Resources." *American Political Science Review* 44 (1950):576–593.

March, James G., and Simon, Herbert A. *Organizations.* New York: Wiley, 1958.

Marmor, Theodore R. *The Politics of Medicare.* Chicago: Aldine, 1973.

Masters, Nicholas A. "The Organized Labor Bureaucracy as a Base of Support for the Democratic Party." *Law and Contemporary Problems* 27 (1962):252–265.

Mathews, Tom, et al. "Single Issue Politics." *Newsweek,* 6 November 1978, pp. 48–60.

Matthews, Donald R. *U.S. Senators and Their World.* Chapel Hill: University of North Carolina Press, 1960.

Matthews, Donald R., and Stimson, James A. *Yeas and Nays: Normal Decision-making in the U.S. House of Representatives.* New York: Wiley, 1975.

Mayhew, David R. *Party Loyalty among Congressmen: The Difference between Democrats and Republicans, 1947–1962.* Cambridge, Mass.: Harvard University Press, 1966.

——. *Congress: The Electoral Connection.* New Haven, Conn.: Yale University Press, 1974.

McConnell, Grant. *Private Power and American Democracy.* New York: Knopf, 1966.

——. *The Decline of Agrarian Democracy.* New York: Atheneum, 1969.

McCraw, Thomas K. "Regulation in America: A Review Article." *Business History Review* 49 (1975):159–183.

McFarland, Andrew S. *Public Interest Lobbies: Decision Making on Energy.* Washington, D.C.: American Enterprise Institute for Public Policy Research, 1976.

——. "Recent Social Movements and Theories of Power in America." Paper delivered at the 1979 Annual Meeting of the American Political Science Association, Washington, D.C., 31 August 1979.

McPherson, Charles P. "Tariff Structures and Political Exchange." Ph.D. dissertation, University of Chicago, 1972.

Meltsner, Arnold J. *Policy Analysis in the Bureaucracy.* Berkeley and Los Angeles: University of California Press, 1976.

Michels, Robert. *Political Parties: A Sociological Study of the Oligarchical Tendencies of Modern Democracy.* Translated by Eden Paul and Cedar Paul. New York: Free Press, 1962.

Milbrath, Lester W. *The Washington Lobbyists*. Chicago: Rand McNally, 1963.

Miller, Warren E. "Majority Rule and the Representative System of Government." Paper delivered at the 1952 Annual Meeting of the American Political Science Association, Washington, D.C., 5-8 September 1952.

Miller, Warren E., and Stokes, Donald E. "Constituency Influence in Congress." *American Political Science Review* 57 (1963):45-56.

Mills, C. Wright. *The Power Elite*. New York: Oxford University Press, 1956.

Montjoy, Robert S., and O'Toole, Laurence J. "Toward a Theory of Policy Implementation: An Organizational Perspective." *Public Administration Review* 39 (1979):465-476.

Moynihan, Daniel P. *Maximum Feasible Misunderstanding: Community Action in the War on Poverty*. New York: Free Press, 1969.

———. *The Politics of a Guaranteed Income: The Nixon Administration and the Family Assistance Plan*. New York: Random House, Vintage Books, 1973.

———. *Coping: On the Practice of Government*. New York: Random House, Vintage Books, 1975.

Mueller, John E. "Presidential Popularity from Truman to Johnson." *American Political Science Review* 64 (1970):18-34.

Musgrave, Richard A., and Musgrave, Peggy B. *Public Finance in Theory and Practice*. New York: McGraw-Hill, 1973.

Nadel, Mark V. *The Politics of Consumer Protection*. Indianapolis: Bobbs-Merrill, 1971.

———. *Corporations and Political Accountability*. Lexington, Mass.: Heath, 1976.

Neustadt, Richard E. *Presidential Power: The Politics of Leadership from FDR to Carter*. Rev. ed. New York: Wiley, 1980.

Noll, Roger. *Reforming Regulation: An Evaluation of the Ash Council Proposals*. Washington, D.C.: Brookings Institution, 1971.

O'Brien, David J. *Neighborhood Organization and Interest-group Processes*. Princeton, N.J.: Princeton University Press, 1975.

Olson, Mancur, Jr. *The Logic of Collective Action: Public Goods and the Theory of Groups*. New York: Schocken, 1970.

Oppenheimer, Bruce Ian. "The Effects of Policy Variation on Interest Group Behavior in the Congressional Process: The Oil Industry in Two Domestic Issues." Ph.D. dissertation, University of Wisconsin, 1973. (Later published as *Oil and the Congressional Process: The Limits of Symbolic Politics*. Lexington, Mass.: Heath, Lexington Books, 1974.)

Pincus, Jonathan J. "Pressure Groups and the Pattern of Tariffs." *Journal of Political Economy* 83 (1975):757-778.

Pitkin, Hannah F. *The Concept of Representation*. Berkeley and Los Angeles: University of California Press, 1967.

Piven, Frances Fox, and Cloward, Richard A. *Regulating the Poor: The Functions of Public Welfare*. New York: Random House, Vintage Books, 1971.

———. *Poor People's Movements: Why They Succeed, How They Fail*. New York: Pantheon, 1977.

Pomper, Gerald M. "From Confusion to Clarity: Issues and American Voters, 1956–1968." *American Political Science Review* 66 (1972):415–428.

Posner, Richard A. "Theories of Economic Regulation." *Bell Journal of Economics and Management Science* 5 (1974):335–358.

Pratt, Henry J. *The Gray Lobby*. Chicago: University of Chicago Press, 1976.

Ranney, Austin. "Toward a More Responsible Two-party System: A Commentary." *American Political Science Review* 45 (1951):488–499.

Rein, Martin. *Social Science and Public Policy*. Harmondsworth, Middlesex, England: Penguin, 1976.

RePass, David E. "Issue Salience and Party Choice." *American Political Science Review* 65 (1971):389–400.

Rieselbach, Leroy N. *Congressional Politics*. New York: McGraw-Hill, 1973.

Riker, William H., and Brams, Steven J. "The Paradox of Vote Trading," *American Political Science Review* 67 (1973):1235–1247.

Ripley, Randall B. *Majority Party Leadership in Congress*. Boston: Little, Brown, 1969.

———. *Congress: Process and Policy*. New York: Norton, 1975.

———. *Congress: Process and Policy*. 2d ed., rev. New York: Norton, 1979.

Ripley, Randall B., and Franklin, Grace A. *Congress, the Bureaucracy, and Public Policy*. 2d ed., rev. Homewood, Ill.: Dorsey, 1976.

Rivlin, Alice M. *Systematic Thinking for Social Action*. Washington, D.C.: Brookings Institution, 1971.

Robinson, James A. *The House Rules Committee*. Indianapolis: Bobbs-Merrill, 1963.

Rose, Richard, and Peters, Guy. *Can Government Go Bankrupt?* New York: Basic Books, 1978.

Ross, Robert L. "Dimensions and Patterns of Relations among Interest Groups at the Congressional Level of Government." Ph.D. dissertation, Michigan State University, 1962.

———. "Relations among National Interest Groups." *Journal of Politics* 32 (1970):96–114.

Rourke, Francis E. *Bureaucracy, Politics, and Public Policy*. 2d ed., rev. Boston: Little, Brown, 1976.

Sabatier, Paul. "Social Movements and Regulatory Agencies: Toward a More Adequate—and Less Pessimistic—Theory of 'Clientele Capture.'" *Policy Sciences* 6 (1975):301–342.

Salamon, Lester M., and Siegfried, John J. "Economic Power and Political Influence: The Impact of Industry Structure on Public Policy." *American Political Science Review* 71 (1977):1026–1043.

Salisbury, Robert H. "The Analysis of Public Policy: A Search for Theories and Rules." In *Political Science and Public Policy*, edited by Austin Ranney, pp. 151–175. Chicago: Markham, 1968.

———. "An Exchange Theory of Interest Groups." *Midwest Journal of Political Science* 8 (1969):1–32.

Salisbury, Robert H., and Heinz, John P. "A Theory of Policy Analysis and Some Preliminary Applications." In *Policy Analysis in Political Science,* edited by Ira Sharkansky, pp. 39-60. Chicago: Markham, 1970.

Schattschneider, E. E. *Politics, Pressures and the Tariff: A Study of Free Enterprise in Pressure Politics as Shown in the 1929-1930 Revision of the Tariff.* New York: Prentice-Hall, 1935.

————. *Party Government.* New York: Rinehart, 1942.

————. *The Semi-sovereign People: A Realist's View of Democracy in America.* New York: Holt, Rinehart, and Winston, 1960.

Schultze, Charles L. *The Politics and Economics of Public Spending.* Washington, D.C.: Brookings Institution, 1968.

Scoble, Harry M. "Organized Labor in Electoral Politics: Some Questions for the Discipline." *Western Political Quarterly* 16 (1963):666-686.

————. *Ideology and Electoral Action: A Comparative Study of the National Committee for an Effective Congress.* San Francisco: Chandler, 1967.

Shabecoff, Philip. "Ecologists Disagree on Clean-water Bill." *New York Times,* 20 November 1977, p. 27, col. 1.

Simon, Herbert A. *Models of Man, Social and Rational: Mathematical Essays on Rational Human Behavior in a Social Setting.* New York: Wiley, 1957.

Smith, T. Alexander. "Toward a Comparative Theory of the Policy Process." *Comparative Politics* 1 (1969):498-515.

Stanfield, Rochelle L. "Housing Integration Remains a Distant Dream." *National Journal,* 5 May 1979, pp. 734-738.

Steiner, Gilbert Y. *Social Insecurity: The Politics of Welfare.* Chicago: Rand McNally, 1966.

————. *The State of Welfare.* Washington, D.C.: Brookings Institution, 1971.

Steiner, Gilbert Y., and Gove, Samuel K. *Legislative Politics in Illinois.* Urbana: University of Illinois Press, 1960.

Stigler, George J. "Director's Law of Public Income Distribution." *Journal of Law and Economics* 13 (1970):1-10.

————. "The Theory of Economic Regulation." *Bell Journal of Economics and Management Science* 2 (1971):3-21.

————. "Free Riders and Collective Action: An Appendix to Theories of Economic Regulation." *Bell Journal of Economics and Management Science* 5 (1974):359-365.

Sundquist, James L. *Politics and Policy: The Eisenhower, Kennedy, and Johnson Years.* Washington, D.C.: Brookings Institution, 1968.

Surrey, Stanley S. "How Special Tax Provisions Get Enacted." In *Public Policies and Their Politics: Techniques of Government Control,* edited by Randall B. Ripley, pp. 51-60. New York: Norton, 1966.

Thompson, James D. *Organizations in Action: Social Science Bases of Administrative Theory.* New York: McGraw-Hill, 1967.

Toch, Hans. *The Social Psychology of Social Movements.* New York: Bobbs-Merrill, 1965.

Truman, David B. *The Governmental Process: Political Interests and Public Opinion.* New York: Knopf, 1951.

Tullock, Gordon. *Toward a Mathematics of Politics.* Ann Arbor: University of Michigan Press, 1967.

Vaccara, Beatrice N. *Employment and Output in Protected Manufacturing Industries.* Washington, D.C.: Brookings Institution, 1960.

Van Horn, Carl E. *Policy Implementation in the Federal System: National Goals and Local Implementors.* Lexington, Mass.: Heath, Lexington Books, 1979.

Van Meter, Donald S., and Van Horn, Carl E. "The Policy Implementation Process: A Conceptual Framework." *Administration and Society* 6 (1975):445–488.

Verba, Sidney, and Nie, Norman H. *Participation in America: Political Democracy and Social Equality.* New York: Harper & Row, 1972.

Walker, Jack L. "Protest and Negotiation: A Case Study of Negro Leadership in Atlanta, Georgia." *Midwest Journal of Political Science* 7 (1963):99–124.

———. "Setting the Agenda in the U.S. Senate: A Theory of Problem Selection." *British Journal of Political Science* 7 (1977):423–445.

Warwick, Donald P.; Meade, Marvin; and Reed, Theodore. *A Theory of Public Bureaucracy: Politics, Personality, and Organization in the State Department.* Cambridge, Mass.: Harvard University Press, 1975.

Wildavsky, Aaron B. *The Politics of the Budgetary Process.* Boston: Little, Brown, 1964.

———. "The Political Economy of Efficiency: Cost-Benefit Analysis, Systems Analysis, and Program Budgeting." *Public Administration Review* 26 (1966):7–14.

Wilensky, Harold L. *Intellectuals in Labor Unions: Organizational Pressures on Professional Roles.* Glencoe, Ill.: Free Press, 1956.

Williams, Walter, and Elmore, Richard F., eds. *Social Program Implementation.* New York: Academic, 1976.

Wilson, James Q. "The Strategy of Protest: Problems of Negro Civic Action." *Journal of Conflict Resolution* 3 (1961):291–303.

———. *Political Organizations.* New York: Basic Books, 1973.

———. "Democracy and the Corporation." *Wall Street Journal,* 11 January 1978, p. 14.

Witte, Edwin E. *The Development of the Social Security Act: A Memorandum on the History of the Committee on Economic Security and Drafting and Legislative History of the Social Security Act.* Madison: University of Wisconsin Press, 1963.

Wolman, Harold L. *Politics of Federal Housing.* New York: Dodd, Mead, 1971.

Wolman, Harold L., and Thomas, Norman C. "Black Interests, Black Groups, and Black Influence in the Federal Policy Process." *Journal of Politics* 32 (1970):875–897.

Zald, Mayer N., and Ash, Roberta. "Social Movement Organizations: Growth, Decay, and Change." *Social Forces* 3 (1966):327–341.

Zeigler, L. Harmon, and Peak, G. Wayne. *Interest Groups in American Society.* 2d ed. Englewood Cliffs, N.J.: Prentice-Hall, 1972.

Zeigler, L. Harmon, and van Dalen, Hendrik. "Interest Groups in the States." In *Politics in the American States: A Comparative Analysis,* 2d ed., rev., edited by Herbert Jacob and Kenneth N. Vines, pp. 122–160. Boston: Little, Brown, 1976.

Index